EurographicSeminars

Tutorials and Perspectives in Computer Graphics

Edited by G. Enderle and D. Duce

User Interface Management Systems

Proceedings of the Workshop on User Interface Management Systems held in Seeheim, FRG, November 1–3, 1983

Edited by Günther E. Pfaff

With 69 Figures

Springer-Verlag
Berlin Heidelberg New York Tokyo

Eurographic Seminars
Edited by G. Enderle and D. Duce
for EUROGRAPHICS -
The European Association for Computer Graphics
P. O. Box 16
CH-1288 Aire-la-Ville

Editor:
Günther E. Pfaff
GTS/GRAL
Alsfelderstraße 7
D-6100 Darmstadt

ISBN-13: 978-3-642-70043-9 e-ISBN-13: 978-3-642-70041-5
DOI: 10.1007/978-3-642-70041-5

Library of Congress Cataloging in Publication Data.
Workshop on User Interface Management Systems (1983 : Seeheim-Jugenheim, Germany) User interface management systems. (EurographicSeminars) Bibliography: p.
1. Interactive computer systems–Congresses. 2. Computer graphics–Congresses.
I. Pfaff. G. (Günther). 1951-. II. Title. III. Series. QA76.9.I58W67 1983 001.64'404 85-2831
ISBN-13: 978-3-642-70043-9 (U.S.)

Softcover reprint of the hardcover 1st edition 1985

2145/3140-543210

Editors Introduction

The book contains the proceedings and reports of the "Workshop on User Interface Management Systems", held in Seeheim, Federal Republic of Germany, November 1–3, 1983. The workshop brought together experts in using and developing techniques for managing the dialogue between users and interactive graphics systems. The purpose of the workshop was to produce an agreed report contrasting existing approaches, and outlining directions for future work. Four different areas were defined and addressed at the workshop, namely

a) role, model, structure and construction of a UIMS
b) dialogue specification tools
c) interface of the UIMS to the application
d) user's conceptual model

All participants prepared papers each in one of those problem areas. The papers have been rewritten in the light of the issues discussed during the workshop. Also a subgroup report was produced for each problem area summarizing the results of the discussions at the workshop.

Preface

User Interface Management Systems (UIMS) are the mediators between the user and the application programs. As more and more interactive programs become widely available, methods and techniques of designing and implementing acceptable user interfaces have to be investigated. Since many years, research on the design of user interface management systems is going on. This EUROGRAPHICS Workshop follows from the ACM SIGGRAPH Workshop on Graphical Input and Interaction Techniques of May, 1982 in Seattle (see: Computer Graphics 17(1), 1983), and the IFIP WG 5.2 workshop on Methodology of Interaction of 1979 (see: R. Guedj et al, eds, "Methodology of Interaction", North-Holland, Amsterdam, 1980) held at Seillac, France.

After the Seattle workshop, two more workshops were proposed: one to concentrate attention on the software aspects of the UIMS, and the other to clarify the interdisciplinary relationships required to better understand interaction methodology. The first of these two workshops is the one reported in this book, the other will be held in the USA in 1985.

The UIMS workshop concentrated on the four areas of general UIMS topics (role, model, structure, and construction of a UIMS), dialogue specification tools, interface to application programs, and the user's conceptual model. After initial presentations in these four areas, participants split into four subgroups, each of which was assigned one of the above topics. The three days we respent on discussing issues specific to the subgroup topics, presenting them and the proposed results to the general assembly, and reconvening with refined issues and accepted solutions.

Subgroup alpha (Role, Model, Structure and Construction of a UIMS) was to discuss general UIM topics and to find a link to the previous Seattle workshop. Since "Role" was sufficiently discussed in the GIIT workshop and was agreed here, the discussion concentrated on "Model" and "Structure". It was recognized that the OSI layer model can be applied very well to communication layers in a UIMS. Similarily, the known models of hierachical interaction blocks fit very well to construct a UIMS. A general generic UIMS being a basis for the construction of special UIMS's remains to be elaborated in future activities.

Subgroup beta (Dialogue Specification Tools) concentrated on the issue, how to describe user interfaces with regard to the following questions:

a) how can implementations of user interfaces be automatically produced,
b) how do UI-descriptions relate to human factors,
c) how can user interface description techniques be classified

A model was developed which defines the logical components of a general UIM system.
Subgroup gamma discussed the interface of a UIMS to application programs, especially to CAD applications. Three major problems were identified, namely the configuration of a UIMS with respect to specific applications, the division of the responsibility for graphical output between application and UIMS, and the communication services and functions required by both applications and UIMS.
Subgroup omega finally made an attempt at the formal specification of the User's Conceptual Model (UCM). Several notations were investigated which can be a start-point to integrate also the work of other experts in the field of the user interface problems, such as philosophers, linguists, or psychologists.
The organisation of the workshop was accomplished with support from several sources. The following institutes provided the means and resources for the workshop:

- EUROGRAPHICS Association
- IFIP WG 5.2
- Gesellschaft für Informatik, GI-FA 4.1

Organising an event such as this workshop can only be done with the help of the right team. Thanks are due to the programme and organizing committee consisting of Paul ten Hagen, Herbert Kuhlmann, and David Rosenthal. Special thanks go the workshop secretary, Bridget Astridge, for her help and assistance.
Obviously the success of a workshop like this depends on the participants and their cooperation. This fruitful and highly interesting event was made possible by the following participants:

Mark Apperly, New Zealand
Rudolfo Belliardi, USA
Bertran David, France
Jan Derksen, The Netherlands
Ernest Edmonds, UK
Jose Encarnacao, FRG
Günter Enderle, FRG
Mark Green, Canada
Richard Guedj, France
Herbert Kuhlmann, FRG
Michael Mac an Airchinnigh, Ireland
Jan Matthys, Belgium
Dimitr Novatchev, Bulgaria
Dan Olsen, USA
Günther Pfaff, FRG
John Sibert, USA
Robert Spence, UK
Hugo Strubbe, USA

Henning Hanusa, FRG
Abid Kamran, USA
Robert Kenyon, UK
Fumihiko Kimura, Japan
Gergely Krammer, Hungary
Tapio Takala, Finland
Peter Tanner, Canada
Paul ten Hagen, The Netherlands
James Thomas, USA
Fan Yu-Quing, UK

Darmstadt, January 1985

Günther E. Pfaff

Table of Contents

Part 1

Subgroup Reports

Report on Role, Model, Structure and Construction of a UIMS

H. J. Strubbe

Prime Computer, Inc., 500 Old Connecticut Path, Framingham, MA 01701, USA

1. OVERVIEW OF THE MEETINGS

The role of a UIMS was discussed in some detail at the previous workshop (GIIT). Our subgroup reviewed it and agreed fully without adding new facets. The conclusions will therefore not be repeated here.

Shedding some light on the structure of a UIMS was considered a rather abstract problem, as long as we did not have a good feeling of what services it really expected from and gave to the rest of the system. We wanted to know how it behaves on the outside, before specifying what should go on inside it. We decided to investigate two subtopics instead: "relation between a UIMS and a graphics system", and "relation between a UIMS and an application". The report of the first topic (based on a write-up by G. Pfaff) can be found in chapter 2. The second topic is fully described by ten Hagen (1984) in a separate paper.

Chapter 3 reports on our discussions of a model for a UIMS. By this time it was clear that the title of our subgroup was much too ambitious, so we never even tried to discuss the "construction of a UIMS".

From the initial presentations and from the discussions in our subgroup it became apparent that attempts to use a UIMS (as presented at GIIT) for complex "real" applications lead to all kinds of problems. Additional problems arise when a UIMS is built on top of a standard graphics package like GKS. These problems kept emerging during our discussion and can be characterised by the following catch phrases:

- echo by the graphics system
- device simulation by the graphics system
- semantic feedback
- style-independent output
- external and internal control
- parallelism
- data exchange
- interaction primitives

In chapter 4 these problems will be stated in more detail, while reflecting the opinion of our subgroup (if any). This ties together what would otherwise be a set of remarks on somewhat randomly chosen topics. Note that this list was made after the workshop, so that these topics were never discussed in that context.

2. RELATION BETWEEN A UIMS AND A GRAPHICS PACKAGE

The UIMS is the mediator between the user and the application program. The application should never communicate with the user directly, without the UIMS knowing about it. Moreover in order to construct an optimal Ui/f, the UIMS wants to be in full control of all details of all input and output. If the interaction with the user is graphical in nature, the UIMS can make use of a graphics system (GS). In the ideal case, such a GS would be an integral part of the UIMS. However, with the current graphics packages (e.g. GKS), the best one can do is to build the UIMS around the GS to insure that all input and output will go through the UIMS.

Input and output are basically separated but there exist many mappings between them. This is illustrated in fig. 1. The UIMS should have control over these mappings at all levels. The concept of internal levels inside the UIMS is touched on in chapter 3. As will be explained later, the application can request data from the UIMS. This is symbolised by an arrow pointing from the output to the input.

```
        |                 input stream                    |
+-----> | >-------------------------------------...-> | >-------+
|       |      v           v             ^             |         |
|       |      | GRAPHICS  | UIMS        | UIMS        | APPLIC  |
| USER  |      | SYSTEM    | (some       | (another    | PROGR   |
|       |      |           |  level)     |    level)   |         |
|       |      v           v             ^             |         |
+-----< | <-------------------------------------...-< | <-------+
        |                 output stream                   |
```

Fig. 1. Relation between input and output. The x axis shows "transformations" of the data streams. The y axis shows "mappings" between input and output.

The mapping on the lowest level is done inside the GS. For GKS, which we will use as an example in the following, this mapping is determined by the measures and triggers of the logical input devices (LID's). Currently, they are part of the GKS implementation. However, they should be under control of the UIMS.

The application program generates an output stream in the format of its own logical data. Along its way through the various levels of the UIMS and the GS, the output gets transformed several times until it ends up in the format of visual data for a particular workstation. A similar process applies to the input data. Conceptually, there exists an intermediate representation of the data after each transformation. The following set of representations, used during output in GKS, can be taken as an example: application data, transformed into workstation independent segment storage (WISS), transformed into workstation dependent segment storage (WDSS). The WISS contains a picture in normalised device coordinates (NDC). The WDSS contains a picture in device dependent format.

The UIMS wants to have full control over the types of all these intermediate representations and over the transformations between them.

Such representations can be of the type "implicit", "explicit" or "explicitly stored". Implicit representations are for internal use, and no other level can access them or rely on their physical existence. In the case of an explicit representation, the adjacent levels can modify the transformations to/from it. For this purpose there exist parameter setting functions for these transformations. The application software can invoke these functions and it can inquire about the parameter settings. In addition the user can modify these transformations by interacting with the UIMS. An explicitly stored representation is an explicit representation of which the data physically exist. Moreover other levels are allowed to take this fact into account. This means that changes to the representation can happen locally to that level, without all upstream levels being aware of this fact. Such levels can update their data if an inverse transformation function is available.

Using GKS again as an example, we can state that WDSS has an implicit representation. No GKS function relies on its physical existence. It need not be physically implemented. WISS has an explicit representation. There exist, for instance, segment manipulation functions which modify its content. The transformation between the application data and WISS, and between WISS and the output device can be set and inquired by the user and the application. Finally, the metafile has an explicitly stored representation.

The current graphics systems contain facilities to make the porting of graphics applications easier (e.g. LID's). They do not yet contain the appropriate facilities to make graphical user interfaces easier to write. (A library of) interaction primitives and typical interaction tasks should be defined and built. Both the LID's and the interaction primitives should make optimal use of the physical device characteristics. This can be achieved by letting them use and (re)define some of the basic building blocks of the GS. In addition, the interaction primitives will have to be built inside the GS on the same level as the LID's, rather than being constructed on top of them.

The basic building blocks in GKS are the triggers and measures (including prompts and echos). Their exact behaviour is defined by the system implementor. These blocks are then combined into a few standard LID's, which the application program uses. Obviously, LID's can be tailored to the needs of a particular physical device and a particular program by having the system implementor define special building blocks for each case. This would largely defeat the purpose of a GS. A more practical approach, using the notion of a "privately configured" GKS for each application is discussed by Pfaff (1983).

3. MODEL FOR A UIMS

We introduced the term "instance of a UIMS" to indicate the module that lies between the application and the user as the result of inputting one specific dialogue and style into the general UIMS. We tried to find a model for such instances.

The OSI model assumes the existence of 4 layers underneath the application, i.e. the physical layer, the transport layer, the session layer and the presentation layer. Applying these concepts to a UIMS, as described by Herman et al. (1984), leads to a physical device layer, a context control layer and a single-context layer. The context control layer is often referred to as the windowing layer. The single-context layer contains all the rest of the UIMS, and needs further refinement.

The popular linguistic model, which distinguishes a lexical, a syntactic and a semantic level, is not considered appropriate for this purpose. Its main problem stems from the fact that in graphical interactions commands are not necessarily "entered in full" before feedback or action starts. This point is elaborated by Kamran (1984), based on the analysis of the MOVE command.

A model of an application-dependent hierarchy of interaction blocks was then put forward. Similar ideas underlie the notion of "Dialogue Cells" (see Borufka et al. (1982)), of "Device Model" (see Anson (1982)), and of "Input-Output Tools" (see Van den Bos et al. (1983)). The idea is to break down the application into a hierarchy of logical blocks. For each block, questions can be asked like: what type of input does it accept and under what conditions; does it act on that input or pass it on; does it produce an echo or a prompt; what type of output does it produce and how; etc. It is necessary to define a separate hierarchy for input blocks and for output blocks: input consumed at a particular level does not necessarily produce output at that same level.

It is felt that dialogue specification will become easier if a formal framework is adopted, in which such a set of questions has to be answered for each block. Code that will actually produce the required effects (e.g. prompts, echo, output) has to be incorporated. In addition the relationship between the blocks must be specified. The UIMS could then use these specifications to keep track of which block should be activated in response to the user's input. Such activation then causes the code in the block to be executed, which produces the prompts, echo, output, etc. and might as well trigger the activation of another block.

It is not known if such models are really practical for complex applications. An attempt to use one of these models for a CAD application is described by Matthys (1984). Much more research is needed in this area.

4. PROBLEM AREAS

Echo by the Graphics System

Many graphics systems do not fully specify the echo produced in reaction to the use of an input device. The implementor of the system has some freedom here. The dialogue writer, however, needs full control of the entire interaction with the user. This requires him to have control over the echo too. It has to be possible to put the graphics system in "full duplex mode".

Device Simulation by the Graphics System

The way in which a graphical device is simulated by another one is traditionally left to the graphics package implementor. As such simulation can drastically affect the quality of the user interface, it has to be under control of the dialogue writer. The process of porting an application to a system with different devices will typically go in two steps. Simulation of the old devices on the new ones will lead to an application that works correctly on the new system, but has a less than optimal Ui/f. To improve it, the dialogue writer might have to modify the interaction sequences.

Semantic Feedback

The notion that there is lexical and syntactic feedback which can be given by the UIMS on its own, and semantic feedback which comes from the application when a command is fully specified, often breaks down. Examples hereof were given by Kamran (1984) and Strubbe (1984). In many cases, the immediate feedback (e.g. echo) cannot be given by the UIMS without the help of the application program. It is not clear that it is a worthwhile goal to try and store large amounts of application knowledge inside the UIMS.

Style-Independent Output

Some of the information that the application hands to the UIMS (e.g. a list of options) is interpreted by it and leads to graphical interactions in the style specified by the user. Other information (e.g. the drawing of a building), however, should not be changed by the UIMS, as it is independent of the style of the interaction and carries semantic information. The UIMS defines the relationship between the i/o it sends to the terminal and the information it gets from the application. The application information must be dominant so as to insure the semantic information flow required by a specific application. The problem stems from the fact that the UIMS as well as the application want to produce screen output, and therefore have to cooperate very well. This problem can be avoided if the application hands only "abstract information" to the UIMS, and if the UIMS contains an appropriate formatter. There are doubts, however, whether this is always practical.

External and Internal Control

In some applications the user has full control of the sequence of the interaction (external control). In others, the application dictates that sequence (internal control). It is often a problem to cast a complex application completely in the external mode or completely in the internal mode: an external control application might meet a state from where it cannot continue, unless the user answers a "yes or no" question. In other words, the UIMS has to come into action, sometimes on behalf of the user, sometimes on behalf of the application: "the UIMS is a slave of two masters". These control modes get diffuse at the implementation level. At the user interface level, however, it is desirable to give the user maximal control: "don't force unnecessary sequencing on him".

Parallelism

For applications that execute time-consuming operations it is useful to have application tasks (e.g. a calculation) performed in parallel with user interface work (e.g. browsing through the results of a previous calculation). The problem is to express this parallel behaviour in the dialogue, so that the completion of the (background) calculation will be signalled to the user in a timely way.

Data Exchange

The same data might sometimes be needed at different levels of the system. For instance, some output data (or different representations thereof) might reside inside the graphics system, inside the UIMS and inside the application. This is done for efficiency reasons, i.e. to minimise data exchange and data transformations. (Compare with traditional "cache-ing"). However, modification of data at a lower level must now also lead to modification of the corresponding data at the higher levels. This can be done via properly controlled shared access mechanisms. Alternatively, the higher levels might have to inspect the data at the lower levels and deduct updates from there (via an inverse transformation).

Interaction Primitives

It would be very helpful to the interaction designer if there existed "standard interaction primitives" that were very well suited for building complex user interfaces. The abstractions (LID's) that exist in current graphics systems were mainly designed to enable portability. They are considered inappropriate for building user interfaces. It is unlikely that these interaction primitives can be put on top of a graphics system. However, they might merely extend the GS (and as such share the physical device drivers). An example of such abstract interaction primitive is a "rubberband" function. An appropriate set of these primitives has not yet been defined.

5. REFERENCES

Anson E (1982) The device model of interaction. Proceedings of SIGGRAPH 82. Computer Graphics 3:107-114

Borufka HG, Kuhlmann HW, ten Hagen PJW (1982) Dialogue cells: a method for defining interactions. IEEE CG&A, July:25-33

Herman I, Krammer G, Tolnay-Knefely T, Vincze A (1984) Picture book about user interface management and associated representation kernels. Proceedings of this workshop

Kamran A (1984) Issues pertaining to the design of the abstract interaction handler. Proceedings of this workshop

Matthys J (1984) The input tool model - a personal experience. Proceedings of this workshop

Pfaff G (1983) Construction of operator interfaces based on logical input devices. Acta Informatica 19:151-166

Strubbe HJ (1984) Components of interactive applications. Proceedings of this workshop

ten Hagen PJW (1984) The relation between a UIMS and an application. Separate Subgroup report. Proceedings of this workshop

Van den Bos J, Plasmeijer MJ, Hartel P (1983) Input-Output tools: a language facility for interactive and real-time systems. IEEE Trans. Software Eng. 3:247-259

Report on Dialogue Specification Tools

M. Green

Department of Computing Science, University of Alberta, Edmonton, Alberta, Canada

INTRODUCTION

One of the goals of User Interface Management Systems (UIMS) is the automatic (or semi-automatic) construction of user interfaces. In order to accomplish this a description of the user interface to be implemented must be available. This report addresses three questions related to user interface descriptions. These questions are: what user interface descriptions are required to automatically produce a user interface, how do these descriptions relate to the human factors of user interfaces, and how can the existing user interface description techniques be classified? In order to address these questions an abstract model of a UIMS has been developed. This model does not represent how a UIMS should be structured or implemented, instead it presents the logical components that must appear in a UIMS. Each of these components has a different function, and different description techniques are required for each one. The logical model of a UIMS is shown in fig. 1. This model is similar to ones proposed by Edmonds [Edmonds 1982], Green [Green 1984], and Olsen [Olsen 1984]. Each of the components of this model will now be discussed.

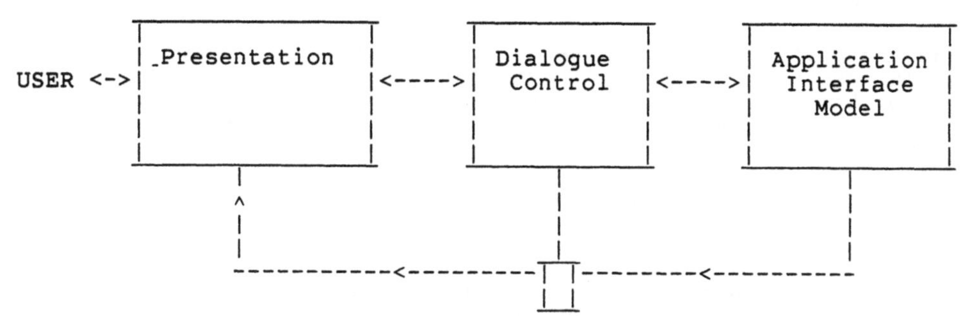

Fig. 1 Logical model of a UIMS

The presentation component is responsible for the external presentation of the user interface. This component generates the images that appear on the display screen, and reads the physical input devices, converting the raw input data into the form required by the other components in the user interface. The user interface employs an abstract representation for the input and output data. This representation consists of a type or name that identifies the kind of data, and the collection of values that define the data item. This representation is similar to that used to represent tokens in a compiler [Aho and Ullman 1977]. For this reason the term token is used for the chunks of information handled by the UIMS. The main purpose of the presentation component is to translate between the external physical representation of the tokens, and their internal abstract representation. In most cases this translation is a simple one-to-one mapping.

The external-internal mapping can be viewed as a dictionary, with one entry for each of the external and internal data items. This entry indicates how the token is to be translated. The presentation component has no control over the contents of the dictionary, it cannot change the external-internal mapping. The dictionary can only be changed by the dialogue control component. The dictionary is a generalization of the physical/logical device bindings that appear in some graphics packages. In terms of Foley's language model [Foley and Van Dam 1982] the presentation component deals with the lexical aspects of the user interface.

The dialogue control component defines the structure of the dialogue between the user and the application program. This component receives a linear sequence of input tokens from the presentation component, and a linear sequence of output tokens from the application. Based on these two sequences of tokens the dialogue control component determines the structure of the interaction, and routes the tokens to their appropriate destinations. The dialogue control component can be viewed as the mediator between the user and the applications program. The user, through the presentation component, makes requests and supplies data to the application program. The input tokens representing these requests and data are examined by dialogue control, and routed to the appropriate routines in the applications program. Similarly the application program generates requests for data and answers to the user requests. The dialogue control component must channel these output tokens to the appropriate parts of the presentation component.

Unlike the presentation component, the dialogue control component must maintain a state and have control over it. The actions performed by this component will usually depend upon the context of the dialogue, therefore, any notations for it must be able to handle dialogue states and state changes. This component can also control the state of the presentation component, thus a means of specifying these state changes is also required.

The application interface model is a representation of the application from the viewpoint of the user interface. This component defines the interface between the UIMS and the rest of the application program. The application interface model defines the semantics of the application. This representation includes the data objects that are maintained by the application, and the routines the user interface can use to communicate with the application. This component contains the information required by dialogue control for routing tokens to the appropriate place within the application. This component also contains constraints on the use of the application routines. This allows the user interface to check the semantic validity of the user input before the application routines are invoked. This information can also be used in error recovery and undoing user actions. This component of a user interface has not appeared explicitly in any of the existing UIMSs. But, most of them have some mechanism for performing some of the functions we have assigned to it. The exact nature of this component will evolve as it is incorporated into UIMSs and used in practice.

HUMAN FACTORS

In this section the relationship between the human factors of user interfaces, and the three user interface components is explored. There are two aspects to this relationship. First, how can human factors experts help us design the three user interface components? By dividing the user interface into three logical components it may be possible to develop better design guidelines, than by considering the user interface as a whole. Second, given descriptions of each component, is it possible to evaluate these descriptions from a human factors point of view?

Starting with the first aspect and the presentation component of the user interface, it appears that name spaces are a key issue. The presentation component is responsible for mapping between the user's symbolism, and the internal representation of the user interface. When the user approaches an application he has a certain set of symbols he uses to name the physical and conceptual objects in the application. In order to have a smooth dialogue the presentation component must deal with the user in terms of these symbols. The design of this set of symbols is where human factors enters the design of the presentation component. We need advice on how the symbols should be designed, how the symbol space should be structured, and the effects of interactions between symbols. Should the symbol space be designed in such a way that all the symbols are obviously disjoint, or is there something to be gained from the interaction between symbols? In order to address these questions advice from experts in human factors and cognitive psychology is needed.

In the dialogue control component the key human factors issue is command and dialogue structure. It is fairly well known that certain command formats and dialogue structures are superior to others, and numerous sets of guidelines have been produced for command language design. It has also been shown that the interaction between commands can have an effect on the usability of a user interface. There is more readily available information on the design of this component than the other two components. But, there are still a large number of human factors issues to be addressed. One of the key issues is the effect of chunking and closure on dialogue design. How can we design a dialogue to take advantage of the user's natural chunking ability? Also, how can we design a dialogue so the closures occur at natural places, and the dialogue does not overload the user's processing abilities?

There is very little we can say about the human factors of the application interface model. The design of this component should be based on the user's model of the application. In many ways this component reflects the user's view of the semantics of the application. It must provide the operations that the user wants to perform in the application. If a particular operator is missing the user must construct a sequence of operators which has the same effect, and this may not always be possible. This imposes a greater cognitive load on the user than invoking a single command.

The design of both the presentation component and the application interface model require a user's model of the application. In this context a user's model is the model the user has of the application. This model exists in the user's mind and he is usually not aware of it. There are two problems with user's models. The first is, how do we determine the model the user has of the application? Since the user is usually not aware of this model, he cannot produce a written version of it. It may be possible to interview the user, and then construct an approximate model from the results of the interview. But, we currently have no way of knowing if this model is correct. The second problem is, given that it is hard to extract the user's model from the user, is it possible to design a user's model, and then transfer it to the user? If this were possible the first problem disappears, and we are left with the problems of designing good user's models and transferring them to the user. The problems of user's modeling are beyond the scope of this workshop, but these problems must be addressed in order to design good user interfaces.

The second human factors issue, the evaluation of user interface descriptions, is motivated by the precise descriptions of the user interface that are produced when a UIMS is used. The main purpose of these descriptions is to facilitate the automatic or semi-automatic production of a user interface. But, when such descriptions exist there is a great potential to use them for other purposes. Some techniques have already been developed for user interface evaluation. The best known of these are the grammar based techniques of Reisner, and the keystroke model of Card, Moran, and Newell. Both of these techniques require a complete description of the user interface. A UIMS should produce a human factors evaluation of a user interface at the same time it was producing the implementation of it. This would give the user interface designer a feel for how the user interface will perform, and where it could be improved. This could lead to a process of user interface debugging similar to the programming language debugging that is currently done with compiler generators.

NOTATIONS

Over the past few years a number of UIMSs have been designed and implemented. All of these systems have, in some form or another, the three user interface components identified in section 1. The designers of these systems have developed notations for these components, largely without knowledge of what other UIMS designers were doing. One of the major goals of this working group was to analyze, and attempt to classify the notations that have been used in UIMSs. The classification scheme presented here is by no means complete, but it does cover most of the existing UIMSs. It is interesting to note that most of the members of this working group already had a classification scheme in mind before the workshop. The classification scheme that resulted from our discussions does not differ radically from any of these preconceived schemes.

Our classification scheme is based on the three user interface components. Each component has its own set of notations. The notations for dialogue control are further divided into three groups.

Presentation Component

For the presentation component the notations must deal with both input and output. At the present time output notations deal mainly with graphical output. The range of these notations should be extended to cover sound, touch, and movement (as in robotics). Most of the notations for graphical output are based on the routines provided by standard graphics packages. Calls to these routines are combined to form the symbols presented to the user. This form of notation is very similar to a programming language, and in most cases the target language of the UIMS is used as the basis for the notation.

This is not an acceptable form of notation, for the following two reasons. First, a textual language is used to describe something that is graphical in nature. As a result the notation is both hard to use and read. Given a collection of subroutine calls it is not an easy task to determine the image they produce on the display screen. What is really required is a graphical notation for the output symbols. One attempt at this can be found in the MENULAY system [Buxton et.al. 1983]. Second, by using a programming language notation the user interface designer is forced to do the work of the UIMS. The user interface designer should produce a high level description of the symbol, and let the UIMS convert it into a program.

A similar situation exists on the input side of presentation component notations. In most cases the input primitives provided by a graphics package are used as the input symbols generated by the user. Most of the UIMSs do not provide a mechanism for combining the input primitives into more complex symbols at the presentation level. Currently this function is performed by the dialogue control component. The range of input primitive should be extended to cover video, voice, and more complicated body gestures (such as character recognition). As of yet no really useful input notations have appeared.

The last issue to be dealt with in presentation component notations is the external-internal mapping. This mapping is controlled by the dialogue control component, but it resides in the presentation component. There are several issues associated with this mapping. The first is whether the mapping is a simple table lookup, or can some form of simple decision making be involved. These decisions could be based on the values of the token. For example, the presentation of an output token may depend upon the magnitude of its values. A detailed presentation would be given for small values, and an overview for large values. If decision making is included in the mapping what form should it take, and how would it be expressed? The presentation component contains the definitions of internal and external tokens. The dialogue control component must be able to reference these tokens in order to establish the mapping between them. How does the presentation component assign a name to the tokens, and how are these names passed to the dialogue control component? These issues must be addressed in any notation for the presentation component.

Dialogue Control Component

The dialogue control component has the most highly developed notations. Since most of the existing UIMSs have concentrated on this component, it has more notations and there is considerably more experience with their use. The notations that have been used for this component mainly fall into three groups. The major difference between these groups is the model the notations have of the user interface. The transition network notations view the user interface as a collection of states, and the user's actions cause transitions between these states. The grammar group views the dialogue between the user and the computer as a language, and uses grammar based techniques to describe this interaction. The event group views the user interface as a collection of events and event handlers. When the user interacts with the computer, one or more events are generated, which are processed by the event handlers, possibly generating more events. This is not a complete classification scheme for dialogue control notations, since at least one well known system does not fit (the Tiger system of Kasik [Kasik 1982]).

The transition network group is the oldest group of notations for dialogue control. This approach to user interface management dates back to at least 1968 with the work of Newman [Newman 1968]. This style of notation has been used in a number of systems since that time, and a considerable amount of experience has been gained in its use. A pure transition network, consisting solely of states and transitions between these states, is not powerful enough to handle a wide range of user interfaces, and tends to be hard to use. This is due to the fact that most user interface have a large number of states, with a large number of possible transitions between them. As a result, several schemes have been developed for partitioning the network. One approach is the user of subnetworks. A subnetwork is an independent transition network having its own set of states and transitions. A subnetwork can be used to replace any of the states or transitions in another network. Once a subnetwork has been entered it retains control of the dialogue until one of its terminal states is reached. When this happens control returns to the point, in the calling network, where the subnetwork was invoked. Thus, compound dialogues can be built up from smaller dialogues, each represented by a subnetwork. An extension of this approach is recursive transition networks or RTNs, where the subnetworks are capable of invoking themselves recursively. Experience with transition networks indicates that RTNs are necessary to handle the types of user interfaces that arise in practice. An example of a notation based on RTNs is SYNICS [Edmonds 1981].

Experience with transition network based systems indicated that a multi-threaded implementation is desirable. This allows the user to interact with several networks at the same time. This can be used in help processing, where there is a separate network for the help command. The user can invoke the help network without fear of losing his place in the original dialogue.

The grammar based notations use techniques from programming languages for both the description, and implementation of the dialogue control component. These notations are based on using context free grammar to describe the dialogue between the user and the program. As with transition diagrams, pure context free grammars do not form an ideal notation for the dialogue control component, so numerous extensions have been made. Most of these extensions give the dialogue designer more control over the order in which the user's input is parsed. For example, it may be possible to specify that the ordering of the symbols in a production is arbitrary. This allows the user to enter these symbols in any order. Other extensions deal with error detection, error recovery, and the ability to undo parts of the dialogue. It should be noted that the descriptive power of RTNs and context free grammars is the same. There is some indication that RTNs may be easier to use than context free grammars. Two examples of grammar based notations are SYNGRAPH [Olsen and Dempsey 1983] and DIALOG [Derksen 1983] [Borufka,. et.al. 1982]. Closely related to this approach is the work of van den Bos [van den Bos 1980].

The event model is not as well known, or as highly developed as the other two groups of dialogue control notations. Since the event model is not widely known a brief description of it is presented here. The event notations are based on the concepts of events, and special procedures called event handlers. In may ways events are similar to the input and output tokens discussed in section 1. Each event has a name and a collection of data values. An event is generated each time the user interacts with an input device. These events are processed by one or more of the event handlers associated with the input, or display device involved in the interaction. An event handler is a procedure that performs a set of actions based on the name of the event it receives. These actions include passing output tokens to the presentation component, passing input tokens to the application interface model, performing some calculation, or generating new events. The collection of events processed by an event handler can be viewed as a state. The set of event handlers active (able to receive events) at any one time defines the legal user actions at that point in the dialogue. This set can be changed by disassociating an event handler with a particular device, or associating an new event handler with a device. An event may be sent to more than one event handler. In this case each event handler is responsible for one aspect of the event's processing, such as the different levels of feedback, error checking, and routing to high levels of the user interface. The event model is in many ways similar to object oriented programming as in Smalltalk [Goldberg and Robson 1983].

Most of the event based notations have the appearance of programming languages. This is mainly due to the procedural nature of the event handlers. These notations need some way of describing both the events, and how the events are processed. In most notations both of these components are combined into one description, that of the event handler. That is, each event handler defines all the events it can receive, even if these events are used in several event handlers. This results in self contained event handlers, at the price of increasing the redundancy of the descriptions, and possibly introducing inconsistencies. The description of an event handler contains one section for each of the events it can process. The section for an event starts with a description of the event itself, followed by the sequence of actions required to process the event.

Application Interface Model

Since the application interface model has not explicitly appeared in an existing UIMS, there have been no notations developed for it. In most UIMSs the application procedures called by the user interface form an implicit application interface model. While this identifies the application procedure used by the user interface, it tells us very little about the application, and these calls are usually embedded in other descriptions making them hard to find. The application interface model must contain certain information about the application. To be useful the application interface model must cover at least the following three areas. First, it must contain a description of the application data structures that are of interest to the user and the user interface. The description of these data structure is at an abstract level, and implementation details are usually not important. The UIMS only needs to know the information that is stored in the data structures, and how it can find it. Second, there must be a description of the application procedures available to the user interface. This description must include the name of the procedure, and the operands it expects. This part of the description defines the interface between the user interface and the application. Third, the constraints on the application of the operators must be outlined. These constraints include any pre-conditions for the operators, and any ordering restrictions on them. This allows the user interface to filter out some of the semantically illegal operations before they reach the application. While this is the minimum amount of information that must be included in the application interface model, there are several other things that would be useful. One of these is the effects, or post-conditions of the operators. This allows the user interface to anticipate the effects of commands, provide automatic help, and automatically perform some undo processing. Another useful component of an application interface model is procedures for performing standard tasks in the application. These procedures could be used by the user interface to guide naive users, and provide sophisticated help facilities.

Since notations for the applications interface model have not been developed, a classification scheme for them cannot be presented. Instead, several possible notations are presented, along with several of the issues that arose in our discussions. One possible notation is objects and operators. The objects correspond to the data structures in the application program, and the operators correspond to the application procedure available to the user interface. A notation of this kind, called UML, is described in [Green 1981] and [Green 1984]. In order to handle a wide range of user interfaces this type of notation must treat object descriptions as type definitions, and allow the creation of arbitrary numbers of object instances. In a number of applications a network of objects is required, so notations that only support object hierarchies are not desirable. Another issue related to this type of notation is the parameters to the operators. An operator definition will contain a number of implicit parameters, but should these be the only objects available to the operator? Should there be global objects that represent the context of the interaction? If there are, how are these global objects defined and referenced?

Another possible notation for the application interface model is based on relations (as in relational database [Date 1981]), and first order logic. This idea was prompted by the work done by Garret and Foley in graphical databases [Garret and Foley 1982]. The relations are used to represent the data structures in the application, while statements in first order logic model the effect of the application procedures.

Two issues that must be addressed by any notation for this component are invariants, and sequential relationships between application procedures. Invariants state properties of the application that are always true. There are two reasons why they are a useful part of the applications interface model. First, they form a concise description of general properties of the application. In most cases these properties could be described by other means, but this will usually entail a large amount of redundant material. Second, the UIMS can use them to detect errors in user input, and as the basis for guiding the user through interaction sequences. One issue related to invariants is whether they should be passive or active. A passive invariant describes some property of the application, while an active invariant takes an active part in the computation. That is, either the application, or the UIMS will perform whatever actions required to maintain the truth of an active invariant.

Some of the procedures in the application cannot be performed in arbitrary sequences. For example, a file cannot be processed until it is open, therefore an open call must always precede any read or writes on the file. This is an example of a sequencing constraint.

INTERRELATIONS BETWEEN COMPONENTS

Figure 1 shows the interfaces between the components in our model of a user interface. These interfaces represent the flow of information or control between the components. In order to completely describe the user interface, the nature of these interfaces must be understood.

There are two issues related to the interface between the presentation component and dialogue control component that effect user interface notations. One of these issues is the form of the tokens flowing between these components. The are a number of ways in which this flow can be viewed. In one view, dialogue control treats the presentation component as a collection of logical devices. In this view there are problems related to the definition of device classes, and device characteristics. One device characteristic is the type of the value produced by the device. Most graphics packages have a fixed set of types that can be used for device values. In the case of the presentation component, a fixed type structure may be too restrictive. On the other hand, the full type definition facilities of modern programming languages may be more than is required here, and needlessly complicate the interface between these components. Work needs to be done on the set of types required to support the communications between these two components. A related issue is the handling of picks. In existing graphics packages there is one type for all pickable objects. This type usually refers to the display file segment containing the object selected, and not the object itself. With the presentation component, each pickable object type could have its own device type, and the pick would contain a pointer into the application data structure identifying the object selected. This would relieve the dialogue control component of determining the object selected by the user. Another important device characteristic is its mode (as in the GKS model of graphical input [Rosenthal et.al. 1982]). What are the interpretations of event, sample, and request modes at the level of the presentation component? If the logical device view is not taken, some of these issues disappear. Another view of this interface is to treat the output of the presentation component as a simple stream of tokens, without any information on the devices that produced them (either logical or physical). In this view the problem of device modes does not occur, but the type problems remain.

Another important feature of this interface is the manner in which dialogue control exerts its control over the presentation component. Dialogue control is responsible for the state of the presentation component, it controls the external-internal mapping. How much information does dialogue control need in order to adequately perform this function? It must at least know the names of all the internal and external tokens, otherwise it will not be able to define the mapping. But, does it need more detailed information about these tokens? For example, should the physical devices associated with the external tokens be available to dialogue control? Or, is there a set of general device properties that would serve its needs? Another issue is whether dialogue control or the presentation component is responsible for enabling or initializing devices. The presentation component deals directly with the devices, so there is some argument for having it responsible for device initialization and control. On the other hand, dialogue control is responsible for the state of the presentation component, so it knows when the devices should be enabled. It may be necessary to share this responsibility between these two components.

At the present time there are far more issues associated with this interface than there are answers. More experience with UIMS implementations is required before a more detailed description of this interface can be produced.

The major issue associated with the interface between dialogue control and the application interface model, is the access dialogue control has to the application data structure. In particular, can dialogue control directly access the application data structure without informing the application? An argument can be made that dialogue control must always call an application routine whenever it wants to change the application data structure. This isolates the user interface from the implementation of the application data structure, and ensures that all modifications to the data structure are legal. On the other hand, this approach can be too inefficient for some applications, and places the burden of error recovery and undo processing on the application. This was an issue at the previous workshop is Seattle, and still appears to be unresolved. One possible, but inefficient, solution is to give the UIMS its own copy of the application data structure. The UIMS is free to modify this data structure without informing the application routines. At key points in the dialogue (determined by dialogue control) the UIMS copy of the data structure is used to update the application copy. In this approach error recovery and undo processing can easily be accomplished by restoring the UIMS copy of the data structure from the application's version.

There are two issues associated with the interface between the presentation component and the application interface model. The first issue deals with picking. The result of a picking operation should be some object in the application data structure that is currently displayed on the screen. The presentation component is responsible for the allocation of screen space, and the appearance of everything on the screen. But, it does not know about the application data structure. When a pick occurs the presentation component knows the coordinates of the pick, but it doesn't know how to relate these coordinates to the contents of the application data structure. Some form of cooperation between the two components is required to determine the object the user selected. There needs to be some correlation mechanism between the coordinates in the presentation component, and the data structure maintained by the application.

The other issue involves the flow of output data from the application to the presentation component. In theory, all the information from the application, that is to be displayed, must go through dialogue control. In most cases dialogue control is not interested in the actual data, it assigns the data a format or template, and passes it on to the presentation component. Since dialogue control does not need to process this data, it could be directly transferred to the presentation component, saving some processing time. This flow of data is represented by the arc flowing from the application interface model to the presentation component in fig. 1. Dialogue control has control over this flow of information, it assigns the formats to the output data, and establishes the pipe line between the application and the presentation component. Once the pipe line has been established, dialogue control does not take part in the information transfer. This approach is particularly effective when large amounts of data must be transferred from the application to the screen.

SUMMARY

In this report we have presented some of the issues pertaining to the notations used in UIMSs. At the present time there are a small number of implemented UIMSs, so there is some experience to draw upon. This is the first workshop of this nature where there has been a significant number of participants with implementation experience. This experience seemed to raise more issues than it resolved. The conclusion that can be drawn from this is there is still a considerable amount of work to be done in notations for UIMSs.

One of the major problems encountered by this working group was the inability to compare different UIMSs. The systems discussed in this group have been used to produce user interfaces for different application areas, with different interaction styles and requirements. This makes it very difficult to compare the ease of use (for the user interface designer), and the quality of the resulting user interface. This problem could be partially solved by constructing a standard set of user interface problems. Each of the UIMSs could be used to solve these problems, and the results used as a means of comparison. This set of problems could be viewed as a benchmark test for user interface management systems. Along with developing the problems, techniques for measuring ease of use and the quality of the user interface must also be developed.

REFERENCES

[Aho and Ullman 1977] Aho A.V., J.D. Ullman, *Principles of Compiler Design*, Addison-Wesley, Reading Mass., 1977.

[Borufka, et.al. 1982] Borufka, H.G., H.W. Kuhlmann, P.J.W. ten Hagen, "Dialogue Cells: A Method for Defining Interactions", IEEE Computer Graphics and Applications, vol.2 no.5, p.25, 1982.

[Buxton et.al. 1983] Buxton W., M.R. Lamb, D. Sherman, K.C. Smith, "Towards a Comprehensive User Interface Management System", SIG-

GRAPH'83, p.35, 1983.

[Date 1981] Date C.J., *An Introduction to Database Systems*, Addison-Wesley, Reading Mass., 1981.

[Derksen 1983] Derksen J., "Een ontwerp van programmeergereedschap vocr dialoogsystemen gebaseerd op dialoogcellen (Tools for dialogue systems based on dialogue cells)", TNO-IBBC rapport nr. B1-83-62/68.0.0004, 1983 (in Dutch).

[Edmonds 1982] Edmonds E.A., "The man-computer interface - a note on concepts and design", Int. J. Man-Machine Studies, vol.16, p.231, 1982.

[Edmonds 1981] Edmonds E.A., "Adaptive Man-Computer Interfaces", in Coombs M.J., J.L. Alty (ed.), *Computing Skills and the User Interface*, Academic Press, London, 1981.

[Foley and Van Dam 1982] Foley J., A. Van Dam, *Fundamentals of Interactive Computer Graphics*, Addison-Wesley, Reading Mass., 1982.

[Garret and Foley 1982] Garret M.T., J.D. Foley, "Graphics Programming Using a Database System with Dependency Declarations". ACM Transactions on Graphics, vol.1, no.2, p.109, 1982.

[Goldberg and Robson 1983] Goldberg A., D. Robson, *Smalltalk-80: The Language and its Implementation*, Addison-Wesley, Reading Mass., 1983.

[Green 1984] Green M., "Design Notations and User Interface Management Systems", in this volume, 1984.

[Green 1981] Green M., "A Methodology for the Specification of Graphical User Interfaces", SIGGRAPH'81, p.99, 1981.

[Kasik 1982] Kasik D.J., "A user Interface Management System", SIGGRAPH'82, p.99, 1982.

[Newman 1968] Newman W.M., "A System for Interactive Graphical Programming", SJCC 1968, Thompson Books, Washington DC., 1968.

[Olsen 1984] Olsen D., "Presentational, Syntactic and Semantic Components of Interactive Dialogue Specification", in this volume, 1984.

[Olsen and Dempsey 1983] Olsen D., E. Dempsey, "SYNGRAPH: A Graphic User Interface Generator", SIGGRAPH'83, p.43, 1983.

[Rosenthal et.al. 1982] Rosenthal D.S.H., J.C. Michener, G.Pfaff, R. Kessener, M. Sabin, "The Detailed Semantics of Graphics Input Devices", SIGGRAPH'82, p.33, 1982.

[van den Bos 1980] van den Bos, J., "High-level graphics input tools and their semantics", in Guedj, R.A., et.al. (eds.), *Methodology of Interaction*, North Holland, p.159, 1980.

Working Group Members:
Jan Derksen, Ernest Edmonds, Mark Green, Dan Olsen, Robert Spence

Report on the Interface of the UIMS to the Application

G. Enderle

SEL AG, Helmuth-Hirth-Strasse 42, 7000 Stuttgart 40, Federal Republic of Germany

SCOPE AND GOAL

The goal of the workshop was to find, evaluate, and describe models, principles, methods, and tasks for the design of User Interface Management Systems. This working group concentrated on aspects of this overall goal that are related to the interface between the application and the UIMS.

One application was given specific attention: Computer Aided Design (CAD). CAD is an application that, on one hand, relies on Computer Graphics as one basic component of the whole system. On the other hand, CAD is also an application area where a favourable user interface is of special importance. The application is the most relevant part of the interactive system. If we look at the application-UIMS interface from the viewpoint of the application, we can identify certain requirements which a UIMS must fulfil to serve the application in an optimal way. A problem of specific interest at the application-UIMS interface is the division of responsibility for graphical output between the application and the UIMS.

PROBLEM AREAS

Three major problem areas related to the application interface of a UIMS were addressed:

- The configuration of a UIMS with respect to a specific application,

- The responsibility for creating and managing graphical output,

- The services and functions available at the communication interface between the application and the UIMS.

In order to gain a common base for the discussion of these questions, an overall structure of the interactive system had to be agreed on. In all problem areas, special attention was paid to CAD aspects.

STRUCTURE OF USER INTERFACE MANAGEMENT SYSTEMS

The application-UIMS interface can be situated at different places within the overall system depending on the design of the structure of the system. A discussion of problems related to an interface can only be successful on the base of an agreed system structure. However, since it was not the goal of this workshop to select and prescribe one specific system structure, the application-UIMS interface was identified in several UIMS system structures. An attempt was made to address the problem areas in a way that the principles and solutions stated can be applied to all UIMS structures.

Two of the UIMS structures were the result of the Seattle Workshop on Interactive Techniques: External control and Internal control. Figures 1 and 2 show these structures with the application-UIMS interface.

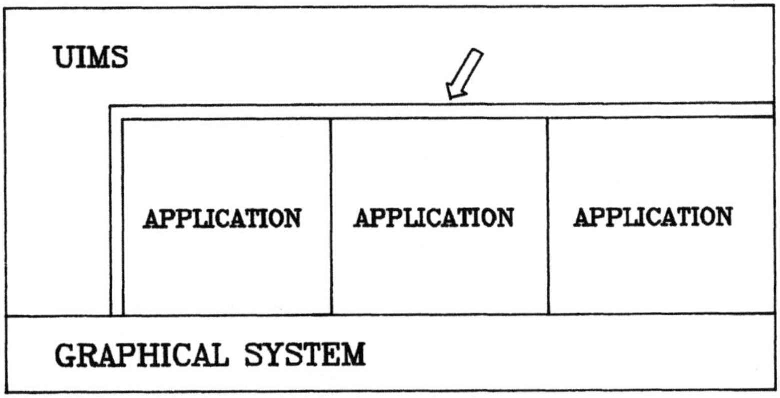

Fig. 1. External control

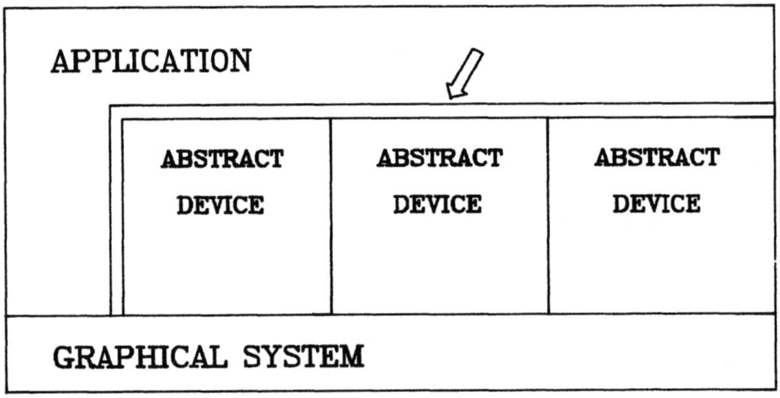

Fig. 2. Internal control

A third structure was identified where the application, the UIMS and the graphics package are on one level. They are parallel processes that are synchronized by means of multitasking facilities. The processes exchange information between them, one of the interfaces is the application-UIMS interface (see Fig. 3).

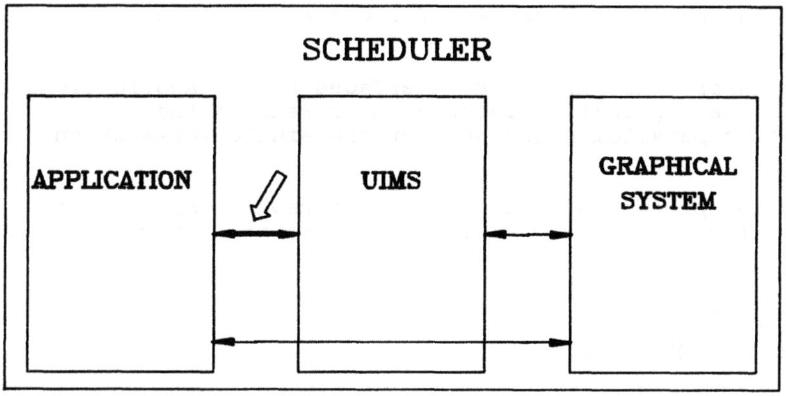

Fig. 3. Parallel processes

In the course of describing the parallel system structure, an interesting new question was identified, that deserves more investigation in the future: Multiple parallel interactive processes. This means that one user, at one workstation, deals with different independent applications. In many cases, such a technique presents itself to the user by a number of windows on a screen, where every window is associated with a different application process running (see figure 4). The user selects the one process with which he wants to communicate, e.g., by moving the cursor into one of the windows.

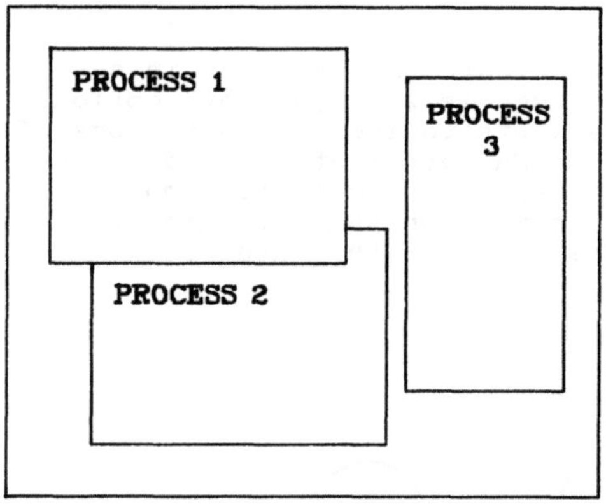

Fig. 4. Windows associated with different application processes

How does a UIMS handle this type of parallel processing? There are (at least) two obvious possibilities:

- Every application has its own UIMS and one interface to this own UIMS. In addition, one "Master UIMS" coordinates and manages the overlaying of the parallel processes for one workstation (see Fig. 5).

- There is one "Super UIMS" that has interfaces to all applications. It handles all the application interfaces as well as the overlaying of the parallel processes for the single workstation (see Fig. 6).

This type of parallel processing will add considerable complexity to the interactive system. Complexity will increase if it is required that

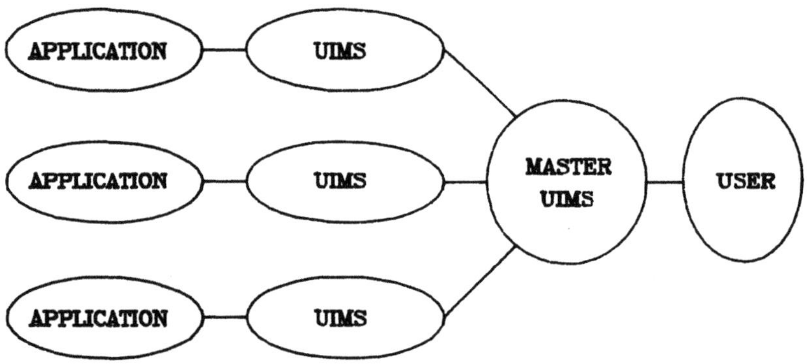

Fig. 5. Parallel application processes and UIMS's, one Master UIMS

the different application processes communicate. An example: in a typesetting application with a "what you see is what you get" option, the user identifies a block of text. He wants to include this block of text in a drawing under construction in a CAD application by dragging it across the boundary of the two processes. Clean concepts and principles are needed for handling this situation and retaining a favourable user interface. There remains work for the future.

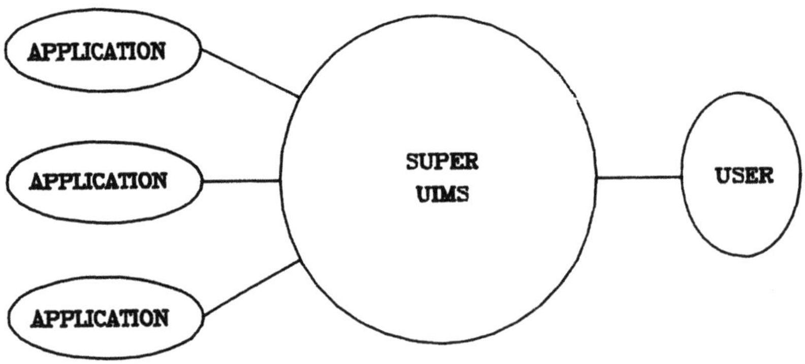

Fig. 6. Parallel application processes, one Super UIMS

TWO GRAPHICS MODES

In the course of evaluating the properties and functions of the interface between the application and the UIMS, two modes of graphics output could be identified that are related to the role of the graphics for the application within the interactive system:

I. Direct graphics: These are direct representations of the application data base that is being created and modified by the interactive process. Examples are:

   - Painting systems and film animation, where a graphical representation in many cases is the only result of the interactive process.

   - CAD systems, where normally one of the results of the design process is a number of drawings, graphical representations of FEM-nets or of results.

   - Business graphics systems, slide production systems.

II. Symbolic graphics: These graphics are used to support the interactive process and enhance the user interface. They are not the final result of the application. There are many examples for this category:

   - Simulation systems, which may have as their primary result the record of a sequence of events, actions and reactions that are a mapping of the real world processes to be simulated.

   - In a computer chess game, graphics are used to display the state of the game to the user, the result of the game, however, is the sequence of moves.

Of course, certain applications which primarily use direct graphics, may well use symbolic graphics for handling the interaction. In the following chapters we will see that the support of the two graphics modes will have different properties and UIMS requirements.

CONFIGURATION OF A UIMS WITH RESPECT TO A SPECIFIC APPLICATION

One question in this area is whether or not it is possible to design a UIMS as a universal tool that can be used for many types of applications. If such a tool can be designed that can be configured and adapted to several kinds of applications, the next question is which are the parts of the UIMS that have to be changed in the configuration process. The following application oriented components of the dialog specification have been identified ("dialog" is the term describing the actual interactive process when the user is communicating with the system, "dialog specification" are those parts of the UIMS that define the set of possible dialogs):

- menues, screen layout, tablet layout;

- error messages to be displayed to the user;

- help messages to be displayed to the user;

- prompts (text prompts, graphics, acoustics);
- icons (icons are graphical symbols that are defined at UIMS configuration time, they are used for user communication);
- list of task names (e.g., application subroutines to be called by the UIMS, UIMS subroutines to be called by the application);
- list of variable names (they define the address space common to the application and the UIMS);
- mechanism for UIMS/application communication (message passing, global common, subroutine parameter passing);
- selection of interaction techniques (the UIMS should offer a number of such techniques that can be selected at configuration time);
- constraints on graphical output (e.g., only drawings of a certain scale might be allowed on certain output devices);
- constraints on graphical context (e.g., colours assigned by the application have specific meanings, they are not to be changed by the UIMS);
- constraints on graphical input (e.g., locator values are only allowed on a grid).

Besides the dialog specification, the responsibility for output can change if the application changes (see next chapter).

GRAPHICAL OUTPUT

There are a number of questions when dealing with the generation of graphical output within an interactive system. The first question is which component is responsible for graphical output, the UIMS or the application. Especially, which component is responsible for the mapping of application data structure to the graphical representation? In the other direction, who does the mapping of graphical input to the application data structure for picking? If data has to be passed between application and UIMS, should that be done by sharing data structures or by duplicating data structures? The following are suggestions that were agreed on with the aim of keeping application related functions within the application while grouping general user interface management functions within the UIMS. This should allow the design of a UIMS as a universal tool that can be configured to a specific application without changing the whole structure of the UIMS.

The responsibility for graphical output depends on the type of the application. The application is responsible for creating the graphical output for direct graphics. This output is created at the run-time of the interactive process. The mapping of application data structures to a graphical representation is the task of the application program. For symbolic graphics, the UIMS will generate graphical output. The basic tokens of this output (the icons) are designed at configuration time. The mapping of application data structures to a graphical representation is done by the UIMS (e.g., the state of a chess game is mapped to the picture of a chessboard with pieces). For both modes of graphics, the management of the output (device control, window management) is done by the UIMS

For direct graphics, the application data structures often have to be made available to the UIMS, so it can control output generation and picking. How this access is achieved is a software engineering problem that needs not to be dealt with in this UIMS-related context. A duplication of data structures should be avoided (to avoid consistency problems). For modification of application data as a result of a user request, the UIMS should activate a service of the application for the UIMS. One such service could be to ask the application for permission to change a value, changing the value, and notifying the application that the value has been changed. All data that is only related to the functions of the UIMS are contained in a UIMS data structure that cannot be accessed by the application.

PICKING

The responsibility for interpreting a pick input is also dependent on the type of objects being picked. For direct graphics objects, interpreting the pick input is done by the application. The setting of the pick context (the scope of the picking) is done by the UIMS using application data. For symbolic graphics, both the interpretation of the pick input and the setting of the picking context is done by the UIMS.

THE COMMUNICATION INTERFACE BETWEEN APPLICATION AND UIMS

The communication interface between the application and the UIMS defines a set of services (tasks performed by one component at the request of the other component) and protocols (syntax for the communication needed to accomplish services) that allow cooperation between the two processes. Naturally, these protocols differ for different system structures (see chapter 2). For external control, the interface will always be controlled by the UIMS, for internal control by the application. For parallel processes, the control of the communication interface can be symmetrical, functions can be invoked in either way. The following is a list of functions irrespective of the system structure:

- Services of the UIMS for the application and corresponding protocols,
- services of the application for the UIMS and corresponding protocols,
- handling feedback loops over the application,
- managing areas like graphics output context (e.g., window management), error handling, help on application errors, undoing, backing out, journaling, checkpointing and restarting.

Table 1 shows the services which have been identified. Services of the UIMS for the application are most important for internal control structures. Services of the application for the UIMS support external control structures. For parallel processes, both types of services are necessary.

Table 1: Services at the application - UIMS interface

Services of the UIMS for the application	Services of the application for the UIMS
* Give a value matching constraints	* Give a value (e.g., for use in help functions)
* Switch input sources (e.g., between user and journal)	* Give a value to be used instead of user input
* Tell the user a value	* Perform graphics update
* Display some graphics	* Set application state variable to a given value
* Handle an application error	* Grant permission to change application data
* Set output context	* Give pick support
* Set dialog scope	* Give task status
	* (Re-) Set task status to a (previously saved) state
* Undo something	* Undo something

CAD/CAM ASPECTS

There are certain characteristics that are specific to CAD applications and similar application areas. Since one final result of a CAD/CAM application is a graphical representation (scaled and dimensioned drawings, representations of 3D objects, of FEM nets, and of results of calculations), it primarily uses direct graphics. The graphical representations are so specific to the application that they are part of the application. Also the contents of the interactive technique library can be very specific to the application. They need redesigning as the application changes. Therefore, they must be considered part of the application. In the CAD area, many constraints are imposed on the user and the UIMS by the application (e.g., prescribed scalings or the conformance to standards). In a CAD application, feedback loops will be executed in more cases with the application involved than in other areas.

CONCLUSIONS

It seems that it is possible to design a User Interface Management System as a general tool that can serve a range of different applications and still serve the user and the application in an excellent way. In a configuration phase, the UIMS will be adapted to the needs of the application without redesigning all or major parts of it.

The one universal tool is not yet existing, however, in this workshop a number of principles and functions have been identified that can serve as guidelines for setting up such a general UIMS. Working group GAMMA addressed in particular problems related to the interface between the application and the UIMS and functions and services needed at that interface. Special attention was given to the area of CAD/CAM. This is a very complex application. If the ideas outlined in this report could be demonstrated to work in the context of a CAD/CAM application, this would be good evidence that such a configurable UIMS could serve a wide range of other applications as well.

Report on the User's Conceptual Model

M. Mac an Airchinnigh

Department of Computer Science, University of Dublin, Trinity College, Dublin, Ireland

INTRODUCTION

The members of Working Group Omega originally belonged to Working Group Beta and, therefore, their deliberations ought to be seen in the context of that Working Group. Already at Seillac II (Guedj et al. 1980), the issue of the user's conceptual model (UCM) received serious attention. We felt that the time was ripe to make an attempt at the formal specification of such user conceptual models. As a starting point we take the following definition of a UCM:

> A UCM is the set of all concepts and conceptual relations possessed by a (human) user with respect to some set of entities. To each UCM there corresponds a universe of discourse that is the expression of those concepts and conceptual relations.

The M-notation, introduced in (Mac an Airchinnigh 1984), may be used as a basis for further development. Specifically, a user *u* possesses a conceptual model *M* of some application domain *a*. This UCM may then be denoted by *M(u,a)*. It must be emphasised that such UCMs exist solely and entirely in the minds of their owners! The next step is to consider how to represent such UCMs. The following section contains the details. Let *u*, *c*, *a* denote a user, a computer system, an application domain, respectively. Then the following figure shows some of the M relations:

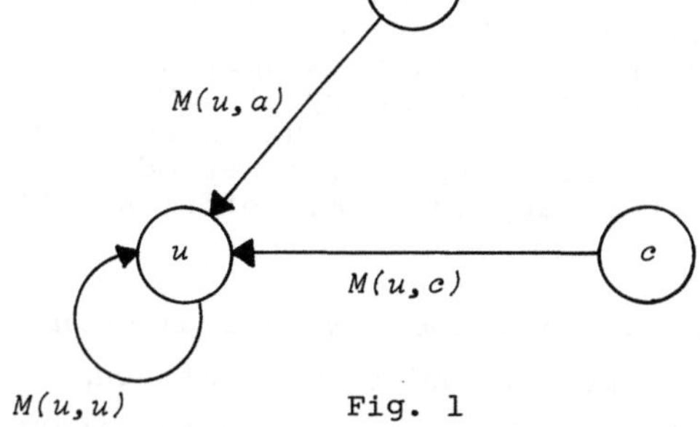

Fig. 1

M(u,u) denotes a UCM that *u* has of herself, *M(u,c)* denotes a UCM that *u* has of the computer system *c*, and *M(u,a)* denotes a UCM that *u* has of some application domain *a*. Diagrams such as that of Fig. 1 are always subject to misinterpretation. The reader is cautioned against reading too much into any of the diagrams presented in this Working Group report. For example, with respect to Fig. 1, the following extra relations hold:

- c may be considered to be a member of a;
- u may never be considered to be a member of a.

The latter relation may be deemed to be an axiom of the theory of UCMs.

Although originally presented in the context of Ada[1] and Ada packages, the categorisation of users into designers, implementors, and end-users with respect to a software component, is thought to be useful (Mac an Airchinnigh 1984). These categories and their relationships to a software component may be illustrated by a figure such as the following:

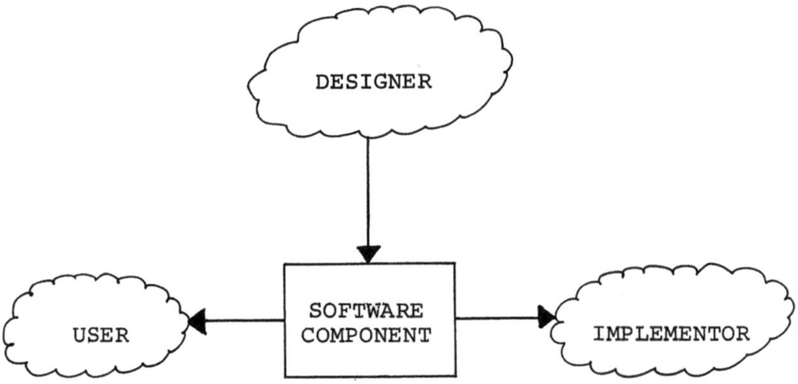

Fig. 2

The direction of the arrows is intended to indicate the information flow. To try to avoid misinterpretation, the section on Categories of Users is a further elaboration of this.

UCMs are not the concern of computer scientists only! They have been and are the subject of research by philosophers, linguists, and psychologists. We believe that we can build on the work of all these people now and thus advance the theory of UCMs one step further. As a starting point, we adopt the subjective approach, i.e. introspec-spection, in our construction of a theory of UCMs. The approach of Jacques Hadamard (1945) in his work on "The Psychology of Invention in the Mathematical Field" illustrates the method. However, we are aware of the dangers of this approach (Schneiderman 1980). The method itself is simple:

- I, as a user, think about what I am doing;
- I reach conclusions and form hypotheses;
- I express these hypotheses using an accepted terminology;
- The formulated hypotheses are subjected to peer review and are either accepted or rejected.

1 Ada is a registered trademark of the U.S. Government, ALO.

Therefore, the theory of UCMs that we propose, is to be subject to critical review by philosophers, linguists, psychologists, and computer scientists. As a basis for the terminology in which to express our hypotheses, we have chosen the conceptual graph notation (CG-notation) of (Sowa 1983). There is a section in the report devoted to this topic. We would hope that such an embryonic theory of UCMs will form a basis for research and discussion at future Workshops.

We believe that the time is ripe for the development of a terminology that will, in a sense, be a standard for use by researchers in the field of human-computer interaction. In the context of this Seeheim Workshop, we felt that terms such as "dialogue", "interaction", "feedback", etc., needed to be defined more precisely. This working group spent time on trying to formulate such definitions. The pen-ultimate section of the report contains some of the results.

THE M-R-C NOTATION

The Working Group refined the original M-notation. $M(u,e)$ denotes the UCM that user u has of entity e. Such a UCM exists only in the mind of the user u. This immediately implies that only human beings can possess UCMs! We hypothesise that given some formal system F and associated notation, we can find a representation R of M. We denote such a representation by $R(M,F)$. Of course, we may only be able to find an R that approximates M, using F. The formalism that we have chosen is the CG-notation. However, for this representation to be useful in a "computable" sense, we have to be able to encode such a representation R. Let P be a computer programming language and S a set of semantics. Then $C(R,P,S)$ is said to be an encoding of the representation R, using the programming language P and semantics S. Again, it is possible that we will only be able to achieve a C that is an approximation of the R. These relationships between M, R, and C, may be expressed in terms of the descending chain:

$$\begin{array}{ccccc} M & \triangleright & R & \triangleright & C \\ \| & & \| & & \| \\ M(u,a) & & R(M,F) & & C(R,P,S) \end{array}$$

Fig. 3

The symbol "$\triangleright$" denotes the relation "is approximated by". A User Interface Management System (UIMS) would be expected to use a set of $C(R,P,S)$ in the specification, implementation, and maintenance of human-computer dialogue. The construction of R from M must proceed by the method of introspection mentioned above. Hence, the extent to which R is a valid representation of M, depends on agreement by con-sensus. The theory of UCMs is, therefore, the theory of the constructability of $R(M,F)$. The members of the Working Group spent much of their time addressing this issue.

CATEGORIES OF USERS

A typical scenario, involving the designer d, the implementor i, and the end-user u, with respect to some application domain a, will try to convey the meaning intended by Fig. 2 above. The designer has a UCM $M_1 = M(d,a)$. Using CG-notation, we represent this model by

$R_1 = R(M_1,F)$. The designer d then produces a software component using a programming language P and semantics S. We denote this by $C_1 = C(R_1,P,S)$. (In general, there may be two distinct but related encodings: $C(R_1,P_1,S_1)$, which is an encoding of the representation R_1 of the designer's conceptual model using programming language P_1 and semantics S_1. Here P_1 is a programming language used for the implementation of the knowledge representation language F. However, a second and perhaps different programming language P_2 with semantics S_2 may be used for the target language of the software component specification. This is encoding $C(R_1,P_2,S_2)$.). Rather than distinguishing between these different encodings, we will continue with the more simplistic approach. The implementor i, upon receiving C_1, is able to form her own UCM of the application domain. We denote this model by $M_2 = M(i,a)$. Analogous forms R_2 and C_2 are also constructed. C_2 is said to be the implementation of the software component. The end-user u, who has the UCM $M_3 = M(u,a)$, also has access to C_1 which is essentially the set of objects and operations upon those objects that may be carried out by u. Ideally, $C_1 = C(R(M(d,a),F),P,S)$, which is the intended expression of $M(d,a)$, will be in agreement with $M(u,a)$. Experience tells us that some iteration of the above process will be required to attain even the appearance of agreement. The theory of UCMs says that by constructing $R_3 = R(M_3,F)$ and $C_3 = C(R_3,P,S)$, we ought to be able to determine the degree of agreement between M_1 and M_3 by considering C_1 and C_3 only! Although the symbols F, P, S have been used above without subscripts, one may, in general, consider sets of formalisms F, programming languages P, and semantics S.

CG-NOTATION

Working Group Omega decided that one could use the CG-notation as a basis for the construction of the representations R of UCMs M. This is not intended as an endorsement of the CG-notation for this purpose. Rather, the Working Group members feel that it is a suitable basis for research and experimentation. Essentially, the "meaning triangle" of Ogden and Richards, as given in (Sowa 1983), expresses the fundamental relationships between REFERENT (object, extension), CONCEPT (intension, thought, idea, sense), and SYMBOL (word). It is essentially another way of expressing ideas first propounded by Aristotle. This meaning triangle, which is fundamental to CG-notation, is given below in Fig. 4. Perception maps extensional objects to intensional concepts, and speech (expression or articulation) maps concepts to words. The relationship between word and object is an indirect mapping (thus the dotted line), derived from the two direct mappings of perception and expression (ibid.).

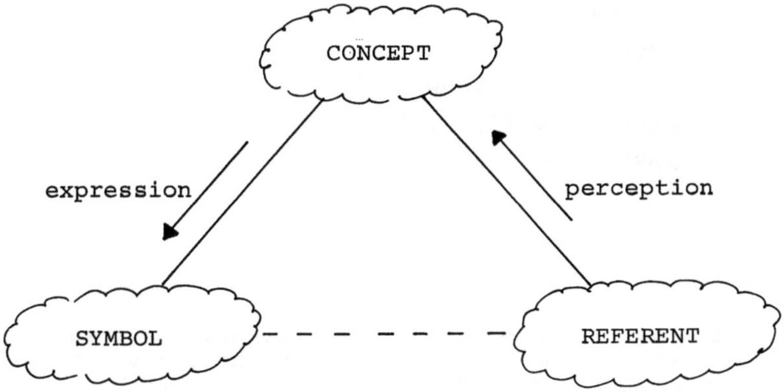

Fig. 4

CG-notation employs two distinct kinds of entities: concepts and conceptual relations. Concepts are represented by type labels - words enclosed in square brackets. Essentially, the type label is analogous to the woolly diagram of (Mac an Airchinnigh 1984). Thus, the concept of "horse" may be represented by [HORSE]. Type labels are also used to represent conceptual relations. In this case, round brackets are used. (STATE) and (LOCATION) denote conceptual relations. For example, the sentence "a cat sits on a mat" is represented by:

[CAT] → (STATE) → [TO_SIT] → (LOCATION) → [MAT]

Fig. 5

Note that we have departed somewhat from the convention used by Sowa himself. In particular, we use the infinitive of a verb to express the underlying concept. This decision was an immediate consequence of our work in developing related conceptual graphs in natural languages other than English. As well as the two dimensional form of CG-notation, the so-called display form, Sowa provides a linear form supported by a formal grammar. Using this latter form, the above conceptual graph would appear as:

```
[CAT] -
   (STATE) → [TO_SIT] -
                  (LOCATION) → [MAT]
```

Fig. 6

The reader is referred to (Sowa 1983) for further details.

One of the most basic conceptual relations is that of "naming". For example, a specific colour, denoted by [COLOUR:#0], may have the names "dubh", "schwarz", "noir", "black", etc. We represent this by the conceptual graph:

```
[COLOUR:#O] -
    (NAME) ——> ["dubh"]
    (NAME) ——> ["schwarz"]
    (NAME) ——> ["noir"]
    (NAME) ——> ["black"]
                 :
```

Fig. 7

The symbol "#O" is called an individual marker. As a second example, consider a PERSON who may be identified by the individual marker #772941 and who has the name "Mary". We represent this by the conceptual graph:

[PERSON:#772941] ——> (NAME) ——> ["Mary"]

Fig. 8

More formally, we may define the conceptual relation of "naming" as follows. Let NAME be a type label for a dyadic conceptual relation. Let ENTITY and WORD be type labels for concepts. Let a and b be any concepts such that

a ——> (NAME) ——> b

Then the following conditions must hold:

- type(a) is a subtype of ENTITY: type(a) $\leq$ ENTITY.
- type(b) is a proper subtype of WORD: type(b) $<$ WORD.

The word type(b) is called a name of referent(a). In the context of (interactive) computer graphics, we use a variety of different names: "echo", "feedback", "dialogue", "interaction", etc., for entities that we think we understand. Use of CG-notation will aid us in being more precise about the names that we use.

To test the applicability of CG-notation in the formal development of UCMs, the Working Group members were given the task of providing conceptual graphs for seven concepts taken from appendix B of (Sowa 1983) in the natural languages Dutch, German, French, and Russian. At the conclusion of the Workshop, other participants were invited to provide the concept TO_COMMUNICATE in Hungarian, Finnish, Portuguese, and Irish. The following section contains a list of these conceptual graphs together with the names of the respective contributors. These graphs are not intended to be definitive. Rather, they are deemed to be a starting point for further discussion and refinement. In particular, it is hoped that a kernel of such conceptual graphs which are of immediate interest to workers in the field of human-computer interaction, be available for use in future Workshops.

TO_COMMUNICATE

The following list of conceptual graphs in linear form is intended to capture the concept TO_COMMUNICATE. Each graph is headed by the natural language used (in English) and the name of the contributor. Readers who understand some of the "foreign" languages used will be able to judge for themselves the appropriateness of the conceptual graphs. Any syntactic errors that appear therein are probably my own and not those of the contributors.

DUTCH, J. Matthys

MEEDELEN < GEVEN

Meedelen is informatie geven; dit gebeurt via een (kommunikatie) medium, zoals gebaren, gesproken woord, telefon, post.

[MEEDELEN] -

(UITVOERDER) → [BEZIELD]

(ONTVANGER) → [BEZIELD]

(MIDDEL) → [ENTITEIT]

(VOORWERP) → [INFORMATIE]

ENGLISH, J. Sibert

TO_COMMUNICATE < TO_GIVE

To communicate is to give information; the instrument is a means of communication, such as mail, telephone, speech or gesture.

[TO_COMMUNICATE] -

(AGENT) → [ANIMATE]

(RECIPIENT) → [ANIMATE]

(INSTRUMENT) → [ENTITY]

(OBJECT) → [INFORMATION]

FINNISH, T. Takala

TIEDOTTAA < ANTAA

Tiedottaminen on tiedon antamista; väline, kuten posti, puhelin, puhe tai ele, on keino tiedottaa.

[TIEDOTTAA] -

(TIEDOTTAJA) → [ELIÖ]

(VASTAANOTTAJA) → [ELIÖ]

(VÄLINE) → [ESINE]

(KOHDE) → [TIETO]

FRENCH, R. Guedj

COMMUNIQUER < MISE_A_DISPOSITION

Communiquer est la mise à disposition d'un destinaire d'une information. Le support de cette information ou moyen de communication est, par example, le télèphone, une lettre, etc.

[COMMUNIQUER] -
(DESTINAIRE) ⟶ [ETRE_VIVANT]

⋮

<u>GERMAN</u>, H. Hanusa

VERMITTELN < GEBEN

Vermitteln ist das Geben von Information mittels eines Medium.

[VERMITTELN] -
(MITTLER) ⟶ [LEBEND]
(EMPFÄNGER) ⟶ [LEBEND]
(MITTEL) ⟶ [EINHEIT]
(GEGENSTAND) ⟶ [INFORMATION]

<u>HUNGARIAN</u>, G. Krammer

KOMMUNIKÁLNI < ADNI

Kommunikálni annyit jelent, mint információt adni. Az eszköz a kommunikáció eszköze, mint amilyen a levél, telefon, beszéd vagy a mozdulat.

[KOMMUNIKÁLNI] -
(KÜLDŐ) ⟶ [ÉLŐLÉNY]
(FOGADO) ⟶ [ÉLŐLÉNY]
(ESZKÖZ) ⟶ [ENTITÁS]
(DOLOG) ⟶ [INFORMÁCIÓ]

<u>IRISH</u>, M. Mac an Airchinnigh

FÁISNÉIS_A_THABHAIRT < TABHAIR

Tugtar agus faightear fáisnéis. Is é ní beo a thugann an fháisnéis agus ní beo a fhaigheann an fháisnéis. Tugtar an fháisnéis ar ghléas éagsúil - mar shampla, an post, an teileafón, labhairt, agus geáitseáil.

[FÁISNÉIS_A_THABHAIRT] -
(GNÍOMHAIRE) ⟶ [BEO]
(FAIGHTEOIR) ⟶ [BEO]
(GLÉAS) ⟶ [EISEACH]
(ÁBHAR) ⟶ [FÁISNÉIS]

<u>PORTUGUESE</u>, J. Encarnação

COMMUNICAR < DAR

Communicar é dar informação; o instrumento é um meio de communicação, como por exemplo correio, telefone, voz ou gestos.

[COMMUNICAR] -

(AGENTE) ⟶ [VIVENTE]

(RECEPTOR) ⟶ [VIVENTE]

(INSTRUMENTO) ⟶ [UNIDADE]

(OBJETO) ⟶ [INFORMAÇÃO]

<u>RUSSIAN</u>, D. Novatchev

ОБЩАТЬСЯ < ДЕЛАТЬ_ДОСТУПНЫМ

Намеренно делать доступной определенную информацию. Это определение ограничивает область обчения только в сфере одущевленного. Средствами обчения могут быт: почта, телефон, речь,...

[ОБЩАТЬСЯ]-

(ПРИЧИНИТЕЛЬ) ⟶ [ОДУШЕВЛЕННОЕ]

(ПОЛУЧАТЕЛЬ) ⟶ [ОДУШЕВЛЕННОЕ]

(СРЕДСТВО) ⟶ [ОБДЕКТ]

(ДЕЙСТВИЯ) ⟶ [ИНФОРМАЦИЯ]

CONCLUSIONS

It is time to begin work on the formal specification of UCMs. We must build on the work already done by philosophers, linguists, psychologists, and computer scientists. As computer scientists, we will co-operate and collaborate with others in this endeavour. We propose that the theory of UCMs form a major work item at future Workshops.

We do not endorse the M-R-C notation. However, we do think that it provides a basis for further developments. Use of the notation will assist in the expression of ideas and concepts with respect to users, computer systems, and application domains.

We do not endorse the CG-notation. However, we do think that it is a good basis for the formalism F of the M-R-C notation. We hope that it will be used as a means of communicating the concepts and conceptual relations that are especially relevant to the users of interactive (computer graphics) systems. We would hope that the languages English, French, German, Russian, will be used for the expression of all concepts and conceptual relations. This is to be regarded as a minimal requirement. Other languages are not excluded. By so doing, we would expect to make progress towards the development of a canonical form for dialogue specification.

It has been the experience of the Working Group members that it is very difficult to define properly some very general concepts such as ENTITY and OBJECT. Also there are many words which have much "overloaded" meaning. It is necessary to examine and measure the expressive power of CG-notation. We would emphasise the fuzziness of conceptual graphs. In order to derive a more concrete expression of a given concept or conceptual relation, with respect to a given category of users, for example, it may be necessary to extend the CG-notation by incorporating a "weighting" factor.

As an immediate work program, we propose that the following concepts be analysed:

- ACT, ACTION, INTERACTION, TRANSACTION;
- OBJECT, ENTITY;
- WORKSTATION, WINDOW, VIEWPORT, TRANSFORMATION.

REFERENCES

Guedj RA, ten Hagen PJW, Hopgood FRA, Tucker HA, Duce DA (eds) (1980) Methodology of Interaction. North-Holland Publishing Company, Amsterdam

Hadamard J (1945) The Psychology of Invention in the Mathematical Field. Dover Publications Inc., New York

Mac an Airchinnigh M (1984) The Model of the User's Conceptual Model of ... In: these proceedings

Shneiderman B (1980) Software Psychology - Human Factors in Computer and Information Systems. Winthrop Publishers Inc., Massachusetts

Sowa JF (1983) Conceptual Structures - Information Processing in Mind and Machine. Addison-Wesley Publishing Company, London

Part 2

Role, Model, Structure and Construction of a UIMS

Issues Pertaining to the Design of a User Interface Management System

A. Kamran

Institute of Information Science and Technology, Department of Electrical Engineering and Computer Science, School of Engineering and Applied Science, The George Washington University, Washington, DC, USA

INTRODUCTION

We reported at the GIIT Workshop our experiences in designing and implementing a prototype Interaction Handling Package called the Abstract Interaction Handler (AIH). In keeping with the terminology that has evolved since that Workshop, this paper will refer to the AIH as a User Interface Management System (UIMS). This paper reports our experiences and realizations beyond the Seattle Workshop [GIIT83]. We have been proceeding in two directions.

1) We have been implementing Interactive programs on top of our Interaction Handling package for the purpose of testing the usefulness of our model of a UIMS as a tool for designing good interaction.

Building tools for Interaction Dialog design as an application of the Interaction Language has shed light on:

(a) The suitability and power of the Interaction Language (as defined in [KAMR83])

(b) The functional separation of the application part and the interaction part of an interactive program.

2) Through experience with our UIMS, we have been constantly involved in addressing the larger issues -- those of defining and understanding more clearly, the domain of Interaction.

In addressing these issues, we have a better understanding of the interface between the Interaction Handling part (UIMS) and the set of semantic modules (application). Also, through the implementation of Interaction Techniques [KAMR83], we understand more clearly the interface between the graphics package and the Interaction Handler.

1. Problems with Basing the UIMS - Application Interface on the Linguistic Analysis Model

A grouping of actions in terms of the task types (data types) of the Interaction Language (IL) results in the expression of a command. A combination of one or more commands realize a user-level task. For instance, a user's desire to rearrange a room in a room layout application will be accomplished through a number of tasks of moving furniture around. These tasks will be mapped onto commands in the Interaction Language. Let us consider a sample command: "MOVE OBJECT FROM TO." This command can be represented in the current Augmented Transition Network (ATN) model of the IL as illustrated in Figure 1.

If we make the separation between the UIMS and the application based directly on the linguistic (semantic - syntactic - lexical) analysis model [FOLE82], giving only semantic control to the application modules, then the whole process represented

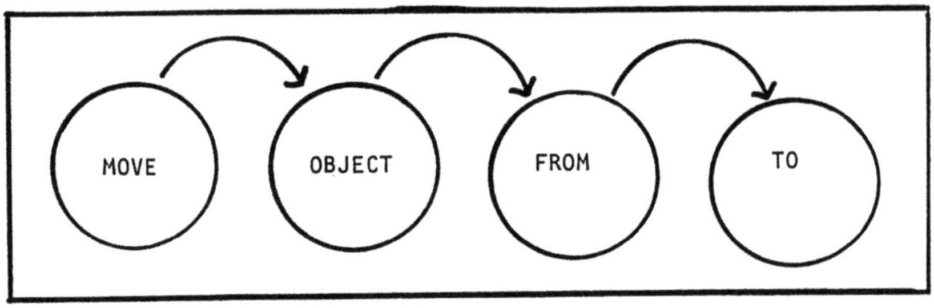

Figure 1. Representation of the command "MOVE OBJECT FROM TO" in current ATN model of the IL.

in Figure 1 would be in the domain of the UIMS. Only at the completion of the command (which the UIMS should be able to recognize) would the control be given to the appropriate application module for the purpose of realizing the specified command.

In interactive programming, a number of factors have to be considered in applying the linguistic analysis model as the basis of separation of functionality. One of the main factors to be considered is feedback. In most cases, immediate feedback is desired at the lexical, syntactic and semantic levels while the command is still being formulated. Let's consider the example command of Figure 1. It is desirable that the user receive immediate feedback, even as the command is being parsed. Assume that the user is using a keyboard to type in the command. Each letter of the alphabet is echoed as the user combines these lexemes to form the first word of the vocabulary "MOVE." The parse for the recognition of this word is part of syntax. If, for instance the user types in a word that is not in the vocabulary, it is desirable that the Interactive System give immediate feedback rather than wait for the whole command to be typed in. At least it should have the capability to handle immediate feedback. At times, a user might be able to avoid continuous syntactic feedback in the sense mentioned above. For instance, if the user is using a keyboard to type in the example command of Figure 1, the system can work in a mode where syntactic parsing begins only when the user indicates a completion of the command specification (e.g., by pressing the RETURN key). Having continuous feedback is generally dependent on the interaction device available as well as the style of interaction. Thus, there are two ways of analyzing the specification of a command like "MOVE OBJECT" as illustrated in Figure 2.

(STEP 1)	(STEP 2)
LEXICAL parse and feedback <MOVE OBJECT>	SYNTACTIC parse and feedback <MOVE OBJECT>
CASE 1	
SYNTACTIC and LEXICAL parse and feedback <MOVE>	SYNTACTIC and LEXICAL parse and feedback <OBJECT>
CASE 2	

Figure 2. Discrete feedback model and continuous feedback model of the command "MOVE OBJECT."

For Case 1, the lexical level parsing and feedback for all the tokens in the command sentence will be complete before the syntactic level parsing and feedback for the sentence commences. An example of this style of interaction is a user typing in a complete command using a keyboard and submitting the command as a whole for syntactic parsing by pressing the RETURN key.

Case 2 illustrates another style of interaction where syntactic parsing and feedback for each token in the command sentence would happen as soon as that token is specified as opposed to waiting for the whole sentence to be specified as in Case 1. We can term Case 1 as the "discrete" (in time) feedback model and Case 2 as the "continuous" (in time) feedback model. Both cases can be be extended to include semantic level feedback. For our discussion, the lexical and syntactic levels will suffice. In interactive graphics applications, many interaction techniques require a "continuous" feedback model as illustrated in Case 2 of Figure 2 and described in the following discussion.

Let us now consider the complete command of Figure 1 again. We will analyze this command in the context of an interactive graphics application in which a number of objects are displayed on a screen and a number of interaction techniques are available for moving these objects from one position on the screen to another. This variety of interaction techniques makes it possible for the end-user to specify the command in different ways. In the simplest case, the user can use an interaction technique that employs a keyboard in a discrete feedback mode, to type in the complete command. In this case the command may be echoed (lexical feedback) as it is typed in, but parsing at all levels and the higher levels of feedback are initiated only after the command is completely specified. This style of command specification is analagous to batch programming and can be supported in the context of a UIMS - application separation based on the linguistic analysis model.

A more interesting case is an interaction technique that employs an interaction device (e.g., light pen) which allows the user to specify the command in Figure 1 by selecting the command from a menu, then "picking" the object on the screen and dragging it from its current position to the desired location. Such an interaction technique relies on continuous feedback as illustrated in Case 2 of Figure 2. In this case, the three levels of feedback are not "discrete" in time and "collapse" into a single form of feedback that we refer to as dynamic semantic feedback. That is, the semantic feedback (the object moving on the screen from the current location to the desired location) begins while the command is still being specified. The same feedback can be viewed as syntactic feedback by interpreting it as dynamic confirmation of syntactic validity. It could similarily be viewed as lexical feedback (the echoing of command as it is specified).

From this analysis, we realize that in the general case of command specification, because of a desire to have continuous feedback capability, the functional work at all three levels (semantic, syntactic, and lexical) is interdependent. That is, unlike discrete feedback, which can be independent at each level, continuous feedback at the lexical input level requires help from the syntactic level and continuous feedback at the syntactic level requires help from the semantic level.

It seems obvious now that as long as we are considering command analysis as "pure" input (i.e., without feedback), the linguistic analysis model is directly applicable and we can relatively easily handle the functional separation, and therefore the interface specification between the lexical and syntactic levels on the one hand and the semantic level on the other. However pure input is a concept that belongs to the batch programming era. When we speak of interaction, continuous feedback to the end-user is a dominant aspect of any command analysis requiring continuous communication between the three levels of the linguistic model. As we saw in the previous discussion, the distinction between the three linguistic levels is "fuzzy" in the case of feedback and depends on the way one interprets the feedback. Secondly, irrespective of where we draw the line of separation between the UIMS and the application, the interface between the UIMS and the application needs to be able to provide feedback across the interface continuously. This interface is further complicated when we consider some of the ensuing issues that relate to this interface.

The conclusion we reach from looking at fitting sample commands to the linguistic model is that the nature of the interactive graphics domain is different from pure linguistics, and if we are exporting a linguistic model of analysis to interactive graphics programming (especially in the context of UIMS-application separation), we need to do so with the realization that it may not always work [HALA82].

2. "ERROR" AND "UNDO" Handling: Its Effect on the UIMS -- Application Interface

For the purpose of the discussion, we will consider communication between the syntactic and semantic levels as equivalent to communication between the UIMS and the application.

Irrespective of whether feedback is "discrete" or "continuous," a communication protocol must exist between the UIMS and the application modules for the purpose of indicating the semantic level rejection of a command specified by the user. In order to achieve this, the application modules and the UIMS should be able to back up to the point in the command specification sequence, just before the error was made (in continuous feedback mode, this error detection could come from the semantic modules). In the example command of Figure 1 in Section 1, this would happen if the user is "dragging" the object to the new location and in doing so, attempts to drag the object to an area of the screen where the object cannot be placed. The detection of this error is clearly the domain of the application, since the application has already begun executing the command (it could also be recognized by the syntax if the interaction technique has access to the necessary information, but that again is not the point).

On the other hand, in the "discrete" feedback mode, error recovery is easier since the application does not start modifying its state until it has complete verification of the syntactic correctness of the command. In both modes of feedback, the application must have the ability to restore itself to the state before the error was made, while the UIMS must be able to go back to that point in the dialog with the user, right after which the error in command specification was made. This problem has been addressed to some extent in the traditional keyboard oriented interactive systems. However, when dealing with interactive computer graphics, the problem becomes much more complex, especially in UIMS research, because continuous feedback is being provided to the user at all levels (semantic, syntactic, lexical). Recovery from errors in this case entails not only restoring the internal state of the interactive system, but also restoring the external representation (the display) to the corresponding state, through all levels of feedback. It is important to note here that detection of an error is not the issue here. To provide good interaction, the dialog designer must be able to specify how an error is indicated to the user as well as where the dialog is to resume after the error. The more specifically one can categorize errors, the more focused the feedback to the user can be. Thus, the handling of errors by the UIMS requires a dynamic communication across the interface with the application that indicates the recognition of errors and their nature.

Undoing a command entails fulfilling the user's desire to undo the effect of a correctly (semantically) specified and executed command. This problem gets more complex if the user desires to undo more than one command. As it is currently not possible to algorithmically compute the inverse of all commands and the accompanying feedback, it seems that the UIMS will have to rely on either a state vector or a record of incremental changes to a previous state vector. In addition, since the external representation of a state of the Interactive System is handled both by the UIMS and the application modules, a mechanism has to be devised to coordinate this feedback across the UIMS - application interface.

3. Some Limitations of Our Interaction Language

We are addressing two problems in working with our Interaction Language, dealing with the ATN model of the language.

The Interaction Language (IL) of our UIMS is modeled as an Augmented Transition Network (ATN). Because the power of an ATN based language is primarily in the augmentations to the transition network, support for powerful structures in the language is encapsulated in these augmentations. Since the IL was prototyped as a Finite State Machine (FSM) equivalent, the augmentations did not add any memory capability to the language. Because of this FSM grammar capability, we have encountered a number of limitations in the IL in designing complex dialogs.

Another major limitation of our IL is that it permits only a rigid sequencing of tasks. The sequencing of user-level tasks (which is influenced by the nature of the application) should, in general, be flexible and adaptable to the needs of individual users. The User Interface Designer (also referred to as the Dialog Designer) should be able to "program" this flexible sequencing and any restrictions on it, using the Interaction Language. Hence, in the terminology used at Seattle [GIIT83], "External" control is a necessary capability, though in one extreme, an interactive system can be implemented with sequencing of tasks embedded in the application, essentially making the control flow "Internal." Control structures that can accommodate flexible sequencing are thus a required functionality of the Interaction Language.

4. Interaction Handling and the Graphics Package

The underlying software environment has also influenced the design and functionality of our UIMS. The specification of the interface between the application program and the input devices via a graphics package, such as the SIGGRAPH CORE [GSPC79] or GKS [GKS84] has in many instances severely limited the quality of interaction that a UIMS can provide to the user. The source of the problem probably lies in the historical baggage that we are carrying around in UIMS research. Logical input devices were abstractions defined primarily for portability and functional interchangeability of physical devices. They were primarily meant for the convenience of the application writer, not for the user of the application.

So that the abstractions closely approximated existing physical input devices (which were packaged with output devices e.g., CRT with Keyboard), they included some output as well. The amount of output involved in the implementation of a logical input device increases even more when the logical device has to be simulated on a physical device that it does not closely approximate. Now if the UIMS has to have control over the quality of interaction, it is imperative that input and output devices be combined together under control of the UIMS. The use of logical input devices as defined in CORE and GKS take this flexibility away from the UIMS.

In summary, if we are going to build UIMS on top of existing software tools, these tools must be chosen carefully such that they don't affect the functionality of the UIMS.

5. Conclusion

This paper discusses some ideas concerning UIMS reserach being conducted by our research group at The George Washington University. We are developing a more comprehensive model of a UIMS that takes advantage of UIMS research to date and answers our concerns with our original model. A more complete report of our research efforts beyond those reported at Seattle [KAMR83] will be forthcoming in the ensuing months.

ACKNOWLEDGMENTS

A number of people have contributed ideas or helped develop ideas expressed in this paper: James Acquah, James Foley, Rodolfo Belliardi, and John Sibert. Lucy Moran, who edited this paper, and helped with the illustrations. James Foley, who reviewed the initial and final drafts. Zora Carrington, who prepared the final camera-ready copy and patiently included last minute changes. The work reported on this paper was partially supported by the United States Department of Energy under grant DOE E-AS05-83ER13122.

REFERENCES

CARE82 Carey, T., "User Differences in Interface Design," University of Guelph, Canada IEEE COMPUTER, November 1982, pp. 14-20.

FOLE74 Foley, J.D., and Wallace, V., "The Art of Natural Graphics Man-Machine Conversation," Proceedings of the IEEE, April 1974.

FOLE82 Foley, J.D., and van Dam, A., "Fundamentals of Interactive Computer Graphics," Addison-Wesley, Reading, MA 1982.

GIIT83 GIIT Workshop Report, Computer Graphics 17(1), January 1983.

GKS84 "Special GKS Issue," Computer Graphics, February 1984.

GSPC79 "Status Report of the Graphics Standards Planning Committee," Computer Graphics 13(3), August 1979.

HALA82 Halasz, F., and Moran, T.P., "Analogy Considered Harmful," Proceedings of Human Factors in Computer Systems, March 1982, Gaithersburg, Maryland, pp. 383-386.

KAMR83 Kamran, A., and Feldman, M.B., "Graphics Programming Independent of Interaction Techniques and Styles," Computer Graphics 17(1), January 1983, pp. 58-66.

Components of Interactive Applications

H. J. Strubbe

Prime Computer, Inc., 500 Old Connecticut Path, Framingham, MA 01701, USA

INTRODUCTION

It is felt that the way in which interactive applications are currently being written leads to a lot of duplication of effort: everybody writes a screen handler, an integer validation routine, a menu system, etc. To avoid this, we want to break applications down into components that can be reused later. Two applications with a similar user interface (Ui/f) should be able to use the same Ui/f component. One application with two different Ui/f's should have only one application component. All Ui/f components should be built on top of the same display component.

Example: i) An airline reservation system and an electronic mail system could both have a similar "forms" Ui/f. ii) Options for a command could be specified via typed keywords or via menu choices. iii) A chess program could have a graphical Ui/f for use on a personal computer (PC), and a command line Ui/f for use via a terminal and telephone line.

A deeper analysis of the third example indicates how we may partition applications. The second example has often been used in the past as a model. However, its two Ui/f's are too similar. The results suggested by its analysis are not sufficiently general.

ANALYSIS OF A CHESS PROGRAM

Consider an imaginary program, that is designed to teach you how to play chess. Two different Ui/f's are described for it.

1. The personal computer Ui/f. (see fig. 1)

A picture of a chessboard is shown on the screen, with all the pieces drawn in their current positions. Whenever the cursor touches one of your pieces, all positions to which that piece can legally move are highlighted on the screen. In addition, in each position a number is displayed that indicates the stategic importance (successfactor) of a move to that position. All these effects are considered as immediate feedback. Once you have decided which piece to move, you position the cursor over it, and you depress a mouse button. The piece becomes highlighted as the starting point of the move. As long as the mouse button is down, the cursor is assumed to indicate the destination of your move. As such, a position which is legal for the starting piece and which is nearest to the cursor becomes highlighted. When the mouse button is released, the move is visually recorded and, after a certain time, the program produces a counter move.

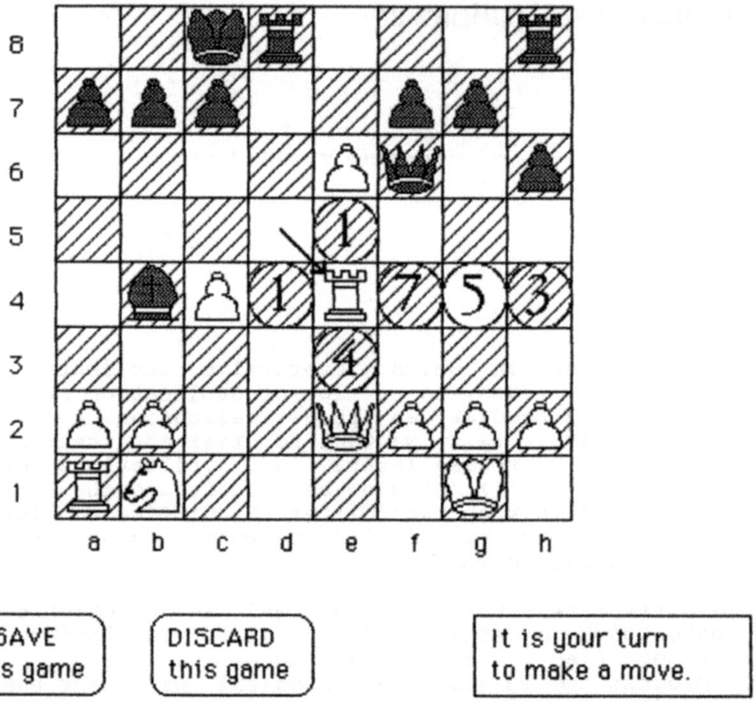

Fig. 1. Example of the PC chess user interface

```
8       bQ bR          bR
7 bP bP bP       bP bP
6             wP bK    bP
5
4    bB wP    wR
3
2 wP wP       wK wP wP wP
1 wR wN             wQ
  a  b  c  d  e  f  g  h

>TRY FROM e4 TO e5
Successfactor=1.
>MOVE FROM e4 TO h4
Move registered. Counter move is a7 to a6.
```

Fig. 2. Example of the teletype chess user interface

2. The teletype Ui/f. (see fig. 2)

A symbolic representation of a chessboard is printed out, line by line, indicating the position of all pieces. Using some coordinate system, you can now enter one of the following commands:

TRY FROM position1 TO position2. The program tells you if the move is legal, and if so, what its successfactor is.
MOVE FROM position1 TO position2. The program tells you if the move is legal, and if so, calculates a counter move. A new chessboard is printed which includes your move and the counter move.
OPTIMAL MOVE FOR position. The program computes all legal moves starting from that position, and returns the one with the highest successfactor.

THE APPLICATION COMPONENT

The previous example was devised in order to clarify the separation between the application domain and the Ui/f domain. The example suggests strongly that the Ui/f component cannot fulfill its task unless it contains (or has access to) a lot of chess expertise. For reasons of encapsulation and modularity, we group ALL the chess expertise into one place, which we call the "chess object" (the word object is used here in SMALLTALK sense).

The chess object consists of a database (which contains the current game in some convenient representation), chess rules and chess strategies. It can answer questions and perform actions on the chess data. Such operations are often called "methods". A few examples are:

LIST_CURRENT_GAME. returns list of (piece, position).
CHECK_IF_LEGAL_MOVE FROM position1 TO position2.
returns TRUE or FALSE.
COMPUTE_SUCCESSFACTOR_OF_MOVE FROM position1 TO position2.
returns number.
DETERMINE_LEGAL_MOVES_FOR_PIECE AT position.
returns list of positions.
RECORD_MOVE FROM position1 TO position2. returns TRUE or FALSE.
MAKE_COUNTER_MOVE. returns FROM position1 TO position2.
LIST_PIECE AT position. returns piece.
CREATE_NEW_GAME. returns game_pointer.

It is important to note that this chess object can be used equally well by the PC Ui/f as by the teletype Ui/f. The visual layout of the board, the representation of the pieces, etc. are considered part of the Ui/f component and are not known to the chess object. In general, an application object should not do any terminal/screen i/o. Formatting of its data is done by the Ui/f component.

To summarise, the application component is an object in SMALLTALK sense. It contains all the knowledge about the application domain. The Ui/f component contains all the knowledge about the communication with the user: screen layout, commands, input devices, etc. The application object does not do any i/o that interacts with the user.

This approach is in contrast to some Ui/f Management Systems (UIMS's), where the application part is concerned with semantic actions alone (e.g. Kamran and Feldman 1983). In our example, the semantic action produces the counter move.

In such UIMS's, immediate feedback, error checking, context dependent help, etc. (lexical, syntactic, etc. actions) are handled by the UIMS on its own. This requires it to have a certain knowledge of the application domain. In simple cases, for instance when an integer has to be entered, such knowledge can be compactly handed to the UIMS. In our example, however, the amount of knowledge needed to produce the feedback is enormous. Moreover, as machines get faster, the feedback and validation that can be done instantaneously will get more complex and more application dependent. We feel it is not useful to devise more complicated mechanisms that hand more feedback data to the UIMS. We would rather investigate structures that allow the Ui/f component to easily access the knowledge inside the application component.

THE USER INTERFACE COMPONENT

As we believe in the external control model (event-driven interaction), our Ui/f component consists of a set of procedures, each one of them "attached" to an image on the screen. When the user positions the cursor over an image (possibly while depressing a key), the procedure attached to that image is invoked with as argument the type of the event (cursor movement, the key which was pressed, etc.). These procedures interact with the application object and with the display component, which is responsible for communication with the user.

Most calls to the application object produce a quick answer, as needed for immediate feedback. They can be implemented as synchronous subroutine calls. Sometimes, however, the requested application action is known to take a long time. In that case, the Ui/f component makes a different call, which activates the application in background mode. Some kind of Inter Process Communication mechanism has to be used so as to activate the Ui/f component again, when the background activity terminates. The impact of time-consuming operations has rarely been addressed in UIMS's.

To summarise, the Ui/f component is always inactive, apart from when it is woken up by one of the following events: activity on an input device, or completion of a background process. A responsive Ui/f requires that the execution time of all the Ui/f procedures be very short.

STRUCTURING THE USER INTERFACE COMPONENT

It is often felt that the dialogue writer should not specify the interaction with the user down to the lowest details. For instance, we would prefer him to specify that he wants an adjustable potentiometer on the screen, while leaving open the details of how exactly the user changes its value. This saves work for the dialogue writer and leads to uniformity of the system.

A set of Standard Interaction Primitives (SIP's) could therefore be constructed. This set is under control of the Ui/f expert, and is tailored to the local equipment. Examples of SIP's are: display a standard potentiometer and attach to it a standard routine to adjust its value; display in standard form a menu with text or icons and attach to each item a standard highlight routine and the appropriate action procedure. These SIP's should be highly parametrised so as to be as generally applicable as possible.

In the above, we assumed that the application object communicates data with the Ui/f component (Ui/fC) in a way that is independent of the Ui/f style. Therefore, the Ui/fC typically has to format these data according to the style chosen by the user. The result is then passed on to the display component in order to be drawn on the screen. From the point of view of modularity, it is useful to think in terms of a "formatter object", which is responsible for displaying the application data. The formatter should be able to work in background mode. Note that not all output of the Ui/fC passes through the formatter. In our PC chess example, the formatter would be able to draw the board and the pieces. However, the icons to discard the game, to save it, etc.. are not produced by the formatter.

The display of these additional images is requested by the third part of the Ui/fC, which we call the "interaction logic". Its task is to analyse the responses of the user and the return values of the application object. Based on these, it steers the interaction by invoking the application object, by writing onto the screen and by reading the input devices. The construction of this interaction logic is often a complex task. The literature on UIMS's suggests that in such cases one might want to write a dialogue specification in some special-purpose language and a corresponding interpreter. In particular if the Ui/f is in an experimental stage and under constant revision, this approach might be very effective.

To summarise, the Ui/f component consists of three parts: the interaction logic, the formatter object, and a set of standard interaction primitives. As a whole, it communicates with the application object and the display component. (see middle of fig. 4)

THE DISPLAY COMPONENT

Interactive systems typically have multiple viewports on the screen. We assume that the user can do a fair amount of manipulation of these viewports without the need for the application program to intervene (e.g. reposition them, pan them over a full-screen sized image).

This can be accomplished by giving each application program the ability to write into (one or more) virtual screens. A "painter", directed by a "viewport manager", displays parts of all these virtual screens onto the physical screen. The painter can be built on top of any convenient graphics system. The user communicates with the viewport manager in order to change the mappings of the virtual screens onto the physical screen. The painter is able to display the resulting image on the physical screen without the help of the application program.

Upon user input, an "input analyser" determines, with the help of the viewport manager, which viewport the user is pointing at. In addition, it distinguishes between commands for the application programs and for the viewport manager itself. (see fig. 3)

To summarise, application writers organise output of their programs inside virtual screens. They are not concerned with the positions of these virtual screens on the physical screen.

Many applications use a "point and command" interaction style. This implies that they have to determine at which object within the virtual screen the user is pointing. Once that object has been identified, an action typical for that object and for that command is executed. Identification of the touched object has to be done very fast, as it is usually part of the feedback action. A structure for the virtual screen was devised that makes this identification as efficient as possible. The above sequence of events occurs in many application programs. It is therefore useful to extract the common logic out of them, and to put it inside the display component.

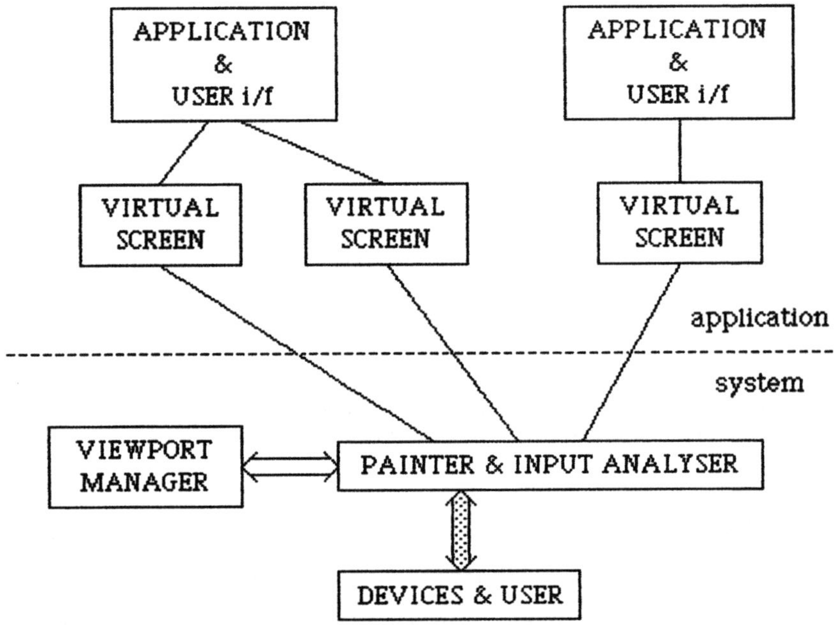

Fig. 3. Structure of a multiple viewport system

THE DISPLAY TREE

In our model, the only way the Ui/fC can communicate with the user is via a "display tree". This tree represents the structure of the 2-dimensional virtual screen image. Each leaf represents an object on the screen. A leaf contains an input procedure, an output procedure and links to their arguments. Execution of the input procedure performs the action associated with touching (and sending a command to) the corresponding object. These input procedures are the "attached procedures" discussed in an earlier section. The set of all of them is the Ui/f component. Execution of the output procedure paints the leaf object on the screen.

Images that are displayed near to each other (in particular, if they build up a composite object), are grouped into nodes. Images that are logically related are grouped similarly. The resulting tree is an appropriate structure for a fast search to find the touched node upon an input event. For output, the nodes are convenient places for specifying graphical attributes.

Each leaf contains the coordinates needed to position it on the screen and an output procedure with output data. If a leaf becomes visible on the screen, its output procedure gets invoked. In order to aid clipping, each node contains an upper limit on the size of its image. In addition, each node contains an input area routine, an input procedure and an application link. The input area of a leaf is defined as the "sensitive" area on the screen inside which cursor hits are routed to that leaf. By including the input area in the display tree, the system can now determine, without any help from the application, which leaf was touched by the cursor. The routine which traverses the display tree, while comparing the cursor coordinates with the positions and sizes of the nodes, is called the resolver. Note that this resolver is part of the display system, and not of the application. In order to speed up the resolver, each node contains an upper limit on the size of its input area. If a hit on a leaf is found, the system invokes the attached input procedure with the application link as argument. This argument can be used by the application program as a means to identify the touched leaf.

So far, the non-leaf nodes have only been introduced as a mechanism to speed up input and to organize output. Often, however, the application possesses an intrinsic hierarchy that can be reflected in the display tree. Consider, for instance, a wine shop inventory program, which deals with bottles that are grouped into cases, and cases that are grouped into shelves. Such a program might define a "remove bottle", "remove case" and "remove shelf" command. This can be implemented by requiring the user to specify a "scope" (i.e. bottle, case or shelf) before giving the "remove" command. The internal structure of the application becomes clearer if not only the bottles (leaves) have an attached input procedure, but the cases and shelves (nodes) as well.

To summarise, the visual interaction style uses the virtual screen as a medium that presents output and receives input. Each virtual screen is represented by a display tree. The nodes contain input procedures, which perform the actions that constitute the application, and output procedures, which paint the application images on the screen. The application programmer merely writes these procedures and attaches them to the nodes. The display system invokes them automatically, as needed.

The display trees are encapsulated inside a display tree object. The Ui/fC's interact with it by requesting it to create, connect, or delete leaves or nodes of a tree. In addition, it can be instructed to attach to the nodes input procedures with their application links, and output procedures with their data.

The complete structure of an application can be seen in figure 4. More details about the display trees and the description of some applications that use them can be found in Strubbe (1983). The entire display component together with the standard interaction primitives and all the tools to construct the interaction logic can be considered as a UIMS.

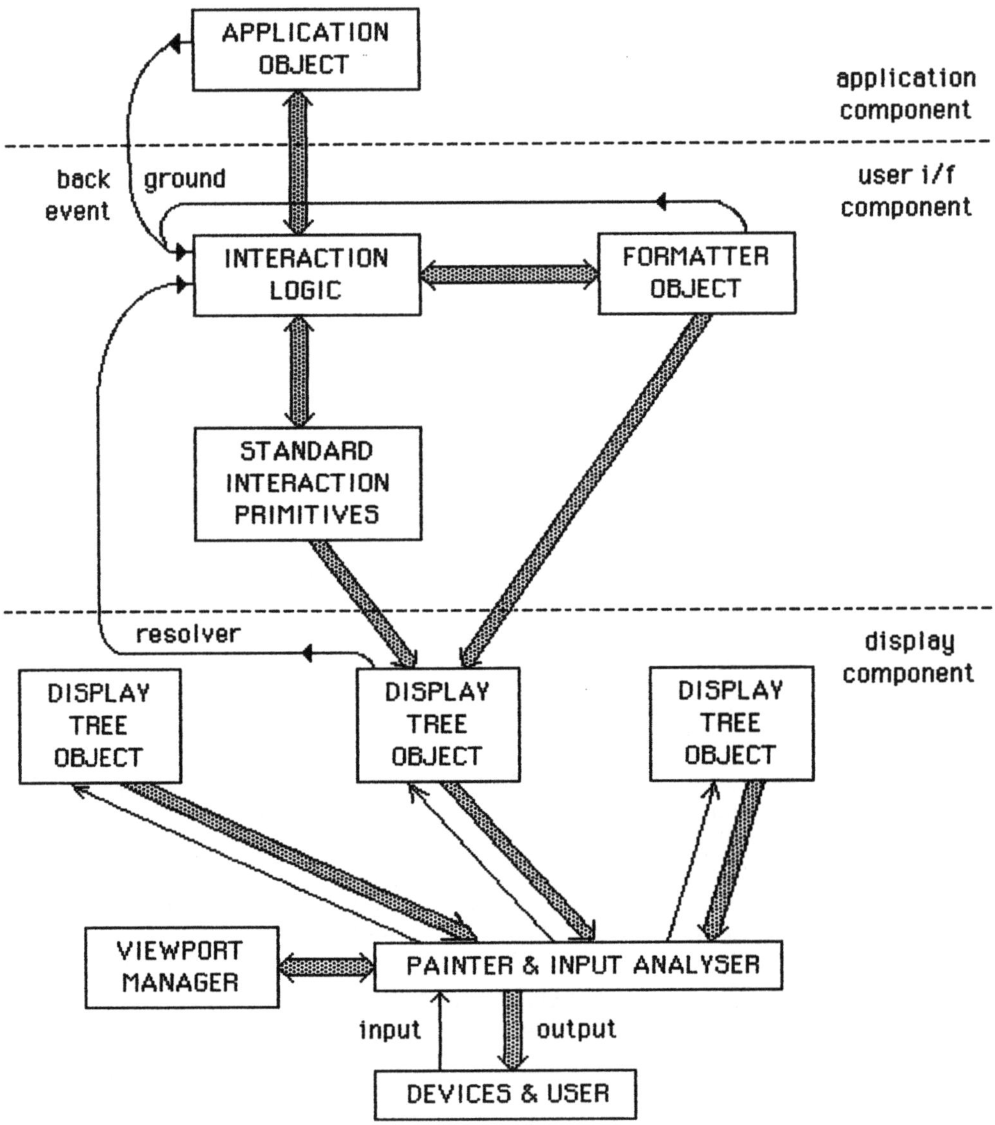

Fig. 4. Structure of an interactive application

APPENDIX: CONSIDERATIONS AFTER THE SEEHEIM WORKSHOP

This paper draws attention to problems with the UIMS's that were discussed in the GIIT workshop. These same problems were addressed during this workshop by several other papers, in particular by Kamran (1984). A list of the problems most widely being investigated is given in the summary of this workshop.

The approach outlined in this paper is much more applicable to "class 2 applications" than to "class 1 applications" (these terms are defined in the workgroup summary). For the latter class, the formatter, as described in this paper, contains the major part of the program. It is therefore usually considered as part of the application, and not of the Ui/f component.

Some workshop discussions pointed out that a typical interaction sometimes requires external control and at other times internal control. The event-driven model, as advocated in this paper, can easily give the illusion of internal control when desired. This is achieved by temporarily replacing the "active" attached procedures of most objects on the screen by "warning" procedures, that remind the user of the action he is required to take before he may proceed.

In complex applications (for example, where several input devices are being used simultaneously), the interaction logic will need to be highly structured. A discussion of various structures is given in the summary of this workshop in the section "model for a UIMS".

REFERENCES

Kamran A (1984) Issues Pertaining to the Design of the Abstract Interaction Handler. Proceedings of this workshop.

Kamran A and Feldman M B (1983) Graphics Programming Independent of Interaction Techniques and Styles. Computer Graphics, 17: 58-66

Strubbe H J (1983) Kernel for a Responsive and Graphical User Interface. Software-Practice and Experience, 13: 1033-1042

Communication Mediator - A Structure for UIMS

T. Takala

Laboratory of Information Processing Science, Helsinki University of Technology, 02150 Espoo 15, Finland

PREFERABLE FEATURES IN USER INTERFACES

Natural communication between humans includes many features uncommon in man-machine conversations. It is a continuous process of interaction making concurrently use of all our senses. Attention can be focused to something, deviated away and brought back again. Messages are often expressed incompletely, but are still understandable when connected to right context. This is usually not the case in current computer systems. To be more specific, the following four points of discrepancy are observed:

1) multimedia multimodal communication:

Typical current systems use only alphanumeric text as the medium of communication, and even most graphics systems with multiple input devices allow only one of them to be used at a time. It would be more natural to give the user the freedom of choosing any devices, eg. pointing and voice concurrently.

2) continuous communication:

In the conventional "ping-pong" style of dialogue (action-reaction cycle), the user gets bored if the response times of computer are longer than about a second. Even more, if the delay of answer is non-deterministically changing, the user will be frustrated with the repeated waiting and checking of operation completion. Typical examples of commonly acceptable continuity can be found in commercial video games, but not in commercial computer systems.

3) interleaving concurrent tasks:

Instead of formulating every action as a discrete dialogue command, the user should be able to deviate and return again. For example in a CAD system, it would be useful to make data base queries during input phase, to help design decisions.

4) free-formed commands:

The difficulty of learning available commands of computer systems often hinders their acceptability. A program asking the user everything separately, or guiding him through modes by changing menus, is only a partial solution. Better would be a system understanding natural-like language, and possibly even adapting to the user's gestures.

It is a difficult task to accomplish all these desirable features. However, a structured framework for UIMS can help to confront each of the requirements separately. It will not only help in designing new systems, but also in tailoring the user interface of existing systems to the user's needs.

DIFFERENT APPROACHES TO UIMS STRUCTURE

In the following a discourse by increasing sophistication and modularity is made, considering which of the problems mentioned rise in each approach. Also the increasing demands for programming environment are considered at each stage.

The term UIM will be used for User Interface Management contained in an application program, and UIMS for a separate independent System available for different applications.

Unstructured Approach

Lack of programming methodology leads to a single module without any structure. The I/O devices are called directly by the application, and their calls are spread all over the program. This makes the program hard to understand and its portability is poor. Most solutions to communication problems are of ad hoc nature, and the user is usually treated like just another file. Fortunately this kind of systems are nowadays rather seldom made.

UIM With Internal Control

Separating the direct handling of I/O–devices in a module of "logical device" subroutines provides a good portability of application programs. This has been the main emphasis in standardization, first for alphanumeric devices (the ASCII code) and later for graphics (GKS). If more than the agreed standard devices are needed, higher–level virtual devices can be programmed on top of them, and added to the I/O module (Anson, van den Bos, Mudur, etc. 1980). In implementations these logical devices are usually statically defined.

This is the most common approach in current interactive systems. Internal control means that the management of communication devices is handled by an application program. So this is "the machine's point of view": a single application reserves the workstation, and the user is controlled by the machine who makes requests.

The lexical level of communication is defined by the virtual devices, but the syntax of commands is embedded in the structure of application program. Some multimodality can be achieved, if multiple event–type devices are enabled simultaneously. Otherwise all the problems mentioned remain.

UIM With External Control

If an application task is thoroughly analyzed, it can be subdivided into natural subtasks that are relatively independent (Moran, etc. 1980). Programming these subtasks as non–interactive modules callable from a master command analyzer brings us to the external control approach.

In several senses this is "the user's point of view": he is commanding the application, and not just answering interrogations. The operation can be modeless: every subtask can be initiated directly, without navigating through a sequence of submodes. If it can be guaranteed that all the subtasks are small enough, then the response to commands is practically instantaneous, and the user has the feeling of continuous communication. Unfortunately, there will always grow new demands by the users for more powerful commands (eg. macros), the execution of which cannot be made instantaneous.

Because the interface to devices is all collected to one module, it can easily check all the input devices (either in event or sample mode) at every stage, thus giving multimodality. Besides that, even multiple applications can be controlled from the same workstation. For example, most operating systems have this kind of user interface (see next paragraph).

As the syntactical structure of commands is not embedded in the application modules, it is easier to change it. Regular grammars and well known parsing techniques can be used and tailored for each application. There are available tools for automatic generation of such analyzers (eg. YACC and LEX in Unix(TM)).

If free form commands are wanted, they can be defined for example by production rules (Hopgood 1980), or even pattern recognition methods may be used for parsing the input actions.

The problem with external control UIM is that most existing applications are designed with internal control. Their division to subtasks and tailoring for external control may be a hard work (Thomas 1983).

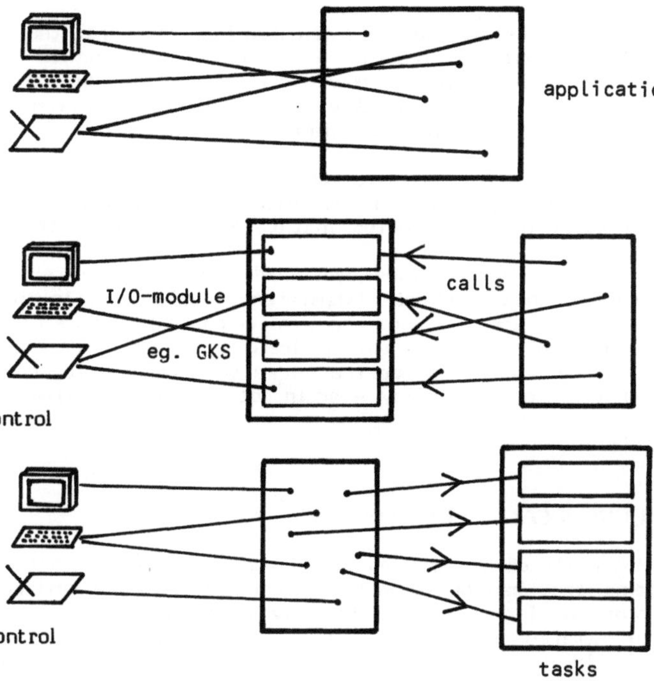

Unstructured system

UIM with internal control

UIM with external control

Job Control UIMS

If the external control UIM is implemented as an independent process, it will be possible to control multiple application jobs concurrently. This is the case of operating system interfaces with a background processing facility.

As the UIMS is not executing the application tasks, it can continuously communicate with the user. During time-consuming operations he can deviate to other applications, or prepare a command for the next operation. Even interrupting a subtask without terminating the whole application is possible.

Because of its generality, the UIMS command analyzer should have dynamic syntax rules. This can be achieved, if it is implemented as a table-driven program, with different production rule tables for each application. These tables can be prepared in a file and loaded at run-time, when needed.

The problems with such a job controller UIMS are in its sophistication: the conventional programming languages are not intended for concurrent processes. Another problem arises with the resource handling: how are the I/O–channels shared for competing requests by applications?

Window Manager UIMS

In up–to–date workstation computers (Star, Sun, Apollo, Blit, etc.) it is realized that a good UIMS should be placed as near the user as possible – in their case at the intelligent terminal. In such systems the problem of I/O resource sharing among applications is solved by spatially separating concurrent jobs on the display lay–out. For each process there exists a dedicated window on the screen, through which all the communication takes place.

As not all input devices are spatially oriented (eg. keyboard), they are to be associated with a window by attention focusing mechanism. For example pointing with a mouse to a window will activate that window and reserve other input devices for its process. For the activated process the window is **transparent,** in the sense that it has virtually direct control of all I/O–devices associated to the window.

Thus the UIMS must have facilities for multiplexing real devices to each process in turn. The application program can be written to use standard logical I/O–devices, but their drivers should be rewritten for multiplexed operation controlled by the UIMS.

If the windows are allowed to be dynamically changing, or perhaps overlapping (with defined priority), then a simple transparent multiplexing in time is not sufficient. Moving a window to another place requires its content to be stored by the UIMS, otherwise all should be redrawn by the application. And a process with partially obscured window cannot be allowed to use the whole window area for drawing, but the UIMS has to filter obscured parts away – again not a completely transparent multiplexing of devices.

SOLUTION PROPOSAL: MEDIATOR UIMS

As a direct control of I/O–devices cannot always be given to the concurrent application programs, they can be completely insulated from the devices by a filtering UIMS mediator process. In our solution the device drivers of application programs are replaced with metafile drivers connected to queuing pipe files. These first–in–first–out pipes (one for input and another for output) of each application are then handled by a common UIMS process.

The UIMS communicates continuously with the user, and mediates his messages to applications by writing them in the input pipe. Correspondingly each output pipe is regularly checked for response, and the appropriate messages mediated to the user.

With this method, the window manager can show the devices to the application programs either transparently or **transformed.** The latter case means that not only virtual device messages, but also higher level constructs (even complete commands) can be used as message units in the pipes. This will be further discussed later.

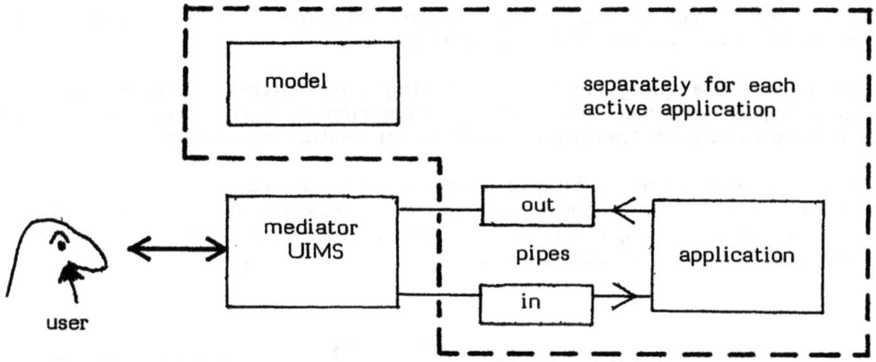

In order to allow dynamic moving of windows by user's control, the UIMS supports a **model** of the data displayed in the windows. Essentially the model consists of a structured segment storage for each window. Then the user communicates with the picture in first place (Rosenthal 1980), and this communication is interpreted and mediated by UIMS to the application.

Much of the facilities of current standard packages can be used as such for constructing this kind of UIMS. The most essential parts are conventional (sampled) device drivers, a structured readable segment storage (Takala 1983), and a commonly agreed metafile format for the pipes.

The hardest demands for programming environment are concurrent processing facilities. Although in principle all messages could be send through pipes, it would be more convenient to have a direct signaling (interrupting) control also. Because of the strictly sequential nature of pipe files, interrupting messages through them could be severely delayed.

AN EXPERIMENTAL IMPLEMENTATION: AGX SYSTEM

A methodology with a simple general metafile format and a standard tool set for processing textual and graphical objects (hierarchical list manipulation, transformation and clipping of graphic primitives, etc.) has been implemented, and recently presented (Takala 1983). It was originally intended to be an interactive geometric modeler (AGX = Advanced GeometriX), but its structure turned out to be general enough for other applications, too.

The model supported by AGX is a tree structure constructed from (mostly) geometric primitives. The whole structure is represented as a linear form of bytes, and can thus be directly transmitted through pipes without any conversions. Driver programs are written for different devices (Tektronix 4012, SUN bitmap display, ADM-3 dumb terminal, Bitpad tablet, etc.). All the tool functions can work either as in-core subroutines, or as concurrent coroutine processes. The representation scheme of data is closed, in the sense that the input and output of all tools is represented in the same format (hierarchical lists). Thus any operations can be done over and over again if wanted. No fixed sequences, like the viewing pipeline in standard graphics, are imposed. Programs are written using C language in a UNIX bsd 4.1 environment, run in a VAX 11/750 machine.

For many applications the model supported by AGX is sufficient as such (for example a page lay-out design system). In such a case the body of the application is essentially contained in the UIMS command analyzer; the executable background processes are just the basic tools of AGX. An extended version of this is a three-dimensional geometric editor intended for CAD applications.

New experiments are going on: One is a simplified window manager using an alphanumeric display terminal instead of expensive high-resolution graphics. The display will be divided in disjoint transparent windows for textual communication.

Another is a student project aiming at graphical interface for the "shell" command interpreter of Unix. This interface will not be transparent, but graphical actions (eg. pointings to icons on screen) are transformed to textual commands for the conventional shell running concurrently at background.

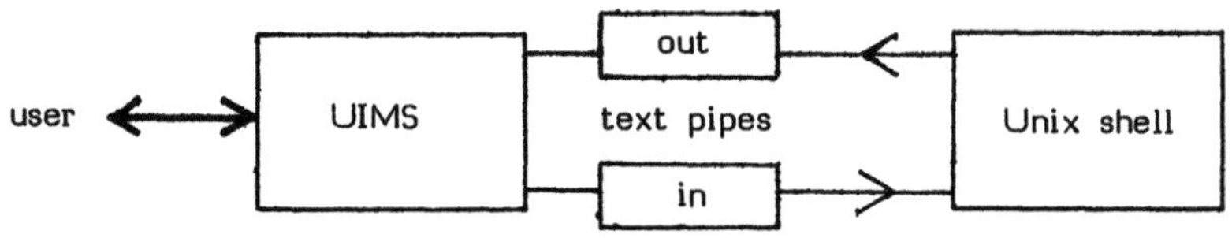

FUTURE DEVELOPMENT OF COMMAND ANALYZER IN UIMS

As in the shell-interface mentioned above, an active command transformer can be placed at each window. This makes it possible to connect any existing application (weather internally or externally controlled) to a UIMS having the good features mentioned in the first chapter.

To be able to transform commands, the UIMS should have knowledge of the actual commands of the application. This will be achieved by representing their **abstract syntax** in a data structure for the analyzer. The analyzer then uses some pattern recognition facilities to extract a command and its operands from the sequence of input actions. If all the items match, then the command is executed (sent as a message to the pipe). This kind of UIMS closely corresponds to the "user agent" of Carnegie-Mellon (Hayes et al. 1981).

The abstract syntax of an application's command language means a list containing a command name and the types of expected parameters for each possible action. In conventional parsing their order and form would be fixed. In flexible parsing however, any unambiguous ordering will be considered valid. If there are extraneous items in the input sequence, they will be saved, as they may belong to another interleaved (shuffled) command.

If some items are missing from a recognized command pattern, they can be filled in either by asking the user, or by taking default values. Intelligent guessing of default values requires keeping track of context where the user is in. This can be achieved by storing all the previous input actions in a "history" data structure. Essentially this structure would be a parse tree, from which the current operating mode and possible previously used parameter values can be resolved.

The abstract syntax of an application, together with the possible real actions matching it, can be represented as a table (for example as a production rule for each action). If these tables are loaded at run-time from a file prepared for each application, then the UIMS command analyzer program can generally be common for all applications. The tables can even be dynamically changing, in order to allow different modes of operation, or personalization to the user's habits.

The three different data structures needed, namely:

(1) the semantic feedback from the application, containing the current state of the process,

(2) the abstract syntax table with possible group structure for modes, and

(3) the parse-tree-like analyzed history of user's actions,

have a close analogy to the Sites, Modes and Trails by Nievergelt (1980), respectively. These are depicted in the data flow diagram below:

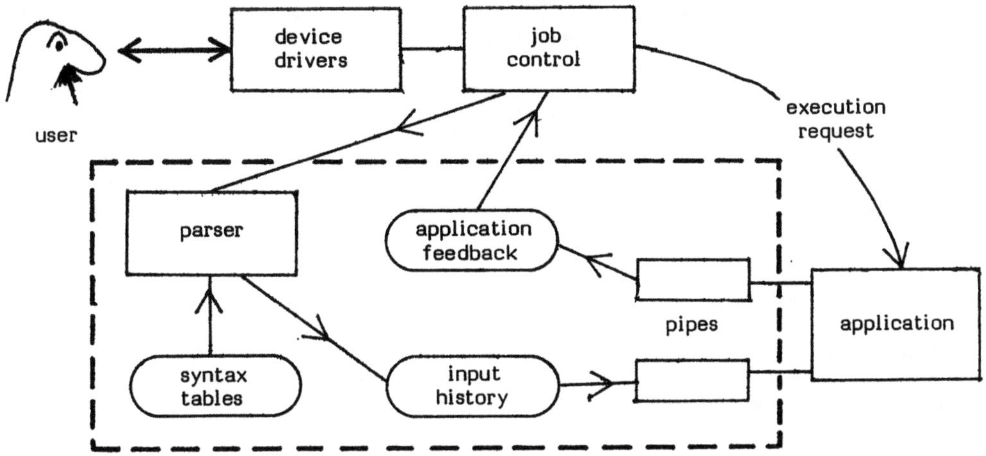

for each active application

CONCLUSIONS

From the user's point of view, high device dependency and modeless operation are benefits, thus suggesting UIMS to be structured with external control. However, portability of existing applications is based on internal control. This discrepancy is solved by placing an externally controlled mediator between user and application. The mediator transforms the user's actions of free format into discrete, well-formed commands (or command sequences) for the application.

In order to allow continuous communication and control over multiple concurrent applications, the mediator UIMS is implemented as a separate process. Commands to and responses from an application are transmitted trough metafile-like pipes.

Intelligent transformation of actions to commands will be facilitated by three dynamic data structures, representing the application's information referred to by the user, the abstract syntax of commands, and the analyzed history of input actions. Flexible adaptation of UIMS to changing users' gestures and to diverse applications will be achieved by making all these data structures loadable from a prepared file and manipulatable at run-time.

EFFECTS OF THE WORKSHOP AND CURRENT RESEARCH STATUS

The main result of the Workshop seems to be the relatively high degree of agreement about the concepts. Terminology, structure of UIMS, and the problems encountered were similar in many papers and discussions. The fact that the graphics system should be an integral part of UIMS will affect the design of subsequent systems and standards. The (still vague) new "interaction primitives" suggest that logical input devices should be implemented in a modular way, preferably distinguishing triggers and measures, and the combination of them by the UIMS.

Our experimental works mentioned are currently finalized: A mediator UIMS with overlapping windows is used with both an alphanumeric terminal and a graphical bitmap display. In each window an independent command interpreter "shell" is run, to which the UIMS transforms the user's actions (mouse pointings) as text commands. After the Workshop, similar work has also been reported elsewhere (Newell 1983).

The next actions to be undertaken are in the analysis of input actions. A flexible parser using production rules, and the tree-like structuring of input **history** (as a manipulatable **model** itself) are to be combined with AGX and the window manager. Automatic generation of UIMS will be facilitated at run-time using the abstract syntax tables. However, good specification tools are needed for them, as was indicated in the Workshop.

ACKNOWLEDGEMENTS

The research work has been done at the CAD project headed by prof. R.Sulonen. I also like to thank the student group Ranta, Kemppainen, Koistinen and Koskivirta, who implemented the experimental UIMS version.

REFERENCES

Anson E (1980) The Semantics of Graphical Input. In: (Guedj 1980)

van den Bos J (1980) High-Level Graphics Input Tools and Their Semantics. In: (Guedj 1980)

Guedj R et al. (eds) (1980) Methodology of Interaction. North-Holland, Amsterdam, New York, Oxford

Hayes PJ, Ball JE, Reddy R (1981) Breaking the Man-Machine Communication Barrier. In: IEEE Computer, Mar 1981

Hopgood FRA, Duce DA (1980) A Production System Approach to Interactive Graphics Program Design. In : (Guedj 1980)

Moran TP (1980) A Framework for Studying Human-Computer Interaction. In: (Guedj 1980)

Mudur SP (1980) Graphic Input Specification in a General Purpose Interactive Graphics System. In: (Guedj 1980)

Newell ME (1983) Perseus(TM) - A Programmable Interactive User Interface in a Multi-Window Environment. In: NACG conference, Nov 1983, Washington

Nievergelt J, Weydert J (1980) Sites, Modes, and Trails: Telling the User of an Interactive System... In: (Guedj 1980)

Rosenthal DSH (1980) Models of Interactive Graphics Software. In: (Guedj 1980)

Takala TI (1983) Standard Graphics as a Geometric Modeling Device. In: Eurographics'83, North-Holland

Thomas JJ (chairman) (1983) Graphical Input Interaction Technique (GIIT) Workshop Summary. In: ACM Computer Graphics, Jan 1983

Some Issues in Future User Interface Management System (UIMS) Development

P. P. Tanner and W. A. S. Buxton

National Research Council of Canada, Ottawa, Ontario, Canada

INTRODUCTION

Much recent research has been directed at the development of better tools to support the design, specification, implementation, and evaluation of human-computer dialogues.[1] Such tools have been variously named "user interface management systems" (Kasik 1982; Buxton et al 1983), "dialogue management systems" (Roach et al 1982), and "abstract interaction handlers" (Feldman & Rodgers 1982). User interface management systems (UIMS's) build upon concepts developed in earlier user interface specification and prototyping systems (Newman 1968; Mason & Carey 1983). The state-of-the-art is now at the point where UIMS packages are becoming commercially available (Rubel Software 1983; Wasserman & Shewmake 1982; Woodmansee 1983).

UIMS's have grown out of an emerging recognition that designing consistently good user interfaces is as difficult as it is important. Virtually all work to date has been based on a few common premises:

- that the dialogue portion of an application can be isolated from the functionality (i.e., that the lexical and syntactic components can be isolated from the application semantics).
- that the ideal tool should render all dialogue styles equally accessible.
- that the UI design must inevitably be intertwined with its implementation, testing, and evaluation.
- that the applications programmer is not necessarily the best person to design the user interface.
- that the tools will render complex interfaces more maintainable, and facilitate portability of software, programmers and end users.

Viewing the dialogue as separable from the application functionality is an appealing notion, since it suggests that the former can be altered with minimum effect on the latter. The analogy made in this regard, by Feldman and Rodgers (1982) for example, is to data base management systems. The UIMS tools, therefore, are tailored to facilitate flexibility and ease in experimentation in the UI implementation, while causing minimum trauma to application functionality. The prime experimental benefit of such tools is, therefore, that they provide environments where alternative designs can be cost-effectively prototyped. The consequence of this is the adoption of an iterative approach to design (Buxton & Sniderman 1980; Swartout & Balzer 1982) which is in contrast to conventional software engineering techniques.

The objectives of such systems go even further, however. By isolating the UI as a separate module from the application and providing adequate tools, it is argued that the design of the UI can be undertaken by a specialist, who is not necessarily a programmer (Buxton et al 1982; Feldman & Rodgers 1982; Foley 1982). Finally, UIMS's facilitate the implementation of UI's that utilize asyncronous I/O. Because of system dependencies, this important mode of interaction is typically difficult for the application programmer to implement.

Existing UIMS's, based on the ideas outlined above, have gone a long way towards meeting their objectives. However, in examining the roots of some of their short-comings, and in planning for

---

* Computer Systems Research Group, University of Toronto, Toronto, Ontario, Canada, M5S-1A4

1. See for example, Ball & Hayes (1980, 1982), Borufka, Kuhlmann & ten Hagen (1982), Buxton, Lamb, Sherman & Smith (1983), Feldman & Rodgers (1982), Foley (1982), Kasik (1982), Olsen & Dempsey (1983), Roach, Hartson, Ehrich, Yunten & Johnson (1982), and Wong & Reid (1982).

the next generation UIMS, certain critical questions arise. For example:

- Is there a point where the separation of the UI and the semantic functionality breaks down? How can semantic feedback, for example, be adequately dealt with in a methodological way?
- Do the systems really push back the complexity barrier and make user interfaces easier to implement, test, and maintain?
- The modules provided in a UIMS will affect UI style through the bias of the path of least resistance. How can we exploit this bias to encourage a preferred and appropriate style of interaction?
- How can we determine sufficiency tests for UIMS's and accommodate currently rare dialogue styles (such as character recognition, voice input, and multi-handed parallel input)?
- To what extent is our ability to build such tools impeded by our underlying programming environment (computer architecture, operating systems, graphics packages, etc.)?
- How can we optimize our computing environment to support effective interaction?

Our prime objective is to encourage research into each of these issues. The rest of this paper will utilize existing UIMS's to discuss them in further detail.

TERMINOLOGY

In this paper the term *user* will refer to the end user of the application system, the person for whom the user interface was designed. The term *interaction programmer*, or simply the *programmer* will refer to the person who designs the interactive dialogue. The *application programmer* is the person who wrote the application, and an *interaction dialogue* is the set of possible user inputs where each input causes some information to be sent to the application, possibly resulting in some syntactic or semantic feedback on the display.

There is conflicting use of the term *user interface manager*. It has been used to refer to a person who manages a UIMS, and to the UIMS itself. For our purposes, the term will refer to the person, and *UIMS* will be used to refer to the system.

THE BEGINNINGS OF A MODEL

Virtually all UIMS's consist of two main modules. The first is a preprocessor which is used to design and implement the user interface. The second is a run-time support package which provides the mechanism that actually executes the UI. These two components are seen in Fig. 1.

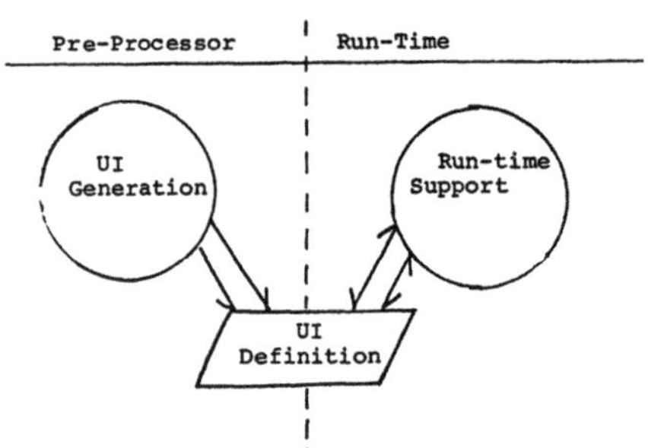

Fig. 1. Main Modules of a typical UIMS

Regardless of how these two modules are implemented they must communicate with each other. In the figure, we assume that this is accomplished through a shared file. It is common for the run-time module to be table-driven, and for the *UI Definition File* to contain the state-transition information.

From this simple model, already several issues arise. For example, it can be seen that the structure of the UI Definition File can have a great influence on both the pre-processor and run-time modules. If it is a regular table, it is relatively easy to build tools to generate and edit it. On the other hand, there are problems of efficiency in implementing large table-driven systems. Perhaps an even more important issue is the model's assumption that the interaction definition takes place previous to run-time, and probably before compile time. An alternative approach would be for the system to be structured such that the UI definition table could be altered at run-time. This is an alternative that will be discussed in a later part of this paper.

SEPARATION BETWEEN THE UIMS AND THE APPLICATION

One of the driving goals of UIMS development has been to separate the programming of the application from the programming of the user interface. The UIMS acts as a framework within which an interface designer constructs the dialogue rules for the user-application communication. The structure of this framework is largely affected by how the UIMS relates to the application code that executes along with it. Two models are described by Rosenthal and Yen (Thomas, Hamlin, et al 1982). Figure 2 shows what they call an external control UIMS, which invokes application modules in response to user inputs. An application would be programmed as discrete functional modules available to the UIMS when required.

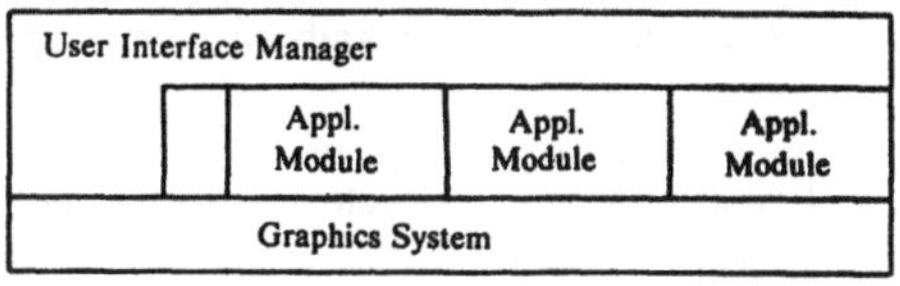

Fig. 2. Structure of External Control UIMS (from Thomas, Hamlin, et al 1982)

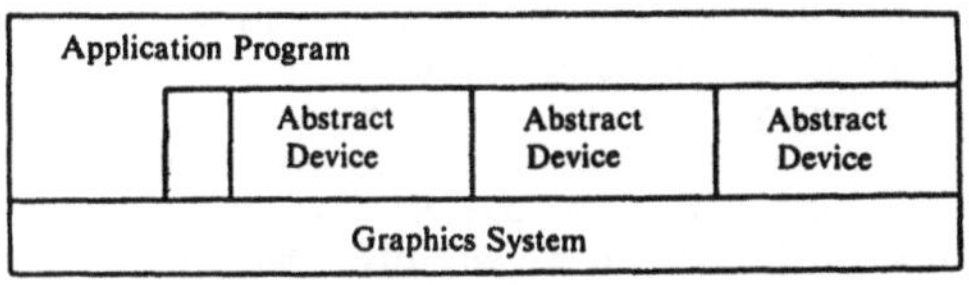

Fig. 3. Structure of Internal Control UIMS (from Thomas, Hamlin, et al 1982)

Figure 3 illustrates what they have termed an internal control UIMS. In this case, the application program is in charge of the flow of control within the package. It requests various abstract devices (e.g. choice, 2D valuator) when they are required by the application. A third model was suggested at the Seeheim workshop. This is a concurrent model, where the UIMS and application run in parallel.

The principal problem with any of these models is that it is not always clear what falls on what side of the line between the application and the UIMS. For example, is semantic feedback a function to be performed by the UIMS or the application package?[2] The UIMS cannot perform semantic feedback when this requires knowledge and manipulation of an application data base. The application cannot perform semantic feedback when such feedback is a function of the particular interaction design.

We have had examples of both cases in our experience with the ACTION package.[3] When used to manipulate control points in sculpted surface generation, ACTION was incapable of generating the required surfaces. This has to be done by the application program. On the other hand, Action was also used to vary parameters controlling a strip-mining simulation. The original application code had been written without any graphics input or output. By peeking into the data base of the application, ACTION was able to plot the position of trucks and status of shovels in the mine. Thus, this system included a module that crossed the boundary between the UIMS and the

2. We distinguish between lexical and semantic feedback. The difference can be seen in the difference "message received" and "message understood".

3. Action is a program package developed at the National Research Council of Canada for adding graphics to simulation and models (Tanner & Evans 1979; Tanner 1979; Tanner Wein & Evans 1981). It was not originally designed as a UIMS. However, many of its design goals were similar to that of a UIMS, and it has recently been used as one. As ACTION was implemented in a different manner than many UIMS's, it provides a convenient foil in comparing system designs. A short description of the ACTION package and its use as a UIMS appears as Appendix A.

application program. Perhaps in future, a finer distinction must be drawn between two classes of graphics: that to be handled by the UIMS and that to be handled by the application. In this case, however, an unambiguous means of assigning responsibilities must be developed which constrains the application by removing some 'direct' control from it.

In many applications, an appropriate way of specifying the data to be operated upon is to draw a circle around it on the screen, or "collect" it by successive "pick" operations. As Olsen and Dempsey (1983) point out, however, this transaction embodies one of the ten unsolved problems of computer graphics, as identified by Sutherland (1966). The pick operation just returns a segment number. How can a UIMS, with no semantic knowledge, possibly know what was intended by the transaction, based on the segment numbers alone? Clearly the UIMS needs some semantic knowledge to enable it to map the graphical information into the user's data model.

Garrett and Foley (1982) present one approach to the pick problem using data base techniques. However, the approach suffers from the fact that it assumes a particular data model, and therefore causes the UIMS to lose some of its desired generality. Also, such an approach will often be too slow for good interaction. We have, therefore, conflicting demands being made by our desire for speed and generality.

Another approach is to have the application supply a "pick service". This, however, must be rewritten for each application, and would be a non-trivial task if it must be able to handle "collected" or "encircled" items, rather than individual picks. Regardless of the approach, the issue must be dealt with. Otherwise, existing UIMS systems will be prejudiced against "chalk-talk" type dialogues which have proven their use, as illustrated in Buxton, Fiume, Hill, Lee & Woo (1983).

There are other areas where problems occur in attempting to separate the UI from the semantic component. One example concerns how the system handles setting and assuming default values. This has a great influence on the UI, and yet it requires a deep understanding of the semantic component to set up. How a UIMS would handle the integration of a spelling checker (Durham, Lamb & Saxe 1983) into a word processor's UI would be another example. Problems of this class will become more pronounced with the advent of knowledge-based, or "expert" systems. Here we see the need for a convergence of UIMS research with that of AI, as already begun in Ball and Hayes (1980) and Sheil (1983).

GLUE SYSTEMS AND MODULE BUILDERS

A major issue in the design of UIMS pre-processor modules is the trade-off that must be made between ease-of-use and generality. On the one hand we want systems that are easy to use, and which are appropriate for the interaction programmer, who may not be a computer programmer. On the other hand, we want general systems that can implement virtually any type of UI. Powerful easy-to-use systems are generally high level, and therefore restrictive. General systems are typically low-level and complex. To date, UIMS preprocessors have tended towards one extreme or the other. Because of their nature, we have chosen to call these two types of systems *glue systems* and *module builders* respectively.

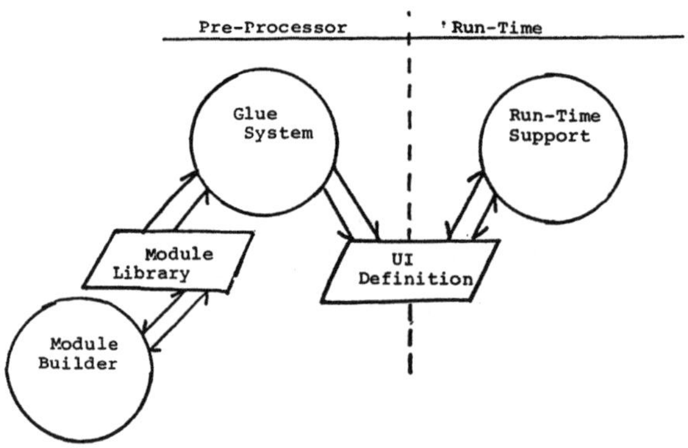

Fig. 4. UIMS with Glue System and Module Builder

MENULAY (Buxton et al 1983) and ACTION (Tanner & Evans 1979) are examples of systems which can be characterized as glue systems. They are tools that permit interactive dialogues to be constructed by using prepackaged modules. These modules, or "dialogue cells", are interactively selected from a library by the interaction programmer. The role of the UIMS, therefore, is to provide access to this library and provide the administrative support required to bind these modules to each other and to the application. The power and range of such systems is largely a function of the range and power of this library. What these systems provide, is a good environment for working on the dialogue at a very high level with minimum complexity.

In contrast, TIGER (Kasik 1982) and SYNGRAPH (Olsen & Dempsey 1983) are examples of systems that are not as well suited to dealing with the "presentation" level of the interface. Where their special strength lies is in specifying and implementing the low level details of the dialogue structure. An example would be defining the interaction modules used by the glue systems. This power derives from their providing a special language for defining interaction dialogues. More training is required to use such systems - one has to learn a new programming language. However, such systems are quite general. The interaction programmer is not restricted to the set of interactive techniques that some user interface manager has provided in some library. Rather, tools to create one's own library are provided.

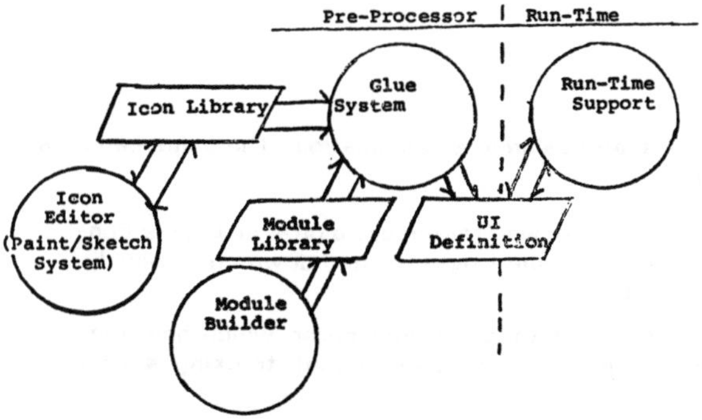

Fig. 5. Layered System with Icon Generator and Library

What is important to note is that the glue systems and module builders can, and probably should, co-exist in a complimentary fashion.[4] In this model, which is shown in Fig. 4, we see that the pre-processor is partitioned into two main modules which communicate through a dialogue cell "module library". Simply, the glue system is used to patch together dialogue cells created by the module builder. (The glue system may be, as in MENULAY, implemented from the low level modules in the module library.) Approaching things from this perspective, and making this distinction explicit, has the advantage that those tasks which should be done by an interaction specialist, who is not a programmer, are isolated in the glue system. Those functions that require a more specialized knowledge of programming concepts are isolated in the module builder.

The layering of the system can be extended one more step. Designing the presentation level of the UI includes the design and layout of icons (which may be used as light buttons and tracking symbols), and other graphics segments used for lexical and semantic feedback. The layout function is naturally handled by the glue system. However, like the design of interaction modules, the design of icons requires a special environment. This module would store graphics in a standard format in a special library, which would be accessed by the glue system (as shown in Fig. 5). One implication of this structure is that a standard format for the graphics exists (such as GKS metafiles).

4. The ideas that appear in this section owe a great deal to conversations with Dave Kasik and Dan Olsen at SIGGRAPH '83.

THE NEED FOR CONCURRENCY: SYSTEM AND USER

A major argument for adopting better tools is to reduce the complexity of thinking about and implementing interactive systems. One of the largest sources of such complexity is in coordinating and structuring all of the many activities that may be active at a given time. We can see this by looking at one of the modules in the module library of the University of Toronto UIMS (Buxton et al 1983). The module is the *graphic potentiometer*, shown in Fig. 6.

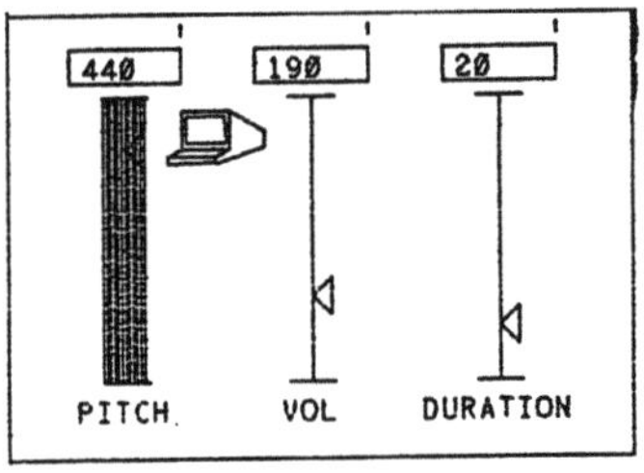

Fig. 6. Graphic Potentiometer Module

This module provides a method for adjusting a scalar value in an application. The value can be set several different ways (analogue and digital):

- by pointing at the "handle" and dragging it up or down (feedback: digital display is continuously updated; potentiometer is highlighted; handle moves up and down continuously; tracking symbol continues to track pointer position)
- by adjusting a continuous transducer, such as a manual potentiometer, which has been "connected" to the module (feedback: as in previous case except tracking symbol remains bound to pointing device)
- by pointing at the digital display, down/up on pointer select button, and typing a numerical value (feedback: terminal icon appears beside the display as prompt to type; digital display is updated; handle is moved to appropriate relative position)

Note that while the user is doing just one thing, changing a value, there are several simultaneous processes involved in the transaction. Examine the feedback for the first method. Even at the coarsest level, there are three processes: monitoring the input device, updating the display, and updating the parámeter being controlled. All of this could be done in a tight inner loop. However, things become much more complex when, for example, the application allows the simultaneous use of two such potentiometers, each connected to a different input device and controlling a different parameter. In many applications (such as process control) this is a typical configuration, and we would want both potentiometers active at the same time. Our simple loop structure becomes strained. Now, if we continue to work with conventional sequential languages, we will have to throw away virtually all the rules of well structured programming in order to realize the desired functionality. The result will be a program which is hard to read, modify, and maintain. If we use sequential languages, a UIMS can help us manage some of the resulting complexity. More potent is to recognize that the use of concurrent programming structures could contribute greatly to overcoming the problem.

We tend to use computers as if we had no feet, only one hand, and no ears. However, our operation of other machinery, such as automobiles or sewing machines, illustrates the complex interactions of which we are capable. A major objective of UIMS design should be to serve as a catalyst in realizing this potential.

SUSPENDED-TIME UI DEFINITION/MODIFICATION

What if during execution of a program we wanted to change something in the UI? For example, we might want to specify a value using a graphical potentiometer rather than by typing. Or, we might want to change the size, position or style of a light button. In section three it was suggested that this could be considered as something that the UIMS should support. During run-time, execution could be suspended and the UI definition table modified. With an appropriate design, this could be done by allowing the glue system to be invoked. This notion of modifying the UI during this "suspended time" is illustrated in Fig. 7. One might argue that the user will never want to modify the UI, or should be restricted from doing so. Nevertheless, the feature would still be worthwhile to the interaction programmer and user interface manager. Namely, being able to modify the UI in the middle of execution will speed up testing and debugging, and therefore shorten the cycle time of each prototype iteration.

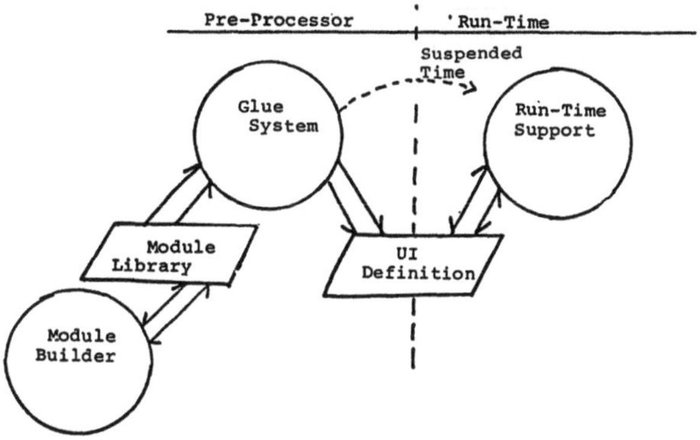

Fig. 7. Suspended-Time Modification of UI

CONTROLLING UI BIAS

Ideally a UIMS should enable the interaction programmer to design any interaction technique with the same ease. This implies that all interaction techniques must be in the UIMS library, ready for the programmer's use. This, of course, is impossible. Some set of techniques must be selected for the library, although others could always be added using the module builder.

It is fair to assume that the interaction programmer will often have a bias towards using existing modules from the library, rather than going through the expense of creating new ones. This is simply the bias of the path of least resistance. Interaction dialogues will, therefore, be flavoured by the interaction library of the UIMS on which they were created. This bias is something that should not be determined by chance. Rather, it should be assumed that the system is biased, and this bias be used to encourage preferred types of dialogue style. The problem for the user interface manager, therefore, is to determine the appropriate degree of generality that must be supported. As a guide, a system should generally support implementing dialogues as diverse as, for example, the selection positioning task described in Buxton (1982): dragging, moving-menu/stationary cursor, character recognition, typing, or function keys.

EVALUATION AND POST-PROCESSING

The UIMS model developed to this point has two main parts, the pre-processor and the run-time module. However, many users of UIMS's develop their UI's using an iterative approach to design (Buxton & Sniderman 1980). Systems are implemented, tested, evaluated, and then reimplemented. The cycle continues until the system is satisfactory, or until time or money are exhausted. The UIMS provides a tool which greatly aids the implementation phase. As a result, the cycle time is shortened. The systems could, however, be extended to aid in the evaluation phase, as well. Namely, they could generate log files of time-stamped data which recorded all interactions during the test phase. This logging would be the responsibility of the run-time module (or more accurately, the graphics package event handler). Another main module would then be added, as shown in Fig. 8. This is the evaluation tool, which aids in the analysis of the time-stamped data. Preliminary work in this area suggests that such tools have great potential in UI design (Buxton 1982; Buxton et al 1983).

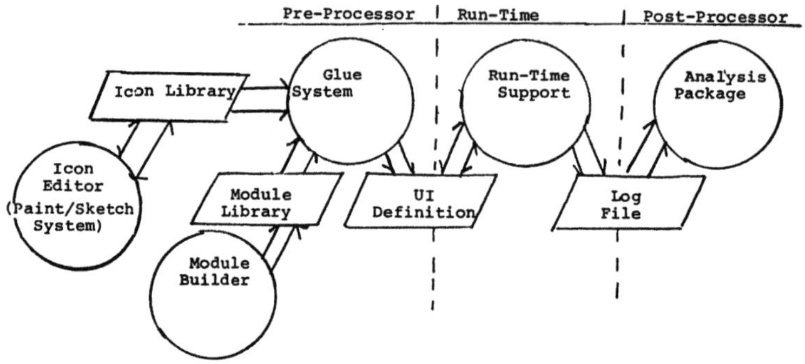

Fig. 8. UIMS model with Analysis Module

PROGRAMMING ENVIRONMENT

There are several components of the computing environment besides the UIMS that affect the UI:

- the available input/output devices
- the graphics support package
- the window manager
- the operating system (O/S)
- and the workstation architecture.

The interplay among these components is complex and not well understood. For example, a UIMS is supposed to provide control over the UI. However, if the application is run through a window manager, the window system itself will impose its own UI on the user. This UI must be taken into consideration by the interaction programmer, since it can affect that of the application.

The support given by the graphics system and the O/S is another concern. The nature of the UIMS greatly affects the type of support needed. For example, SYNGRAPH (Olsen & Dempsey 1983) looks at its input as a single stream of tokens which it then parses. When semantic feedback is required for constantly sampled input, such as that from a locator, it would be appropriate to consider changes in the locator position as events, allowing the parser to receive its tokens through an AWAIT EVENT type of mechanism. However, this use of sampled devices as event emitting devices is not permitted in GKS (International Organization for Standardization 1983). What is required is the ability to specify a new layer which enables devices to send event reports at specified time intervals or when a normally sampled device changes value by a specified amount.

Going to the opposite extreme, ACTION services each of its active dialogues once during each "tick", (see Appendix A). In this case, all the active devices are sampled to check their current status. Even buttons and changes in the tablet pen status are sampled rather than dealt with in an event driven manner. A polling UIMS needs only the GKS sample device support, and does not need event queues or triggers since event detection and event response are handled by the interaction dialogue specification. It does, however, need special device handlers that save such events as pen pushes so that they may be handled during the next tick.

GKS supports the implementation of simultaneously active parallel input devices. Each input device may have an independent active measure process and a trigger process. However, implementing many communicating processes on most operating systems results in significant context switching and memory overhead. Similarly the external control UIMS shown in Fig. 2 (Thomas, Hamlin, et al 1982), implemented as a set of separate communicating processes, results in the same overhead problem.

An operating system design that may be very appropriate for supporting the many sequential processes of a UIMS is one that would allow fast execution of message passing between processes, rapid context switching, and low per-process overhead. Such a system, Thoth

(Gentleman 1981), has been used for several years at the University of Waterloo. A descendant of Thoth, Harmony (Gentleman 1983a, 1983b), which supports rapid message passing among processes on a multi-processor system has recently been written at the National Research Council of Canada. Both Thoth and Harmony use a small set of message passing primitives to support inter-process communication and I/O. Message passing is very quick, taking about 1ms for a Send-Reply-Receive sequence.

From a UIMS designer's point of view, perhaps the most interesting experience derived from the use of such a system is that gained from the programming of an interactive Paint program (Beach, Beatty, Booth, Plebon & Fiume 1982; Plebon & Booth 1982). Figure 9 shows the organization chart for this multiprocess Paint program. As we shall see, the Paint User Interface bears a certain similarity to a UIMS. The Tablet Administrator takes the place of both the GKS active measure process and the trigger process for the tablet.

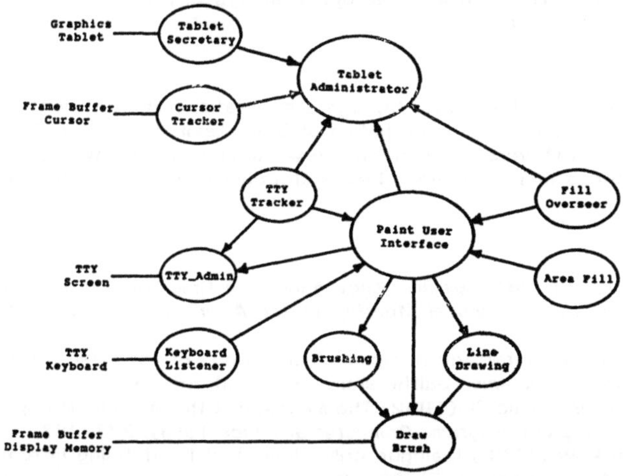

Fig. 9. Organizational Chart for Paint Program (from Beach et al 1982)

The Paint User Interface samples tablet values which can then be sent to active application modules, such as Brushing, Line Drawing, or Draw Brush. The Tablet Administrator can reply to a request for a trigger from the Fill Overseer (if the user pushes a tablet button). The Fill Overseer is a temporary process that, on receiving a tablet trigger, will signal the Paint User Interface to abort the Area Fill process. The Tablet Administrator receives the tablet information from the Tablet Secretary, and sends the tablet X,Y position to the Cursor Tracker to update the echo. The Tablet Administrator is never blocked waiting for the completion of a message passing sequence. Processes that need information from the Administrator request it using a .Send. (After a process issues a .Send, its excution is blocked until it receives a reply.) The administrator gives the information using a nonblocking reply. Gentleman (1981) includes a good description of the organization of interactive and real time programs written with Thoth.

Using such an operating system makes it natural to program parallel processes to process parallel input. Going one step further, a Harmony-type O/S could control a multi-processor system that includes the processors that act as controllers for various devices. For example, the Tablet Administrator could be simply a process on the frame-buffer controller, passing lexical feedback messages to the display controller process with a rapid transmission speed (since the two processes are on the same processor), but passing tablet position values to the application modules on different processors at a slower speed.

This section has only touched on a few of the issues in using message-passing operating systems to support UIMS's. It is an approach that seems well suited for UIMS support; however, very little of the leg work has yet been done. Much effort will have to be spent, and many problems overcome before we will know whether these operating systems are indeed appropriate. At this stage, we believe that experimental implementations of UIMS's on such systems would be a worthwhile exercise.

CONCLUSIONS

Although several UIMS's are now in operation, much work remains to be done. This paper has suggested some areas that require further study. In the process, it has developed a model of UIMS systems which identifies the major components for study. We saw an integrated UIMS as consisting of *specification tools* consisting of a module builder and glue system, *run-time support tools*, and *analysis tools*. We have seen that the UIMS cannot be as isolated from the application semantics as had originally been presumed. We also addressed the importance of supporting concurrent programming structures. As well, we discussed how unrealistic it is to assume that the influence of the UIMS is neutral with respect to the systems it generates. It was suggested that the bias imposed by such systems could be turned towards the encouragement of good design practice.

Major problems that remain to be adequately addressed concern how the UIMS relates to other major components of the computing environment, namely the operating system, graphics support utilities, window manager, and workstation design.

ACKNOWLEDGEMENTS

Several people contributed to the content of this paper through conversations and comments on the manuscript. We would like to acknowledge the contribution of Dave Kasik, Dan Olsen, Ralph Hill, Dave Schiferl, Marceli Wein and Brad Meyers. In addition, we would like to acknowledge the support of the Canadian Natural Sciences and Engineering Research Council for their contribution to the research.

REFERENCES

Ball E, Hayes P (1980) Representation of Task-Specific Knowledge in a Gracefully Interacting User Interface. *Proceedings of the 1st Annual Meeting of the American Association for Artificial Intelligence:* 116-120.

Ball E, Hayes P (1982) A Test-Bed for User Interface Designs. *Proceedings of the First Conference on Human Factors in Computer Systems.* Gaithersburg, Maryland: 85-88.

Beach RJ, Beatty JC, Booth KS, Plebon DA, Fiume EL (1982) The message is the medium: Multiprocess structuring of an interactive paint program. *Computer Graphics* 16(3): 277-287.

Borufka HG, Kuhlmann HW, ten Hagen PJW (1982) Dialogue cells: A method for defining interactions. *Computer Graphics and Applications.* 2(5): 25-33.

Buxton W A, Sniderman R (1980) Iteration in the design of the human-computer interface. *Proceedings of the 13th Annual Meeting of the Human Factors Association of Canada:* 72-81.

Buxton WA (1982) An informal study of selection positioning tasks. *Proc. Graphics Interface '82.* 8th Conf. of the Canadian Man-Computer Communications Society, Toronto: 323-328.

Buxton WA (1983) Lexical and pragmatic considerations of input structure. *Computer Graphics* 17(1): 31-37.

Buxton W, Fiume E, Hill R, Lee, A, Woo C (1983) Continuous Hand-Gesture Driven Input. *Proc. Graphics Interface '83*, 9th Conference of the Canadian Man-Computer Communications Society, Edmonton: 191-195

Buxton WA, Lamb MR, Sherman D, Smith KC (1983) Towards a comprehensive user interface management system. *Computer Graphics* 17(3): 31-38.

Durham I, Lamb D, Saxe J (1983) Spelling Correction in User Interfaces *Comm. ACM* 26(10): 764-773.

Feldman M, Rodgers G (1982) Toward the design and development of style-independent interactive systems. *Proc. 1st Annual Conference on Human Factors in Computer Systems*, Gaithersburg Maryland: 111-116.

Foley J (1982) Framework for the design, evaluation, and implementation of user-computer interfaces. *Proc. Graphics Interface '82*, 8th Conf. of the Canadian Man-Computer Communications Society, Toronto, (abstract only): 1

Garrett MT, Foley JD (1982) Graphics Programming Using a Database System with Dependency Declarations. *ACM TOG*, 1(2): 109-128.

Gentleman WM (1981) Message passing between sequential processes: The reply primitive and the administrator concept. *Software Practice and Experience*, 11: 435-466.

Gentleman WM (1983a) If only the hardware... (A software designer's lament). *Proceedings of the IEEE International Workshop on Computer Systems Organization: 88-95*

Gentleman W M (1983b) Using the Harmony Operating System. *Technical Report ERB-966 NRC No. 23030*, National Research Council of Canada, Ottawa.

International Organization for Standardization (1983) *Information Processing-Graphical Kernel*

System (GKS) Functional Description, ISO/DIS 7942.
Kasik DJ (1982) A user interface management system. *Computer Graphics* 16(3): 99-106
Mason R, Carey T (1983) Prototyping Interactive Information Systems. *Comm. ACM* 26(5): 347-354.
Newman W (1968) A System for Interactive Graphical Programming. *Proc. Spring Joint Computer Conference*: 47-54.
Olsen DR Jr, Dempsey EP (1983) SYNGRAPH: A graphical user interface generator. *Computer Graphics* 17(3): 43-50
Plebon DA, Booth KS (1982) Interactive picture creation systems. *CS-82-46*, University of Waterloo Computer Science Department.
Roach J, Hartson R, Ehrich R, Yunten T, Johnson D (1982) DMS: A comprehensive system for managing human-computer dialogue. *Proc. 1st Annual Conference on Human Factors in Computer Systems*, Gaithersburg, Maryland: 102-105.
Rubel Software (1983) *BLOX Graphics Builder*. Rubel Software, One Soldiers Field Park 605, Cambridge, Massachusetts 02163.
Sheil B (1983) Power tools for programmers. *Datamation* 29(2): 131-144
Sutherland, IE (1966) Computer Graphics: Ten Unsolved Problems. *Datamation* 12(5): 22
Swartout W, Balzer R (1982) On the inevitable intertwining of specification and implementation. *Comm. ACM* 25(7): 438-440.
Tanner PP, Evans KB (1979) ACTION, a graphics aid to interacting with models and simulations. *Proc. 6th Conf. of the Canadian Man-Computer Communications Society*, Ottawa: 49-61.
Tanner PP (1979) ACTION, a graphics aid to interacting with models and simulations. M. Sc. Thesis, Carleton University. Available as ERB 920 from the National Research Council of Canada, Ottawa.
Tanner PP, Wein M, Evans KB (1981) Dynamic illustrative graphics for simulations. *DISPLAYS Technology and Application*, 2(5): 245-250.
Thomas JJ, Hamlin GH, et al (1982) Graphical input interaction technique workshop summary. *Computer Graphics* 17(1): 5-30
Wasserman AI, Shewmake DT (1982) Rapid Prototyping of Interactive Information Systems. *ACM Software Engineering Notes*. 7(5): 171-180
Wong PCS, Reid ER (1982) FLAIR-User interface design tool. *Computer Graphics* 16(3): 87-98
Woodmansee, G. (1983) Visi On's Interface Design. *Byte* 8(7): 166-182.

APPENDIX A: ACTION Package

Introduction

In the late 70's, there was considerable work done at the National Research Council of Canada (NRC) on a program package used to provide an interactive environment for computer simulation,. The system was to provide facilities for users to monitor the progress and control various aspects of simulations (Tanner & Evans 1979; Tanner 1979; Tanner Wein & Evans 1981). This package was basically an externally controlled UIMS (Fig. 2). Actually the ACTION package was not designed to be a UIMS. NRC had, at the time, many computer models and simulations that had been programmed without any thought of graphics. They wanted to provide an environment where illustrative or symbolic dynamic graphics could be quickly and easily attached to these simulations without much reprogramming. For such an environment to be considered friendly, all of the tools would have to be easy to use, and require little apprenticeship to learn their use. Mistakes would have to be easily repairable, and perhaps most important to the current discussion of UIMS's, experiments in interaction design would be quick and easy to undertake.

Switchboard Model

The ACTION package, which ties together a simulation with graphics output and input devices, is modelled on a telephone switchboard. This switchboard can link input device values with simulation variables, or simulation variables with graphical transformations of picture segments.

The requirements for the ACTION environment encourage a unique style of language. As the simulation and the ACTION package can run asyncronously, one has, on one hand, a simulation executing at some speed, making available some set of parameters that change over time, while on the other hand there is a set of input devices also producing time-varying values. The language must tie pairs of these values together or connect values to graphical transformations. For example, if the switchboard program contains a statement of the sort

OILTAX=POT(1)

the parameter OILTAX (perhaps in an energy model), would be tied to the value of the first potentiometer. This means that OILTAX would be reset to the current value of the first pot at some request rate, usually equivalent to the CRT frame update rate. If the program were to include the statement

POSITION_XY(CAR, TABLET)

the picture segment CAR would be tied to the position of the tablet pen.

In a switchboard, at any one time, several connections are being made simultaneously. Moreover, a short time interval later, those same connections are still being made unless something has changed the mode of the system. An ACTION program defines this single state switchboard. The complete ACTION program is executed once during each "tick" (the display update rate, 50-500ms depending on the complexity of the displayed image and the model). During each tick, every link in the switchboard is checked, data is passed from input devices to the model, and the picture segments on the display are modified according to the values of the simulation variables.

We can carry this model further to make it the base for a UIMS. Interaction dialogues can also be thought of in this switchboard context. At any one time, one or more interactions are possible; perhaps the user can make a selection from a menu, grab and drag an object across the screen, as well as changing object colour using both a two-dimensional valuator for the hue and saturation and a single-dimension valuator for the lightness component.

A UIMS could be constructed in which each of these possible dialogues is a separate routine or module. Then, like the ACTION language, the routine for each currently possible interactive dialogue would be run in its entirety, around 20 times per second. In the example above, a UIMS routine for a menu, one for the dragger, a third for the 2D valuator, and a fourth for the single-dimensional valuator would be simultaneously active. The user could be moving the picture segment with the dragger while simultaneously changing colour.

The dragger routine supports an interaction which allows the user to pick an item with the tablet puck, and drag that item while the puck button is depressed. It then anchors the item at its current position when the button is released. This interaction "chunks" several interactions into one logical sequence. Using our switchboard model, this could be implemented with the following few lines of code:

```
initialize:
    pick_seg = 0;
    on_echo(drag);

run:
    if pick_seg = 0
        pick_seg = pick(tablet_image);
    else if tablet_image(status) = down
        move (pick_seg, tablet_image(mouse));
    else
        pick_seg = 0;
terminate:
    off_echo(drag);
```

The following definitions hold for the example:

- *pick_seg* is a picture segment pointer when set to some non-zero value.
- *drag* is the name of a picture segment to be used as an icon.
- *pick* is a function that returns a segment pointer if an item is picked and returns a 0 otherwise.
- *tablet_image* is that area of the tablet corresponding to the image window on the screen.
- *tablet_image(mouse)* is an x,y value giving the displacement of the tablet pen since the last check on the displacement (i.e. mouse mode).

If the tablet puck is close to a picture segment, and the puck button is depressed, then pick_seg is set to point to that segment. The function will move the selected segment as the tablet puck moves (here the tablet is used in mouse mode; only changes in the position of the tablet are used to move the segment, absolute positions of the tablet are unimportant). It should be noted that the current version of ACTION cannot execute the above code, but this is a logical extension of the current implementation.

This dialogue routine would be run once per tick, as would the other currently active dialogue routines. Statements can, of course, be added to the dialogue routines to handle information flow to and from the application and to invoke application modules in response to some input.

Graphics Editor

Like MENULAY, ACTION does have an interactive graphics front end. Since ACTION is basically a glue system where interactive techniques are available as function calls, the graphics editor is directed mainly towards aiding the programmer define parameters for the function calls, the graphical editor engages in a menu-based question and answer session which allows the user to respond to such questions as "which picture segment is to be the parameter for your MOVE function call". A valid response could be a picture segment pick using the tablet puck, or the name of the picture segment could be typed in.

User Experience

The ACTION package has been used successfully to add both the graphics and user interaction to several event driven simulations that were not designed to use graphics. All output was originally destined to the line printer, and no thought had been given to allow user input. More recently, the package has been used to add user control to vary model parameters in a sculpted surface package. However, ACTION was not designed to be a general purpose UIMS. Major revisions (or a complete rewrite) would be required for it to reach that state. It has a small number of predefined interaction tools, it has neither tablet nor screen window handler, and requires a more powerful user language to define and glue tools. However, the current facility has given us some insight into the needs and possibilities of UIMS's.

Architecture for A User Interface Management System

J. J. Thomas

Battelle Pacific Northwest Laboratories, Battelle Boulevard Richland, Washington, WA 99352, USA

ABSTRACT

The term User Interface Management System has been coined to represent a set of software tools for the construction and control of the interaction dialogue between the user and the computational resource. This set of software tools will have a significant impact on the structure of applications in the future. Its advantages include faster and more reliable application development, consistent user interfaces across application domains, and easily modifiable user interfaces. Also, the user interface management systems are an essential experimental tool for research in the human computer interface. This paper describes a brief history of UIMS and an architecture for a specific UIMS to provide an adaptable user interface.

BACKGROUND

The needs and concepts leading to the current UIMS's have been discussed for many years (Foley 1981; Swartout and Bolger 1982; Buxton and Sniderman 1980). These needs along with the current state of technology lead to a team of researchers from Lawrence Berkley Laboratory, Harvard Holmes, Pacific Northwest Laboratory, James Thomas, and GWU (Foley, Feldman, Kamran, Rogers), to focus attention for an 11 month dedicated effort on the construction issues leading towards UIMS systems. The output was an implementation of a simple UIMS. This UIMS could provide consistent interaction styles across two application domains; first, SEEDIS, a geographical information system from Lawrence Berkely Laboratories, and second, ALDS (Thomas and Hall 1983), a tool for the statistical analysis of large data sets. During this effort, several others joined in concert in offering approaches to UIMS's. These included Grif Hamlin of Los Almos Scientific Laboratories, Dave Kasik of Boeing Computer Services, and Bill Buxton from the University of Toranto.

To help establish the concepts within the UIMS, Grif Hamlin and Jim Thomas proposed a workshop on Graphic Input Interaction Techniques to be sponsored by ACM SIGGRAPH. This workshop was held in Seattle on June 2-4, and is documented in a dedicated issue of ACM/SIGGRAPH Computer Graphics, January 1983. At this workshop, the term UIMS was coined and given its identity as a significant research area seen to have a major impact on application developments in the future. The unanimous agreement of the workshop participants indicated the concepts were understood and could provide a focus for further research.

This unanimous agreement also indicated that others had recognized the importance of the underlined concepts of UIMS and had been working in related fields for quite some time. The majority of the time at the GIIT workshop was spent in further defining the concepts of the UIMS. This established a clear understanding and pointed out: (1) the need for continued interdisciplinary research, (2) the lack of tools for the construction and usage of UIMS systems, and (3) a focus on further research areas.

At SIGGRAPH 82, David Rosenthal proposed that Eurographics sponsor a workshop on UIMS. Also at that time, Frank Moses, Army Research Institute and Jim Thomas proposed a workshop on Understanding User Task Interfaces: Styles and Techniques. These two workshops were proposed to concentrate attention on the software aspects of the UIMS and to clarify the interdisciplinary relationships required to better understand interaction methodology.

Since then, research has continued in several areas of UIMS. This paper discusses one area, the architecture of UIMS specifically to allow for an adaptable (dynamically changing) user interface management system. That is, its primarly goal is to allow the system to change and adapt its interaction style to the user's needs rather than requiring the user to adapt to the computer's needs.

ARCHITECTURE

The basic task of the UIMS is similar to language translator systems. That is, the input dialogue is translated into a language controlling the application modules. Therefore, it is not surprising to see that the components of a UIMS have similar components to that of traditional language translators (Aho 1979). A key difference between language translation and the UIMS is that most language translation is one way (towards code generation). UIMS, on the other hand, can provide communication at any level within the UIMS from the interaction feedback tied directly to the interaction technique to an application control training set.

Figure 1 illustrates the architecture for the proposed UIMS.

Interaction techniques are the processes for requesting the response and handling of that interaction. Note that an interaction technique involves a prompt, a language input, an input process, as well as an interaction feedback. Any of these four components of an interaction technique may be null but all must be addressed in defining interaction techniques.

An example interaction technique subdivided into four stages would be function key interaction. The prompt may be the back lighting of the key. The language input is the action of pushing the key and the resulting event. The input processing, the identifications of the function key, and the feedback may be the blinking back lighting signaling the selection.

The interaction techniques will be chosen based on several factors. These include devices available, tasks to be completed, user familiarity with techniques, etc. Since these techniques are separate from the application, changing or adapting these interaction techniques to fit the situation is achievable.

FIGURE 1

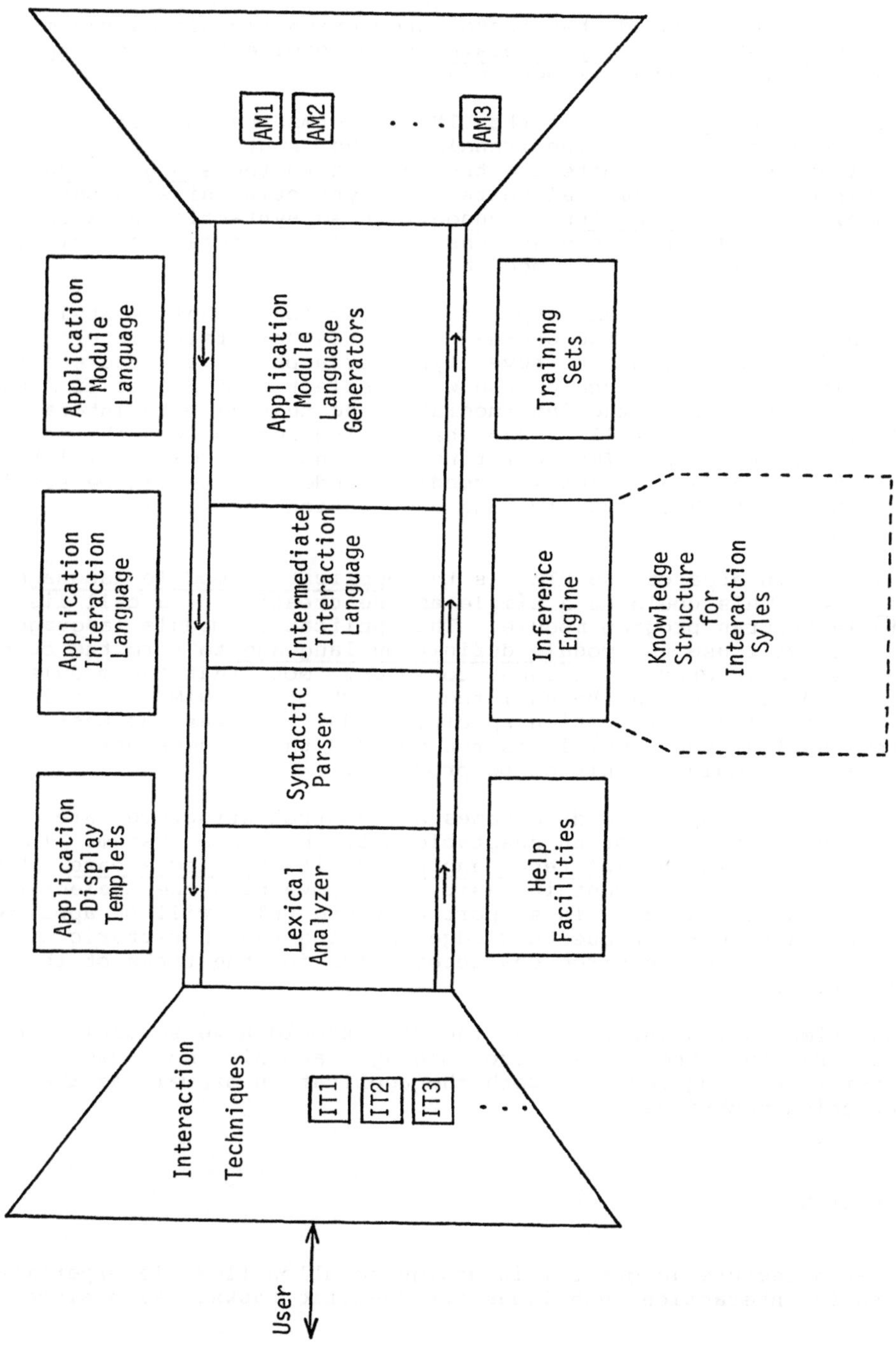
AM1
AM2
AM3
Application Module Language
Application Interaction Language
Application Display Templets
Application Module Language Generators
Intermediate Interaction Language
Syntactic Parser
Lexical Analyzer
Training Sets
Inference Engine
Knowledge Structure for Interaction Syles
Help Facilities
Interaction Techniques
IT1
IT2
IT3
User

There are likely to be a library of interaction techniques. Some researchers are starting to identify such libraries (Martin 1973; Green 1982; Foley, Wallace and Chan 1981). At the GIIT Workshop, a call was made for a classification schema for those interaction technique catalogs.

It should also be noted that these interaction techniques can make use of Application Display Templates to determine both the output format as well as input responses.

The lexical analysis part of the UIMS performs the interaction technique identification and translates the input language into the lexical units. These units are then passed to the syntactic parser. This parser combines lexical units into syntactic units as defined as the application interaction language. These syntactic units can be a combination of several interactions to form a response to a single request from an application module.

The syntact parser has as output an interaction technique style independent language. The George Washington University interaction handler [Thomas 2] contains seven types of a phrase structure interaction language. One such phrase was a select N of a list of M elements. The design of the intermediate code that is both interaction style independent as well as application independent was the most difficult part of the UIMS to refine. Extensive research will be required before generalized intermediate code formats can be specificied having both interaction and application independent characteristics.

The last main area of the UIMS is the application module language generator. This could be a simple as the creation of a call list for a single Fortran program module. The application module language generator will use the module definition language to form the output commands and interpret the input commands. Note that the module language definition may be an integral part of the UIMS if it is intended to be an application specific UIMS. However, as most systems evolve over time, it is recommended that a separate application module definition be provided.

Several other supportive data bases and control structures are necessary to provide for an adaptable user interface system. The most important is the inference engine and its knowledge base. The inference engine must contain basic rules governing the selection of interaction techniques. In support of these rules will be application interaction technique knowledge defining the characteric of the techniques and the required characteristics for the tasks of the application.

At any time during interaction, the UIMS should have several levels of help ranging from simple error messages and hint messages to extensive training sets for both the application as well as the interaction techniques.

CONCLUSION

This architecture is general in design to allow flexible experimentation in interaction techniques for specific tasks. Also since adaptable user interfaces are not common, a more general structure must be proposed. As research continues, the architechture is expected to evolve.

REFERENCES

Aho AV, Ullman JD (1979) The principles of compiler design, Addision Wesley

Buxton W, Sniderman R(1980) Interaction and the design of the human-computer interface, Proceedings of the 13th Annual Meeting of the Human Factors Associations of Canada, pp 72-81

Foley JK, Wallace VL, Chan PM (1981) The human factors of interaction techniques, IIST Report 81-03, Department of Electrical Engineering and Computer Science, The George Washington University, Washington D.C.

Green M (1982) A catalog of graphical interaction techniques, GIIT Workshop, Seattle, Washington

Green M (1982) Towards a user interface prototyping system, Proceedings of Graphic Interface 1982, Toranto, pp 37-45

Martin J (1973) Design of man-computer dialogue, Englewood Cliffs, N. J. Prentice Hall

Stwartout W, Balzer R (1982) An inevitable intertwining of specification and implementation, Communication of the ACM 25(7), pp 438-440

Thomas JJ, Hall DL (1983) Motivation, statistical database management issues, perspectives, and directions, Second International Workshop on Statistical Database Management, Los Altos, California

Thomas JJ, Hamlin G (1982) Graphical input interaction technique (GIIT), ACM SIGGRAPH Workshop

Thomas JJ, Holmes HH, Rogers GT (1982) A clause-structured interaction handler, Technical Report GWV-IIST-81-20, The George Washington University, Institute for Information Science and Technology, Washington D.C.

Part 3

Dialogue Specification Tools

Design Notations and User Interface Management Systems

M. Green

Department of Computing Science, University of Alberta, Edmonton, Alberta, Canada

INTRODUCTION

The topic of this paper is the design notations required to support User Interface Management Systems (UIMS). For the purposes of this paper a user interface is the software module that stands between the user and the rest of the program. The user interface is the only part of the program that directly deals with the user, all the other modules obtain user input from the user interface and rely on the user interface to present output to the user. Traditionally the user interface has been programmed by hand. The hand construction of the user interface for each new application is costly and has a negative effect on user interface quality. This need not be the case since the same basic user interface structure can be used in a wide range of applications. This leads to the notion of a UIMS, a program that automatically constructs a user interface given a description of it.

The two key questions raised here are: what descriptions are necessary to automatically construct a user interface, and what should these descriptions look like? In order to address the first question a logical model of user interfaces must be developed. This model divides the user interface into a number of conceptual levels that are similar in spirit to the schemas in Data Base Management Systems (DBMS) [Date 1981]. The user interface model used here is discussed in section two of this paper. Each of the conceptual levels requires a description, the nature of these descriptions depends upon the model of the user interface employed by the UIMS. User interface models are similar in spirit to the data models found in DBMS. Some of the user interface models that have been used or proposed are discussed in section three. In the fourth section some of the notations that have been proposed will be examined. The emphasis is placed on how these notations relate to our model of a UIMS.

In this discussion several analogies have been made between UIMS and DBMS. The database area is a good source of motivation for work on user interface management. This field has many similarities to user interfaces, the key ones being the emphasis on applications and the management of large complex software systems. But, some care should be given to the use of this analogy. The designer or developer of a DBMS has a large amount of knowledge to draw upon in the database literature. The models that underlie DBMSs have been thoroughly studied and most of their properties are well understood. There have been a large number of DBMSs implemented and used in production. The experience gained from these implementations is available to the designers of a new DBMS so they can build on the work of others. This is not the case in the user interface field. There does not exist a large body of knowledge on which to base the design of a

UIMS. We still don't understand the nature of human-computer interaction and the proper structuring of graphics programs. While the designer of a DBMS is building on a very firm foundation, the designer of a UIMS is building on shifting sand. As a result he should not be surprised if his edifice collapses.

A LOGICAL MODEL OF USER INTERFACES

The purpose of this section is to present a possible model for the logical structure of a user interface. This logical model identifies the descriptions required to automatically generate a user interface for a given application. The approach taken in the development of this model is to work from the outside in. A very simple model of a user interface is shown in fig. 1.

```
----------          ----------------          --------------------
|        |          |              |          |                  |
|        |--->------|     User     |---->-----|   Applications   |
|  User  |          |              |          |                  |
|        |---<------|   Interface  |----<-----|     Program      |
|        |          |              |          |                  |
----------          ----------------          --------------------
```

Fig. 1 A simple model of a user interface

In this simple model only the two components that must interface with the user interface are shown. On the one side there is a user who conducts a dialogue with the user interface. On the other side is the rest of the applications program which the user interface draws upon to perform calculations and manage data. In order to completely describe the user interface we must have descriptions of both these components. Following Green [Green 1984], the description of the user will be called a task model. A task model is a description of the tasks the user performs with the user interface. It describes the objects the user is interested in and the operations he performs on them. The task model corresponds to the conceptual level in Foley's language model [Foley and Van Dam 1982]. The applications program is described by an application model. This model describes the operations and data objects that are supplied by the applications program. The operations in this model correspond to the procedures or modules that can be called by the user interface.

At this point descriptions of the two components the user interface communicates with are available, but not its internal structure. One way of viewing the user interface is as a function that transforms the tasks of the user into the procedures and data structures of the applications program. This transformation is usually fairly complex so it must be divided into a number of steps. The user interacts with the user interface by performing a sequence of physical actions. These actions include keystrokes, gestures made with a mouse or tablet cursor, adjusting dials, and reading information on displays. The order of the actions determines the commands invoked and the data entered by the user. The descriptions of these actions is called an action model. The action model is what is traditionally viewed as the description of the user interface. The last description required to completely define the user interface is the control model. The control model is a logical description of the user interface. It defines the semantics of the user interface, along with the objects and operations that are required to structure it. The control model is similar to the task model, it can be viewed as a rewrite of the task model in the vocabulary of the user interface. The control model describes all the commands in the user interface in terms of their operands and the effects they have. It also describes the main structuring mechanisms of the user interface, such as menus and command selection. The control model can be viewed as the user's model of the user interface.

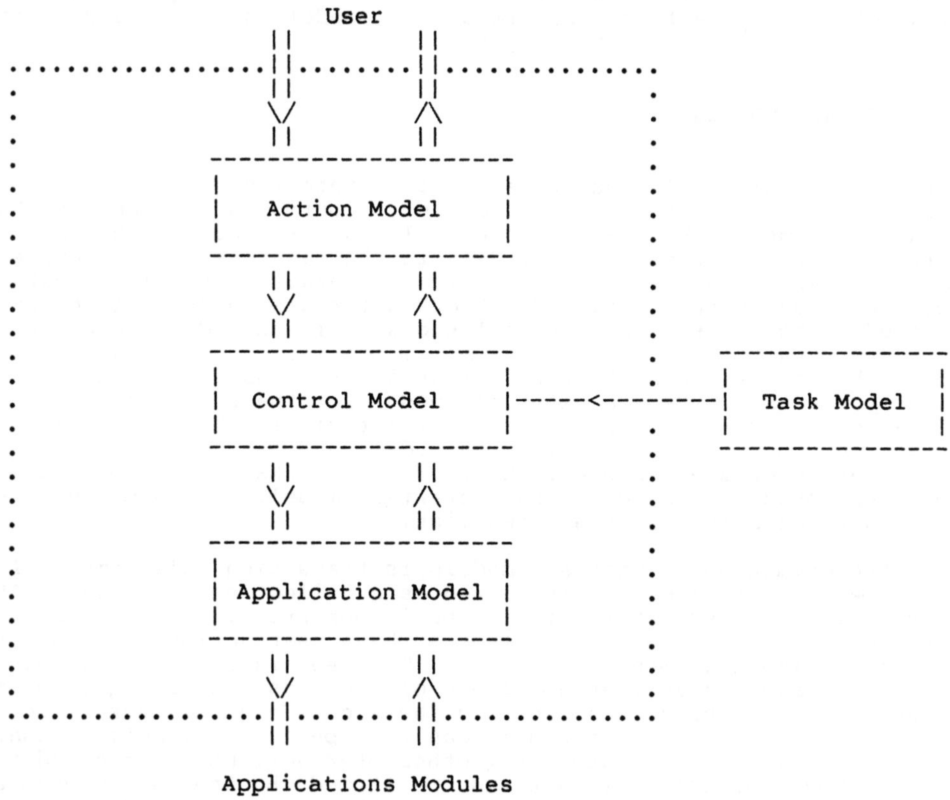

Fig. 2 Logical model of a user interface

The complete model of the user interface is shown in fig. 2. The left side of this figure represents the flow of information from the user to the applications program. The right side shows the opposite flow of information. Each action performed by the user need not result in a call of an applications module. The processing of the action may stop in one of the models and result in some form of feedback to the user. Similarly each action performed by the applications modules need not be the result of a user action. The key to describing a user interface is the definitions of the three models (action, control, and application) inside the dotted box. The implementation of the user interface is the set of mappings between these models. These mapping define the application program calls that result from the actions performed by the user.

The model of a user interface presented in fig. 2 has a number of important properties. The layers in this model isolate the user from the details of the applications program in the same way that a DBMS isolates the user (programmer) from the physical structure of his data. This allows several user interfaces to be used with the same applications program, and the same style of user interface can be used with several applications. In doing this only one or possibly two of the models need to be changed. This model also places a structure on the UIMS. This structure can be used as a guide in the design of user interfaces and UIMSs. The model in fig. 2 serves as the basis for the rest of this paper.

USER INTERFACE MODELS

In order to automatically generate a user interface an underlying model of user interfaces is required. Continuing the analogy to database systems, each DBMS has an underlying data model. This model is the logical structure of the data in the database. For example, relational databases are based on tables of data, hierarchical databases on tree structures, and network databases on sets of records connected by pointers. The physical storage of the data need not follow the data model, but the data model provides the logical structure of the database and the terminology for the database designer. Similarly, with UIMSs a logical model for the structure of user interfaces is also required. This model determines the structure of the action, control, and application models and the terminology used by the user interface designer. Most of the UIMS generators that have been produced have a user interface model, but this model is usually not emphasized in their descriptions.

One of the common user interface models is transition diagrams. In this model a user interface is viewed as a collection of states. At any one time the user interface will be in one state. The states are connected by arcs, which are labeled by a user action or class of user actions (such as menu selection). The user interface will move from one state to another along one of the arcs connecting them if the user performs the action labeling the arc. When the user interface is in a given state the user can only perform the actions that label arcs leaving that state. All other user actions are treated as errors. The sequence of actions performed by the user causes a sequence of state transitions following the arcs labeled by the user's actions.

In order to process the user's actions, program actions are attached the states and/or arcs of the transition diagram. The program actions are typically procedure calls, messages, or prompts to be displayed to the user. These actions are performed each time the state is entered or the arc is traversed.

There have been three major extensions to this basic model. The first extension is to attach conditions to the arcs to further specify when the arc can be traversed. This can be used to make the available commands depend upon the state of the dialogue. The second extension is a subroutine capability in which a set of states and their corresponding arcs can be treated as a subdiagram. This subdiagram can then be attached to one or more arcs or nodes in the diagram. If the subdiagram is attached to an arc, it is traversed before the node at the end of the arc is reached. If the subdiagram is attached to a state, when the state is reached the subdiagram is entered. The use of subdiagrams decreases the size of transition diagrams and facilitates their construction. The third extension is the addition of memory to the states. This allows the states to remember the most recent path through them and default parameter values.

Some examples of UIMSs that use transition diagrams as their user interface model are [Newman 1968], [Kasik 1976], [Kasik 1982], and [Wasserman and Stinson 1979]. The main advantages of this model are it is easy to implement, and learn to use. The chief disadvantages are it often leads to large transition diagrams which are hard to construct and manage, and it is not as flexible as the other models.

The other common user interface model is based on context free grammars. In this model the actions performed by the user are described by a context free grammar. The user interface is viewed as a parser for this grammar. In order to interface to the rest of the program actions are attached to the productions in the grammar. These actions can be calls to procedures, prompts, or messages to the user. When a production is used in the parse of the user's input the actions attached to that production are executed.

Some examples of UIMSs that use context free grammars as their user interface model are [Olsen 1983], [Olsen and Dempsey 1983a], and [Hanau and Lenorovitz 1980]. The main advantages of context free grammars are their familiarity and the existence of algorithms to produce efficient parsers. Their chief disadvantage is they were developed to describe linear, textual languages so they are not well suited to some of the dialogues that can occur in user interfaces.

These two models account for most of the UIMSs that have been proposed. Both of these models have a significant problem, they only describe half of the dialogue. They do a good job of describing the input produced by the user, but there is no way of describing the output produced by the user interface. As a result the output side of the user interface must be buried in the action routines that are part of the applications program. In order to completely isolate the user interface from the applications code a user interface model covering both user input and output is required. Finding such a model appears to be a difficult problem. One model that partially solves this problem is the event model.

In the event model the user is viewed as a source of events. The user generates events by interacting with one or more input and output devices. A number of properties can be attached to each of the events. Common properties include screen area, image, echo, and action procedure. The screen area defines the portion of the screen the event occupies, and image describes what appears in this area. When the user points at this area and signals a selection the event occurs. The result of the event can be an echo which appears on the screen or the call of an action procedure. The result of an event can also be the generation of other events. A number of events can be grouped together to form a user interface state. At any one time one or more of these states may be active. The occurence of an event can cause new states to become active and other states to deactivate. Note the difference between the transition diagram model where only one state can be active at a time, and this model where multiple active states are possible.

Some examples of UIMSs based on the event model are [Buxton et.al. 1983], [Green 1979], and [Green 1983b]. The event model accommodates graphical output in two ways. First, an event can be tied to graphical objects that appear on the screen. Events can be defined dynamically as the application or UIMS produces images on the screen. Second, the event itself can define its own screen appearance. This is useful when events are used for menu items. The application does not need to draw the menu, the appearance of the menu item is included in the corresponding event definition.

In this section three user interface models have been presented. The advantages and disadvantages of each model have been briefly discussed. As in databases it is likely that no one model will completely dominate the others. Each model will have an application area where it is either the best or the most convenient model. Over the next few years UIMSs based on all three models should be thoroughly investigated to determine their strengths and weaknesses in practice.

USER INTERFACE NOTATIONS

In fig. 2 four models associated with UIMSs are shown. In order to completely define the UIMS three of these models (action, control, and application) are required. The fourth model, the task model, describes the tasks the user wants to perform with the user interface and forms the basis of the control model. The task model is used to direct or guide the design of the user interface (for more information on how the task model is used in user interface design see [Green 1984]). Both the task and application models are independent of the user interface model employed by the UIMS, so their notations can be discussed without reference to a particular user interface model. The control model can be effected by the user interface model, but these effects are mainly limitations on what can be expressed and not upon the notation used. As a result the discussion of the control model notations is also independent of user interface models. The action model is highly dependent upon the user interface model. This dependence is so strong that action model notations used with one user interface model cannot usually be applied to the other models. In the following sections some of the notations that have been used to describe these models are briefly described.

Task and Control Model Notations

There are two notations that can be used for the task and control models. One of these notations, UML [Green 1984], is based on objects and operators, and the other, algebraic specification, is based on the data types in the user interface.

In UML the user interface is viewed as a collection of objects and operators. The objects are the things or entities in the user interface. They are the conceptual or physical objects the user wants to manipulate. The operators are used to manipulate the objects in the model.

An object is described by listing its attributes. Each attribute is given a name, and a type for its value. The type of an attribute value can be either a primitive UML type, the name of another object, or a GUSL module (GUSL is a specification language for user interfaces, it is described in section 4.3 and [Green 1984]). Object definitions in UML are treated like type definitions in most programming languages. There can be many objects of the same type and object instances can be created dynamically. Each UML model contains a set of global object declarations. These are objects, such as menus, that always exist in the user interface and are within the scope of all the operators.

The operators are described by a set of pre-conditions and a set of post-conditions. The pre-conditions are logical statements that describe the conditions that must be true before the operator can be used. The post-conditions are logical statements that describe the effects of the operator. The post-conditions are true after the operator is used.

Examples of the use of UML to produce task, control, and application models are presented in section five. A detailed description of UML and its use can be found in [Green 1984].

In algebraic specification the user interface is viewed as a collection of data types. Each data type has a set of values and a set of functions or operators that can be applied to values of the type being defined. The specification of a data type is divided into two sections. In the first section the syntax of the operators is described. This description consists of the name of the operator, the types of its operands, and the type of its result. The second section consists of a collection of axioms that define the behavior of the operators. Further discussion of the use of algebraic specifications to describe user interfaces can be found in [Guttag and Horning 1980] and [Mallgren 1983].

Both of these notational techniques take the same approach to describing a user interface. They divide the user interface into a number of objects or data types, and then define the operations that can be performed on them. There are two major differences between the two notations. In UML first order logic is used to describe the operators while in algebraic specification algebraic axioms are used. Second, in algebraic specification each operator belongs to one of the data types, while in UML the definitions of the objects and operators are independent. It is not clear whether one of these notations is better than the other. As a result the choice between them is mainly a matter of personal preference.

Application Model Notations

The purpose of the application model is to describe the routines in the application program that are available to the user interface. These routines are called by the user interface to perform the calculations and data manipulations involved in the application. The application model describes the interface between the user interface and the rest of the application.

Any of the existing software specification techniques can be used to produce the application model. All the UIMS needs to know about the application program is the names of the available routines, the parameters to these routines, the results they return, and any other effects they have (such as updating the database or producing a display). This is well within the range of most of the specification techniques that have been developed. Since we have considerable freedom in the choice of notation for this model an intelligent choice would be to use the same notation used to produce the task and control models. This benefits the user interface designer since he has one less notation to learn and remember. It also benefits the implementor of the UIMS since he has one less language to process. The end result of this exercise is one notation for the task, control, and application models.

Action Model Notations

The action model notations are based on the user interface model employed by the UIMS. As a result the three user interface models presented in section three are used as the basis for the organization of this section.

For the transition diagram model the obvious action model notation is some form of network showing the states and arcs. This network can be represented in two ways, either textually or graphically. In the textual representation there is typically one entry for each state in the diagram. This entry lists the prompt or message produced when the state is entered, any application modules associated with the state, and the arcs leaving the state. The description of each arc includes the user action that causes its traversal and the state it leads to. Including all the arcs leaving a state in the description of the state facilitates the consistency checking of the diagram. For example, it is easy to determine if all the arcs leaving a given node are labeled by different user actions. It is also easy to define a general error message for each state that will be used when the user performs an undefined action. Examples of this type of notation are [Kasik 1976] and [Kasik 1982].

In the graphical representation of transition diagrams the states are represented by circles, and the arcs by arrows connecting the circles. This representation can easily be displayed on a graphics terminal and edited interactively. The application modules and user actions can be represented by text strings that are placed on, or close to the states and arcs. Extra information associated with the states and arcs can be hidden and only displayed when the state or arc is selected by the user. Since graphics displays are limited in size this representation forces the designer to use subdiagrams and edit each diagram individually. An example of this representation of transition diagrams is [Newman 1968].

For the context free grammar model the natural notation is a context free grammar. In UIMSs based on this model BNF with extensions to provide better control over the parse is used as the notation for the action model. Examples of the types of extensions used can be found in [Van den Bos 1978] and [Olsen and Dempsey 1983b]. The grammar itself specifies the structure of the dialogue, but does not cover the actions the user can perform. This is handled by making the user's actions the tokens in the grammar. There is then a separate description for each of the tokens. The token descriptions usually include the device involved in the interaction, the type of value produced, parameters to the device, any prompts or icons associated with the action, and low level feedback. Examples of token descriptions can be found in [Olsen and Dempsey 1983a,b]. In summary the action model for a grammar based UIMS consists of an extended BNF grammar for the syntax of the interaction, and token descriptions for each of the possible user actions.

In the case of the event user interface model there is no one obvious notation for the action model. For this user interface model the notation should provide a means of describing each of the events in the user interface, how they are grouped into states, and which states are active at any one time. There are several ways in which this can be done, and like transition diagrams the notations can be either textual or graphical. In the case of textual representations there is one entry in the description for each of the events. This entry describes the circumstances under which the event is generated (the device or screen area involved), the graphical representation of the event, and the application program module that processes the event. Inside the user interace this information is usually stored in a table so the textual representations tend to have a tabular organization. In [Green 1983b] the action model consists of a collection of subroutine calls that define the events. This makes it possible to dynamically define new events while the program is executing. In [Green 1979] the action model takes the form of a very high level program. In this notation the events are defined by programming language structures that allow them to be either attached to input devices or given an internal name so they can be referenced by other events. In this notation the processing of an event can generate new events. It is also possible to group events into tools which serve as user interface states. Tools can be dynamically activated and deactivated.

A good example of a graphical notation for events is the MENULAY program that is part of the University of Toronto UIMS [Buxton et.al. 1983]. In this program the implementor of a user interface works with a graphics display and tablet to define the events in the user interface. The implementor can graphically define the icons for an event and layout the events on the screen. The program actions associated with events are entered through a keyboard in the form of a procedure name or definition. The output of this UIMS is a C program that builds the tables used in the user interface and handles other details of the interaction.

Summary

In this section some of the notations that have been used to describe user interfaces have been presented. The descriptions of these notations are quite brief, they are only intended to give the flavor of the individual techniques and not the details of their use. Further discussion of the use of each of these notations can be found in the references.

The one major problem with all the notations is the lack of experience in their use. The only notations that has been used in a significant number of applications are the ones based on transition diagrams. Unfortunately, these applications are spread over several different versions of the notations and very little has been published on experiences with them. Two important research questions are how well does each of the notations work when applied to real problems, and how do the different notations compare to each other. In order to answer these questions UIMSs based on the different notations must be implemented and used.

EXAMPLE

In this section examples of the descriptions required to produce a simple user interface are presented. The design of this user interface is taken from chapter four of [Green 1984] where it is used as an example of a user interface design methodology. This design methodology produces the task model, control model, and specification of the user interface. As a result at the implementation stage only the action and application models need be produced. The specification could be used as part of the action model saving considerable implementation effort. But, to save some space and provide an example of another notation an event based action model is used instead.

```
OBJECT directed_graph_type;
  ATTRIBUTE name : text;
  ATTRIBUTE nodes : SET OF node;
  ATTRIBUTE arcs : SET OF arc;
END;

OBJECT node;
  ATTRIBUTE label : text;
END;

OBJECT arc;
  ATTRIBUTE start : node;
  ATTRIBUTE end : node;
END;

GLOBAL directed_graph : directed_graph_type;
  name = 'no name';
  nodes = Ø;
  arcs  = Ø;
END;
```

Fig 3 Task model objects

The user interface described here is part of a program used to enter, edit, and display directed graphs. A directed graph is a mathematical structure consisting of a set of nodes and a set of arcs. Each node has a label that is used to identify it. The arcs are ordered pairs of nodes representing connections between the nodes. In this user interface the nodes are represented by circles and the arcs by arrows pointing from the first node in the ordered pair to the second. Note that a transition diagram is a directed graph so this program could be used as part of a transition diagram based UIMS!

UML is used to produce the task, control, and application models for this example. The definitions of the task model objects are presented in fig. 3, and the definitions of the task model operators are presented in fig. 4. In the task model the only objects are directed graph, node, and arc since at this point the user interface design has not been considered. The task model operators correspond to the things the user wants to do with directed graphs. These operations include adding a node to a graph, adding an arc to a graph, removing a node from a graph, removing an arc from a graph, and looking at a particular directed graph.

```
OPERATOR add_node(l : text);
  PRE
    FORALL n : node | n in directed_graph.nodes
      { n.name ≠ l };
  POST
    LET new_node : node | new_node.name = l;
    new_node in directed_graph.nodes;
END;

OPERATOR add_arc(start : text; end : text);
  PRE
    EXISTS s : node | s in directed_graph.nodes
      { s.label = start };
    EXISTS e : node | e in directed_graph.nodes
      { e.label = end };
  POST
    EXISTS s : node | s in directed_graph.nodes
      { s.label = start };
    EXISTS e : node | e in directed_graph.nodes
      { e.label = end };
    LET new_arc : arc | (new_arc.start = s) AND (new_arc.end = e);
    new_arc in directed_graph.arcs;
END;

OPERATOR delete_node( l : text);
  PRE
    EXISTS n : node | n in directed_graph.nodes
      { n.name = l };
  POST
    EXISTS n : node | n in directed_graph.nodes
      { n.name = l };
    FORALL a : arc | a in directed_graph.arcs
      { IF (a.start = n) OR (a.end = n) THEN
           delete_arc(a.start,a.end);
         ENDIF;
      };
    NOT (n in directed_graph.nodes);
END;

OPERATOR delete_arc(start : text; end : text);
  PRE
    EXISTS a : arc | a in directed_graph.arcs
      { (a.start.label = start) AND (a.end.label = end) };
  POST
    EXISTS a : arc | a in directed_graph.arcs
      { (a.start.label = start) AND (a.end.label = end) };
    NOT (a in directed_graph.arcs);
END;

OPERATOR display_graph(name : text);
  POST
    directed_graph.name = name;
END;
```

Fig. 4 Task model operators

```
OBJECT node;
  ATTRIBUTE label : text;
  ATTRIBUTE position : point;
END;

OBJECT work_area_type;
  ATTRIBUTE graph : directed_graph_type;
  ATTRIBUTE size : extent;
END;

TYPE
  command = (add_node, delete_node, add_arc, delete_arc,
             display_graph, exit);

OBJECT menu_type;
  ATTRIBUTE contents : SET OF menu_item;
  ATTRIBUTE size : extent;
  ATTRIBUTE current_command : command;
END;

OBJECT menu_item;
  ATTRIBUTE name : command;
  ATTRIBUTE size : extent;
END;

OBJECT cursor_type;
  ATTRIBUTE position : point;
END;

GLOBAL work_area : work_area_type;
  graph = directed_graph;
  size = extent1;
END;

GLOBAL add_node_command : menu_item;
  name = add_node;
  size = extent3;
END;
              . . .
GLOBAL exit_command : menu_item;
  name = exit;
  size = extent8;
END;

GLOBAL menu : menu_type;
  contents = { add_node_command, delete_node_command, . . . ,
               exit_command };
  size = extent2;
  current_command = Ø;
END;

GLOBAL cursor : cursor_type;
  position = (0,0);
END;
```

Fig. 5 Control model objects

The control model for the user interface is developed from the task model by considering how the user interface is structured. In this example one part of the screen, called the work area, is used to display the directed graph, and the other part contains a menu of commands. A command is selected from the menu by pointing at it with some type of pointing device. Once a command is selected it stays in effect until a new command is selected. The new objects required to support this behavior are shown in fig. 5. The combination of the object definitions in figures 3 and 5 form the set of objects in the control model.

The control model operators are divided into two groups. The support operators defined in fig. 6 are used to manipulate the user interface. These are the operations the user performs to select commands and operands. The command operators shown in fig. 7 directly correspond to the operators in the task model. These operators are the commands in the user interface. The support operators interface with the action model and the command operators interface with the application model.

```
OPERATOR menu_select(c : command);
  PRE
    menu.current_command ≠ exit;
    EXISTS m : menu_item_type | m.name = c
      { cursor.position in m.size };
  POST
    menu.current_command <- c;
END;

OPERATOR select_node(l : text) -> node;
  PRE
    EXISTS n : node | n in work_area.graph.nodes
      { n.label = l };
    | cursor.position - n.position | < radius;
  POST
    EXISTS n : node | n in work_area.graph.nodes
      { n.label = l };
    select_node <- n;
END;

OPERATOR select_arc(s : text; e : text) -> arc;
  PRE
    EXISTS a : arc | a in work_area.graph.arcs
      { (a.start.label = s) AND (a.end.label = e) };
  POST
    EXISTS a : arc | a in work_area.graph.arcs
      { (a.start.label = s) AND (a.end.label = e) };
    select_arc <- a;
END;

OPERATOR select_position -> point;
  PRE
    cursor.position in work_area.size;
  POST
    select_position <- cursor_position;
END;
```

Fig. 6 Support operator definition

```
OPERATOR add_node(l : text; p : point);
  PRE
    FORALL n : node | n in work_area.graph.nodes
      { n.name ≠ l };
    menu.current_command = add_node;
    p in work_area.size;
  POST
    LET new_node : node | (new_node.name = l) AND
                          (new_node.position = p);
    new_node in work_area.graph.nodes;
END;

OPERATOR add_arc(start : node; end : node);
  PRE
    start in work_area.graph.nodes;
    end in work_area.graph.nodes;
    menu.current_command = add_arc;
  POST
    LET newarc : arc | (new_arc.start = start) AND (new_arc.end = end);
    new_arc in work_area.graph.arcs;
END;

OPERATOR delete_node(n : node);
  PRE
    n in work_area.graph.nodes;
    menu.current_command = delete_node;
  POST
    FORALL a : arc | a in work_area.graph.arcs
      { IF (a.start = n) OR (a.end = n) THEN
          delete_arc(a);
      };
    NOT (n in work_area.graph.arcs);
END;

OPERATOR delete_arc(a : arc);
  PRE
    a in work_area.graph.arcs;
    menu.current_command = delete_arc;
  POST
    NOT (a in work_area.graph.arcs);
END;

OPERATOR display_graph(name : text);
  PRE
    menu.current_command = display_graph;
  POST
    work_area.graph.name = name;
END;
```

Fig. 7 Command operator definitions

The application program modules are responsible for storing and manipulating the directed graphs. The manipulations performed by this program are quite simple, so the major part of the application program is a database management system. Each of the directed graphs is stored in a separate database. A database consists of a set of records, each record is identified by a unique record number. In this application two types of records are required, one for nodes and one for arcs. The object definitions shown in fig. 8 represent the data structure used by the applications program.

```
OBJECT database;
  ATTRIBUTE name : text;
  ATTRIBUTE records : SET OF record;
END;

TYPE
  record_number = integer;
  record_type = UNION node_record, arc_record;
  tag_type = (node_tag, arc_tag);

OBJECT record;
  ATTRIBUTE number : record_number;
  ATTRIBUTE tag : tag_type;
  ATTRIBUTE event : event_id;
  ATTRIBUTE contents : record_type;
END;

OBJECT node_record;
  ATTRIBUTE label : text;
  ATTRIBUTE position : point;
END;

OBJECT arc_record;
  ATTRIBUTE start : record_number;
  ATTRIBUTE end : record_number;
END;

GLOBAL db;
  name = 'no name';
  records = Ø;
END;
```

Fig. 8 Application model objects

The operations performed on this database are quite simple. There are only four operations (add a record, remove a record, retrieve a record, and load a database) that are required for this application. The declarations of these operators are shown in fig. 9. These operators represent the four procedures the UIMS can call.

The final description to be produced for the user interface is the action model. For this example it is assumed that the UIMS is based on the event model. As a result the action model must describe all the events in the user interface. The user can generate an event by pointing at any of the commands in the menu, an arc in the work area, or a node in the work area. Thus we must associate events with all of these graphical entities. The events for the menu are always active and are defined before the user interface is used. This type of event is called a static event. In the case of the arcs and nodes their events must be defined when they are drawn, and destroyed when they are removed from the directed graph. This type of event is called a dynamic event. A group of internal events is associated with each command on the menu. These events groups form the states in the user interface. When a command is selected the events for the previous command are deactivated and the events for the selected command are activated.

```
OPERATOR add_record(r : record);
  PRE
    NOT (r in db.records);
  POST
    r in db.records;
END;

OPERATOR remove_record(n : record_number);
  PRE
    EXISTS r : record | r in db.records
      { r.number = n };
  POST
    EXISTS r : record | r in db.records
      { r.number = n };
    NOT (r in db.records);
END;

OPERATOR retrieve_record(n : record_number);
  PRE
    EXISTS r : record | r in db.records
      { r.number = n };
  POST
    EXISTS r : record | r in db.records
      { r.number = n };
    retrieve_record <- n;
END;

OPERATOR load_database(n : text);
  POST
    db.name = n;
END;
```

Fig. 9 Application model operators

A very a high level programming language similar to that presented in [Green 1979] is used to define the events. The states in this notation are called tools. In the action model there is one tool for the menu and one tool for processing each of the commands. When an event is declared (by the EVENT statement) it is given a name and can be associated with one of the input devices. In the case of internal events, the event name is used to generate the event. This notations also provides a mechanism for dynamic event declaration through the function new_event. This function returns an identifier for the event so it can be destroyed at a later point. Only enough of the action model is presented in fig. 10 to get a feel for how this notation works. The remainder of the action model is very similar to the portion shown in this figure.

```
VAR
  current : tool;

TOOL menu;
  EVENT add_node ASSOC tablet IN extent3 DO {
    deactivate(current);
    current = activate(add_node_state);
  };

  EVENT delete_Node ASSOC tablet IN extent4 DO {
    deactivate(current);
    current = activate(delete_node_state);
  };

  EVENT add_arc ASSOC tablet IN extent5 DO {
    deactivate(current);
    current = activate(add_arc_state);
  };

  EVENT delete_arc ASSOC tablet IN extent6 DO {
    deactivate(current);
    current = activate(delete_arc_state);
  };

  EVENT display_graph ASSOC tablet IN extent7 DO {
    deactivate(current);
    current = activate(display_graph_state);
  };

  EVENT exit ASSOC tablet IN extent8 DO {
    "exit program"
  };
END TOOL menu;

TOOL add_node_state;
  VAR
    r : record;
    rn : record_number;

  EVENT position ASSOC tablet IN extent1 DO {
    r = node_record(label, position);
    rn = add_record(r);
    r.event = new_event("EVENT x ASSOC tablet AT position DO
                        { current <- node r };");
  };
  EVENT label ASSOC keyboard;
END TOOL add_node_state;

TOOL delete_node_state;
  EVENT node INTERNAL DO {
    delete_event(node.event);
    remove_record(node);
  };
END TOOL delete_node_state;

            .
            .
            .
```

```
TOOL display_graph_state;
  VAR
    r : record;
    i : record_number;

  EVENT name ASSOC keyboard DO {
    load_database(name);
    FOR i = first_record(db) TO last_record(db) DO {
      r = retrieve_record(i);
      IF r.tag = node_tag THEN {
        draw_circle(r.position);
        r.event = new_event("EVENT x ASSOC tablet AT r.position DO
                              { current <- node r };");
      } ELSE {
        draw_arrow(r.start, r.end);
        r.event = new_event("EVENT x ASSOC tablet IN
                  extent(r.start.position, r.end.position) DO
                  { current <- arc r };");
      };
    }
  };
END TOOL display_graph_state;
```

Fig. 10 Action model

References

[Buxton et.al. 1983] Buxton W., M.R. Lamb, D. Sherman, K.C. Smith, "Towards a Comprehensive User Interface Management System", Siggraph'83, p.35, 1983.

[Date 1981] Date C.J., *An Introduction to Database Systems*, Addison-Wesley, Reading Mass., 1981.

[Foley and Van Dam 1982] Foley J., A. Van Dam, *Fundamentals of Interactive Computer Graphics*, Addison-Wesley, Reading Mass., 1982.

[Green 1979] Green M., *A Graphical Input Programming System*, MSc Thesis, Department of Computer Science, University of Toronto, 1979.

[Green 1981] Green M., "A Methodology for the Specification of Graphical User Interfaces", Siggraph'81, p.99, 1981.

[Green 1982] Green M., "Towards a User Interface Prototyping System", Graphics Interface'82, p.37, 1982.

[Green 1983a] Green M., "A Catalogue of Graphical Interaction Techniques", Computer Graphics, vol.17, no.1., p.46, 1983.

[Green 1983b] Green M., M. Burnell, H. Vrenjak, M. Vrenjak, "Experiences With a Graphical Data Base System", Graphics Interface'83, p.257, 1983.

[Green 1984] Green M., *The Design of Graphical User Interfaces*, Phd Thesis, Department of Computer Science, University of Toronto,

1984 (forthcoming).

[Guttag and Horning 1980] Guttag J. J.J. Horning, "Formal Specification as a Design Tool", Proceedings of the Seventh Symposium on Principles of Programming Languages, p.251, 1980.

[Hanau and Lenorovitz 1980] Hanau R.R., D.R. Lenorovitz, "Prototyping and Simulation Tools for User/Computer Dialogue Design", Siggraph'80, p.271, 1980.

[Kasik 1976] Kasik D.J., "Controlling User Interaction", Siggraph'76, p.109, 1976.

[Kasik 1982] Kasik D.J., "A User Interface Management System", Siggraph'82, p.99, 1982.

[Mallgren 1983] Mallgren W.R., *Formal Specification of Interactive Graphics Programming Languages*, MIT Press, Cambridge Mass., 1983.

[Olsen 1983] Olsen D., "Automatic Generation of Interactive Systems", Computer Graphics, vol.17, no.1, p.53, 1983.

[Olsen and Dempsey 1983a] Olsen D., E. Dempsey, "SYNGRAPH: A Graphic User Interface Generator", Siggraph'83, p.43, 1983.

[Olsen and Dempsey 1983b] Olsen D., E. Dempsey, "Syntax Directed Graphical Interaction", Proceedings of the Sigplan'83 Symposium on Programming Language Issues in Software Systems, p.112, 1983.

[Newman 1968] Newman W.M., "A System for Interactive Graphical Programming", SJCC 1968, Thompson Books, Washington DC., p.47, 1968.

[Van den Bos 1978] Van den Bos J., "Definition and user of Higher-level Graphics Input Tools", Siggraph'78, p.38, 1978.

[Wasserman and Stinson 1979] Wasserman A.I., S.K. Stinson, "A Specification Method for Interactive Systems", Proceedings of Specification of Reliable Software, p.68, IEEE Computer Society, Long Beach CA, 1979.

Parallel Input and Feedback in Dialogue Cells

P. J. W. ten Hagen* and J. Derksen**

*Centre for Mathematics and Computer Science, Amsterdam, The Netherlands
**The Netherlands Organisation for Applied Scientific Research (TNO-IBBC), Rijswijk, The Netherlands

ABSTRACT

In this paper a specification method for interaction is outlined based on a new programming concept called 'dialogue cells'.
The method supports parallel input and separation a dialogue part from the algorithmic part of the application.
Graphics interaction can be fully integrated. Some problems associated with parsing parallel inputs are analyzed.

Keywords: *Interaction, Man-Machine Communication, Computer Graphics.*

1. Introduction.

The programmer of an interactive program has a complex task to perform. In addition to the specification of correct, efficient algorithms he must pay continuous attention to the way the program will manifest itself to the observing user when run and by what means the user can influence the problem solving process. The success of the program depends as much on how easily the user can interact with it as on the efficiency and correctness of the algorithms.

In this paper we will concentrate on techniques for programming the interactive part of a program. We will not attempt to define what constitutes high quality interaction. This is a multidisciplinary subject. Psychologists (perception, cognition), ergonomists, artists, application specialists, etc., all have something to say about this. Very likely no two of them will agree about which are the more important rules and issues.

The techniques that will be presented, and the fundamentals for such techniques, ideally will be such that they can be used or misused for implementing any type of interaction. At best the programmer may discover that the techniques he is using follow some rules of thumb such as:

- give the user value for his efforts. (e.g. keep the amount of work he has to do to obtain some information sufficiently small).
- present only relevant information; remove rubbish.
- don't be ambiguous without reason.

However, no systematic is known. Sometimes one rule prevales, sometimes another. Also, many of the principles can be traded off against each other.

The particular type of interaction needed for a succesful interactive program, may depend on the application or on the available hardware. This implies that a programming method which aims at portability and device independence should not exclude any particular type of interaction.

2. User Interface.

The user interface to a program is the collection of visualisation and manipulation facilities and their interpretation (right or wrong) given to them by the user. Each of these facilities as perceived by the user is made up of four entities: the physical part of a facility, the way it can be used, the way it is controlled by the program, and, its contribution to the interactive process.

The fact that each facility depends on a physical realisation is reason for questioning by many people whether generally good interfaces can be specified in a device independent manner.

Also many people believe that good interfaces cannot be described unless taking into account the general model of the whole program and the role of each interaction facility in such a model. The problems here are that different users may perceive different models and that such models are not a bases for specifying (designing) interaction, because they are difficult to formulate.

The optimists however, consider the capability of human beings to adapt and to use abstractions sufficient in order for interactive systems to be realised on a wide variety of devices and to work with a great variety of user models. The techniques discussed in this paper attempt to support the optimists view.

The attention of researchers and system designers has, with respect to user interfaces, shifted from the conceptual model to the realm of devices and interaction techniques. The recognition that the techniques used are substantial in determining what you can say, or, that communication and expression are as important as understanding has emerged with the use of rich interaction devices.
The computer graphics experts are for the time being also the experts who can build user interfaces. It is through graphics that communicating with computers has become fun. That is to say, it has become a fun for non-experts in programming. Providing good interactive techniques is essential for good and effective interfaces. However, understanding is also essential. Many good interfaces are based on exhibiting that the user is understood (e.g. natural language interfaces). This shows that interactive techniques are ultimately to be coupled with the process of understanding.
This paper will concentrate only on the interactive techniques.

3. Interaction and Graphics.

3.1 Properties of graphics interfaces.

One may wonder what is so special about a computer interface involving graphics.

The first important property of communicating through pictures is the directness. That is to say using pictures removes at least one level of encoding-decoding. Pictures are much closer to the concepts one wants to convey, be it for input or for output. One may consider both the method of constructing a view from a picture description, or constructing a picture description from input activities, as local activities, which have only to do with the syntax of an interaction language. This is a very important justification for situating graphics viewing facilities both for input and output in a local terminal, to be used by arbitrary applications. The fact that the CORE -once proposed- standard and to a lesser extend the GKS standard failed to support picture input at the same level as picture output, had more to do with the state of the art, than with the principles underlying the standard.

A second important property is the non-sequential nature of pictures. Two or three dimensional objects cannot be linearly ordered. Therefore a user cannot be expected to react only to the last item produced. In principle he must be able to act upon every aspect of the information presented.
The program must be prepared to receive input referring to items produced earlier but still visible. It is up to the program to reconstruct the association with the semantic context.

A third property is the opportunity to convey a meaning by changing something rather than adding something new. Hence manipulation and 'gesture' become part of the dialogue.

Last but not least the syntax of a graphics dialogue should allow many degrees of freedom and variable feedback. So that adaptation to user skills becomes feasible.

By no means can one say that today a general solution and method exists for exploiting these possibilities in interactive systems.

3.2 Introducing parallelism.

The specification of complex inputs and interactions, such as those involving pictures, can be adequately done by using parallel programmings concepts. In some cases the parallelism can be convenient. However, for the general case, we intend to show it being necessary.

Modern graphics packages, like GKS, allow for basic input devices to be active in parallel. Each of these input devices has associated with it an interactive (basic) technique to produce the input items of the device. The operator at a workstation can make his own decision about which input to produce next. He might even decide to produce several inputs simultaneously.

On a higher syntactical level more than one picture may be under construction. At that level for a given picture it is immaterial that inputs for another picture were produced as well. The only way to abstract from these irrelevant details is by applying a parallel model. This will simplify and make possible the independent programming of simultaneous picture constructing processes.

A similar argument applies to a user reacting to several pictures presented on a screen. If different processes or subprograms are associated with different pictures, each one is assumed to only process the corresponding reactions. This may imply that these processes are concurrently active.

A user defining a correlation between two items presented may trigger both associated subprograms. This is an example of conveying a message by changing the information as presented. As a result changes on more than one place may occur simultaneously.

The most complex use of parallelism occurs when one tries to maximise user freedom in specifying input sequences. In between given synchronization points all permutations of an input sequence may be acceptable. This means that between these points all mechanisms that can produce symbols for the sequence must be active. If not, then the user is forced to activate every mechanism himself prior to producing an input with that mechanism.

We will present some aspects of a dialogue specification language which facilities for parallelism for the situations mentioned above.
In particular we will describe the problem of parsing input under parallel conditions and how parsers can be built to solve these problems.

4. Dialogues.

In these notes a human-computer dialogue, or dialogue for short, is the exchange of information (commands, results, explanation) between a human operator and an interactive computer program in execution.
As part of writing an interactive program it is specified which information can be exchanged. Besides defining algorithms, a programmer also defines a dialogue language, i.e. he specifies which exchanges can take place at any time and what their effect (=meaning) will be. We can therefore consider a program to consist of two parts: the algorithmic part and the dialogue part. Whether both parts can be mutually separated depends on the program structure.

The state of the art very much is that the algorithmic part of a program is designed before it is implemented whereas the dialogue part is merely designed while implemented.

For a proper method of designing a dialogue language prior to implementation three conditions have to be met:

1. The dialogue part must indeed be a separate program section (not interwoven with the algorithms).
2. The programming method for the dialogues must allow for easily readable dialogue specifications, so that a programmer can conclude what happens at the user interface when reading the program text. This is a 'structured programming' requirement for dialogues.
3. The constructs for dialogue programming must provide complete control over the physical part of the user interface, with or without device independence.

Generally speaking the program structure required for algorithms differs from dialogue structure. For instance, the algorithm may ask for parameters in a format and order quite different from the way most users would naturally provide them.

4.1 The separation of algorithm and dialogue.

A separate dialogue module would provide a number of advantages:

- The algorithmic part is relieved from all details concerning in- an output such as: test whether input is correct, check whether output is possible right now.
- One can alter the dialogue part (e.g. adapt to new hardware), without having to change the algorithms.
- Dialogue specialists can write a dialogue most suitable for a given environment and/or application.
- Interactive techniques may become available as (sub)dialogue libraries.
- A dialogue run time support system may provide facilities for user help, error recovery and audit-trails.

The most simple and maybe adequate method for separating algorithms from dialogues is by introducing dialogue procedures. They would, when called, look quite similar to, say, subroutines.
However, the dialogue procedure itself may be specified by a method or language quite different from the general purpose programming language used for the algorithms.

Dialogue procedures provide a structure different from input- or menu-driven systems. Here the program block- and subroutine structure can be seen as a directed graph (the arrows are the procedure calls or block nestings), the top levels of which are the input handlers.

One can imagine that dialogue procedures in turn can call algorithmic routines, for instance, to do conversions of input data. At run time dialogue and algorithm can be conceptually two cooperating processes which exchange messages (=procedure calls). The language construct that will be presented here for specifying a dialogue can represent dialogues where both processes can cause side effects in the other.
Current practice does not allow for such complicated structures. Especially situations requiring backtracking over algorithms or dialogues cannot be dealt with satisfactory. A better strategy seeks to avoid the necessity of such mechanisms.
As we will see this can be achieved without becoming too restrictive.

4.2 Dialogue Cells

The language construct that will be presented here for specifying a dialogue procedure is called **dialogue cell.**
A dialogue cell is a unit which can completely specify one step in a dialogue. Each step comprises the following parts:

- an action from the user,
- the corresponding external reaction from the system,
- the effect on the internal state of the system
- the environment and conditions in which the action takes place.

Dialogue cells can be organised in hierarchies. This means that a big unit can be built from a combination of smaller units. In a hierarchy the way smaller units are combined can be precisely controlled. The overall action of two combined units is determined by the individual actions and the combining operator. This hierarchy therefore allows at the same time the specification of dialogue syntax (how words combine to sentences), the internal semantics (how a structured state vector is changed component by component), how the effect of changing the visible interface is built from little changes and last but not least how sub-dialogues get activated and deactivated.
The four groups of dialogue cell activities as given here are specified in four separate cell components that make up a dialogue cell.
These components are:

Prompt: The section which initialises the sub-dialogue and activates all sub-cells required. In addition it informs the user that it is ready to accept the input.

The appearance of the prompt can vary from a simple 'continue' sign to a whole new screen set up plus initial message (question) for the user. This means that it can express where the initiative lies, or, who asks the question and who provides the answers.

Symbol: The section which specifies the syntax of an input sentence. It will tell how the input monitor will try to read the input words and when the dialogue cell input is completed.

First of all specifying how the system will read symbols is different from specifying how (and in what order) a user must produce the inputs. Only in strictly synchronous, sequential systems will these two be the same.
Sub-symbols (i.e. 'words' of the sentence) are produced either by the user directly (basic symbols) or are obtained from sub-cells. The mechanisms to provide basic symbols are integrated in the dialogue system as special dialogue cells, so-called *basic cells.*

Echo: The acceptance of a symbol by a dialogue cell causes a message to be sent back to the user.

These pictorial messages (echoes) may remain visible when the dialogue cell is completed (global echo) or may have to be removed (local echo) when the cell is deactivated. Thus the echo mechanism is the basis for dynamic control of the screen.

Value: Each symbol accepted has a value associated with it. This value may with or without conversion contribute to the complex value to be produced by the cell.

Also here a local-and-global value scheme is used which is controlled through the cell hierarchy. The value section contains an extensive mapping mechanism including input validity checks. The result of mapping and checking may be fed back to the symbol section by means of synchronisation tokens which can be used to select among alternatives or end repetitions. In this way attributed grammars can be handled.

4.3 The Basic cycle of a Dialogue Cell

What happens when a dialogue cell becomes active?
The answer is: its four components become (simultaneously) active. However, implicit in the dialogue cell semantics are synchronisation rules and some form of abstract data typing. We will give an informal description here because the understanding is more important than the precise form.

In each of the sections names of sub-cells may be used. It is understood however, that when a prompt part names a dialogue cell it only refers to the prompt section of that sub-cell. A similar rule holds for all other sections.

The next rule is that only symbols appearing in the symbol part of a cell may appear in the other parts. This guarantees that only cells are activated which inputs can be read and also that values and echoes of cells that are to be produced stem from active cells.

An additional very important rule states that symbols can only be read when a cell is active (i.e. the prompt section must be executed before symbol parsing) and the value and echo actions specified for a symbol must be triggered by the parser. This guarantees that value expressions cannot be evaluated further unless all values required become available and all output echoes (e.g. pictures) produced are either prompts or echoes.

A refinement of this rule allows for mutual synchronisation between value and echo, so that the change to the internal state can be visualised. An active cell proceeds for each symbol in the symbol expression through the sequence, $P \rightarrow S \rightarrow V \rightarrow E$. When the last symbol is encountered the cell will deliver a symbol, value and echo to the external environment.
After delivery of the external results the cell is ready for a new complete basic cycle. Whether this will happen or not is controlled by the surrounding cell.

4.4 The activation of dialogue cells.

A dialogue cell, as we have seen, is either activated by the algorithmic part as dialogue procedure (root-cell), or it is activated as sub-cell of a dialogue cell closer to the root-cell. This activation can generally be either synchronous or asynchronous. In the synchronous case a cell is activated just prior to the action by the symbol part to accept this symbol. The activating dialogue cell is forced to wait until the symbol asked for has been produced. The cell is deactivated immediately after its symbol has been accepted. This activation mode is a generalisation of the REQUEST mode defined for GKS input. Similarly the asynchronous activation is a generalisation of the GKS concepts SAMPLE and EVENT.

All asynchronously used sub-cells of a dialogue cell are activated in the prompt section as part of the initialisation. So all these subcells are active simultaneously. This has two important consequences:

1. The user is allowed to produce input long before it is being used and he can produce input in an order quite different from the order in which the symbol part will accept them. This is indicated with the term **early activation.** Symbols produced before they will be used are called **early symbols.**
2. Symbols may be produced in parallel, the symbol expression of many cells may simultaneously attempt to accept the symbol produced for it. Therefore the symbol parsing process goes on in many rules at the same time although ultimately one start symbol will be produced. This requires a so-called dynamic multi-stream parser.

In order for both user and programmer to limit the complexity of this parallel parser a number of restrictions must be imposed on the dialogue cell semantics. These will be discussed in the next section.

Simultaneously active dialogue cells model the actual situation of many graphics workstations, having for instance, a keyboard, menu on the screen and a locator all simultaneously enabled. They then leave it up to the user which one to select.

A dialogue cell activated in SAMPLE mode puts the initiative with the computer program. The program can decide at any time to 'sample' the value produced, even before the user has provided one, or, after the user has provided several, in which case all but the last get lost.

A dialogue cell activated in EVENT mode gives the initiative to the user. Firstly the program is forced to wait if no symbol is yet produced. Secondly, the program is forced to read all symbols produced one after the other from a queue. Unlike GKS, the various event queues of the individual dialogue cells are not merged into one.

5.1 Input Parsing

The symbol part of a dialogue cell consist of a grammar rule. This rule directly controls the input parser. Two kinds of problems with respect to input parsing must be dealt with.
The first one has to do with ambiguous grammars. An ambiguous situation occurs when a symbol is produced which might fit in more than one alternative. Then the parser cannot decide where to continue. In addition, a parallel parse over a non-ambiguous grammar may introduce ambiguities, because more than one active rule (= symbol part of the active cell) may require such a symbol. Ambiguous situations are generally speaking, not wanted in interactive dialogues because they leave the user confused. They either force the system into multiple reaction (try all possibilities for some time) or they postpone one reaction or they choose one arbitrarily. Each of those has its own contribution to confusion to make.

A user who makes an error in an ambiguous situation forces the system to reject, without having the possibility to direct the user where to go.

A dialogue cell system is provided with a strong mechanism to dynamically remove ambiguities. First observe that in order to be able to obtain a symbol, a sub-cell or basic cell must be activated first. The run time system can easily detect by a lock-out mechanism that the subcell is already activated. Disambiguating means that it will in this case activate a different instance of the same cell, which will be guaranteed to manifest itself to the user in a different way (e.g. on a different place on the screen, or with a different cursor and prompt or eventually at a different time (local

synchronisation by priority)).
This mechanism is closely coupled to the resource manager which assigns and deassigns hardware and firmware interaction resources.

This strategy is based upon a principle which is very fundamental. That is the strict separation of type and value. In a dialogue cell type is the realm of the symbol part whereas value is in the realm of the value part.
For instance, a syntax rule which has two alternatives:

A: all letters and digits
B: all punctuation marks and zero.

is ambiguous when a zero is encountered.
In a dialogue cell either A and B would use different (virtual) keyboards or the same keyboard at different times, or there is only one syntax rule (say C), and the value mechanism associates a value with C in all cases. So, the ambiguity is either removed before the activation or it is not a syntactic but a semantic ambiguity.
An additional benefit is that the system is at first instance always prepared to accept all user inputs possible. The inputs it cannot accept are not enabled.

5.2 Syntactic specification

The two types of parallelism have different syntax. The parallelism based on early activations is specified by the **prompt-component** by selecting an asynchronous mode (e.g. SAMPLE and EVENT). A cell which is asynchronously active can only be deactivated through the deactivation of the parent cell.

The parallelism based on syntactic branching (AND- and OR-branches) is specified as part of the **symbol-component.** The activation of synchronous (REQUEST) cells in a given parallel branche is completely independent from the progress in the corresponding other parallel branches.
Through activation of a cell also its prompt section is activated. As a result a whole series of subcells may become active as well. For each active cell the parser (re)opens the corresponding syntax rule in the parse table. A parse cursor is initialised on the first symbol(s) of the rule and the input will be scanned for such a symbol (cf. input pool section 5.3). Simultaneous active dialogue cells produce external echoes and values which will be further dealt with by the parent cell. When exactly this will take place will only depend on the status of the parent cell. The handover of value and echo result is controlled by the input pool.

5.3 The input pool.

When the parallel production of symbols for input is served by only one processor one needs a scheduler to determine which early symbol will next be processed by the parser. We will now show how this arbitration mechanism can influence the behaviour of the system as perceived by the user. The situation we are confronted with is as follows:
Each time an active cell produces a symbol this symbol can either immediately be consumed by the requesting cell (synchronous mode) or it is placed in the cell's corresponding sample or event register. In case the requesting cell is not immediately scheduled, the symbol is placed in the request register.
The input pool is the collection of all request sample and event registers.
Only a subset of the symbols in the pool is candidate for reading by the parser. All others are, one could say, produced too early.
Each time an elementary parse action has been completed, (i.e. the parser moves to the next symbol of the symbol expression), the arbitration unit can be activated to

decide which symbol for which cell to parse next.
The decision procedure chosen, favours high level cells over low level cells, and also favours cells in left branches over cells in right branches, provided the higher level parse pointer has not proceeded beyond those branches. This is achieved by considering the syntax graph which is implied by the dialogue cell hierarchy and appending a preorder code to each dialogue cell, being the preorder code from the node in the corresponding graph. The root will get the highest code. Then the scheduler will search the pool for the symbol with the highest preorder code.

The effect of all this at the user interface is that the highest level result implied by any input is always produced first and also that cells trying to empty an event queue have priority over cells adding a new symbol to the queue.

6. Example

Suppose a user is working with a graphics terminal and wants to specify a text, a position and a rectangular box. These actions may be part of, say, adding legends to a blind map.

The program will arrange the text in such way that it fills the box and next will place the box at the position given.
We will compare three different dialogues for the same problem, both from the point of view of feedback quality and conciseness of dialogue. The second and third solution are given as transformations of the specification of the first solution. In this way also the dialogue cell specification method itself will be illustrated.
In each of the solutions a requirement is to be met saying that the user may choose the order of specifying the values (text, pos., box) at will. At any point in the dialogue he must be able to look at the result of combining the current values of the triple. In addition he may save, discard or change the result.
The three solutions will offer an increasing amount of feedback and support to the user. Among other things this may lead to a simpler, more effective, dialogue.

6.1 First solutions: use a keyword menue

The user is given the possibility to choose any action by presenting him a keyword menue. After selecting a menue item he is prompted for the corresponding action and the result is shown. Then the menue reappears asking for the next action. This is a strictly synchronous approach. Only one activity at the time is possible. Nevertheless, this is a very commonly used way of providing such facilities. In many implementations of similar dialogues the menue is up on the screen continuously. However, sometimes it is usable an sometimes it is not. The improvement of the solution in the first example over this situation is that the menue will only be presented when a selection is expected from the user.
We will now briefly describe the dialogue cell program for this problem. The language syntax can be seen as an extension to the syntax of the programming language C.
The overall structure of the program consists of a list of typedefinitions, resource declarations and dialogue cell definitions. One of the dialogue cells is marked as the main cell. It will be called from the application within which this program is embedded.
The typedefinitions prepare for the use of variables specific to the dialogue program. The resource declarations define resource claims, such as a part of the screen or a particular cursor. They can then be used by the various dialogue cells. Resource declarations are used to partly define a resource strategy e.g., screen layout.

/* This is a comment line

/* Resources

/* A window is defined by its lower left and upper right corner in virtual screen coordinates ([0 ,1]:[0,1]).

WINDOW

w text	=	{ 0.0, 0.0, 0.5, 0.2 }
w menue	=	{ 0.0, 0.2, 0.2, 1.0 }
w box	=	{ 0.5, 0.0, 1.0, 0.2 }
w screen	=	{ 0.2, 0.2, 1.0, 1.0 }

/* Type definitions, including global initialization

TYPEDEF STRUCT

MENUE ptb menue = The 'ptb menue' defined here will be handled over as a parameter to a basic cell called 'menue'. This dialogue cell will allow the user to select a menue item. To this end it will present the menue in a window (also a parameter) on the screen. The activitation of the cell 'menue' will take place in the prompt-section of the calling cell e.g. through the rule: REQUEST menue (ptbmenue, wmenue) ...
The user will initiate each action, either his own or by the system, by a menue choice, as follows:

'text'	for typing a string
'box'	for specifying a rectangular box around the text,
'pos'	for specifying a position for the text in the window wscreen,
'do'	for showing the result of combining text, box and pos,
'keep'	for storing the result in external store (e.d. variables, files),
'next'	for setting up for a new triple,
'stop'	for exiting the dialogue.

Only the first three actions require further input. This input is collected by three subcells called 'text', 'box' and 'pos' respectively. 'do', 'keep' and 'next' will cause interval systems actions whcih also may create further pictorial output.
We will now give the main dialogue cell with explanatory comment lines:

/*
MAIN DICE legend: STRUCT (STRING, LOC [2]) [ ]; SEG [ ]

/* The result produced by legend is an array of structs describing text in a box,
/* represented by: a) STRING, LOC [2] and b) a SEG
/* The first is the internal representation, the second is the picture

PROMPT

/* the prompt section of the dialogue cell body

STRUCT (STRING, Lo [2] tbox = NIL

```
/*   local variable, initialised to undefined
/*   activitation of subcells in REQUEST mode

TEXT tx = NIL

/*   local picture var. of type TEXT.

REQUEST       menue (w menue) (ptb-menue),
         text  (w-text),
         box   (w-box),
         pos   (w-screen);

ECHO OFF menue;

/*   each of the subcells gets a window on the screen
/*   the ECHO OFF switch will make the menue disappear
/*   after each selection

SYMBOL

/*   the symbol section
     CASE menue IN(
          text;
          box;
          pos;
          EXIT;
          CONT;
     ) * CONT;

/*   This expression in a nutshell, contains the whole control structure.
/*   i.e. an endless loop: menue * CONT, with an exit rule (
/*   internal to the loop
/*   the CASE construct which is embedded, allows for
/*   entering the sub-dialogue branches one at
/*.   a time

VALUE

/*   in the value part internal representations are obtained
/*   either locally or globally (through a SEND rule),
/*   from mapping subcell results-values.

     menue ('do')   → tbox = (text, (pos, pos + box));
     menue ('keep') → SEND (tbox);
     menue ('next') → tbox = NIL;

/*   'do' generates the internal representation of the triple
/*   'keep' stores it away.
/*   'next' cleans the variable, if not kept, then it is lost.
/*   this implements a user rejection after checking ('do') the
/*   visual result (see ECHO).

ECHO
```

```
menue ('do')      →   tx = TEXT (fit(text,pos,box));
menue ('keep')    →   CREATE SEG (rect(p,b),tx);
                      REMOVE tx;
menue ('next')    →   REMOVE tx;

/*  'do' generates a picture primitive using a utility routine
    to fit the three parameters, amd producing a TEXT primitive
/*  every picture primitive value assigned
/*  is also visible on the screen
/*  it removes the now redundant tx
/*  'next' removes (if still required) the current tx

END
```

The subcells called are **menue, text, pos** and **box.** They each have a separate window on the screen. This makes it possible, for instance. that **pos** and **box** use the same (hardware) cursor for specifying a position. There can be no confusion about the questions for whom (**pos** or **box**) a position is provided. The system may emphasise this by providing different cursor feedback for the two uses. This will become even more interesting in the next improved version.

6.2 Second solution: continuously active input mechanisms.

The high price for user freedom to be paid in the previous solution is the elaborate way of indicating the next input type through a menue-keyword. In the next solution the system presents all relevant input options simultaneously. The user simply by using the right mechanism (e.g. keyboard for text, cursor in either menue window, pos window or box window) implicitely indicates what he is going to do.
Consequently, the keywords 'text', 'pos' and 'box' can be removed from the menue.
At any time he can still select 'do', 'keep', 'next' and 'stop' with the same effect as in the previous solution.
We will not repeat the complete program here but only give those lines which hav been changed,

```
        Menue dkn menue        =      { 4, ('do','keep','next','stop')
                                      };

        DICE legend ...

        PROMPT ...

REQUEST menue (w menue) (dkn menue);
SAMPLE text (wtext), box (wbox), pos (wscreen)

...
/*  the reduced menue is still used in a synchronous mode
/*  but now this mode will be used to initiate some action
/*  on previously provided other inputs
/*  text, box and pos are immediately (early) activated
/*  and their most recent input as provided by the user is kept in
/*  the input pool.
```

```
/*   While the input is in the pool, its echo remains
/*   on the screen, so that the user can see what he has done.

SYMBOL            CASE menue IN (
                  'do'  : (text AND pos AND box);
                  'stop': $
                       ; CONT
                  ) * CONT;

/*   A 'do' selection in the menue will immediately lead to
/*   simultaneously sampling of the current  text, pos and
/*   box values. The VALUE mechanism will next provide a new
/*   triple echo based on the sampled result.
.
.
.

END

/*   no more changes are needed to achieve this improvement.
/*   in fact the dialogue has been simplified, as is also apparent
/*   from the simplified SYMBOL part, and yet the systems gives
/*   better support.
```

The continuously active cells **text, pos** and **box** will only become deactivated when the calling cell (**legend**) is deactivated. This will occur after a 'stop' selection.

6.3 Third solution: real-time, integrated feedback

In the last solution the triple: **text, box** and **position**, is immediately updated each time one of the three current values changes. The result is dispalyed in the map. This means that instead of having a 'do' keyword in the menue, input of one of the triple values must trigger the do-action.
Depending on how, for instance, the sub-cell **pos** works, one can achieve either a reappearance of the triple each time a user acknowledges a new position in **pos** (i.e.: the triple 'jumps' on the map) or the triple will be 'dragged' over the map into the right position, provided that the position mechanism of **pos** can supply new positions in a 'continuous' mode.
Again we will only give the changes with respect to the first splution.

The entry 'next' in the menue can also be discarded, provided that either an empty string (**text**) or an zero sized **box** (lower left = upper right position) will effectively cause removal of the current triple from the map.

```
MENUE triple = { 2, ('keep', 'stop');
DICE legend ...
PROMPT
EVENT menue (w menue) w triple);
     EVENT text (w text), box (w box), pos (w screen);

/*   all input mechanisms are permanently presented on the screen.
```

```
/*    each, when satisfied by the user may cause some action.

SYMBOL
    (CASE menue IN (
    'stop' :
          ; CONT
       )
    OR (text OR pos OR box)
    ) * CONT;
/*    each of the four subcells are in a parallel OR-construct
/*    which is cyclically kept active until via the menue
/*    'stop' the dialogue is terminated.

VALUE

        (text OR posOR box        →        tbox = (text, (pos, pos + box));
        menue ('keep')            →        SEND (tbox);
        ...

ECHO

        (text OR pos OR box) tx        =        TEXT (fit (text,pos, box));
        .
        .
        .

END
```

In the Value-part and ECHO-part now the occurence of the sub-expression (text OR pas OR box) in SYMBOL will cause the 'do' effect.
The updating of the triple can be done in an efficient way if the corresponding utility can see which parameters have changed since the previous update. (e.g. if only **pos** is changed, the **text** need not be reshaped, but only translated.

The three variants of the solution for the same problem demonstrates the great variety in dialogue forms one can have and at the same time that the specifications method can accomodate this variety. As long as no pertinent rules for user interface programming can be given, this flexible approach seems the best way. The method allows for easy program transformations to obtain a different external behaviour of the system after trial sessions.

7. Conclusions.

In this paper the situation of a user at a powerful interactive graphic terminal has been analysed, leading to the formulation of two kinds of parallel input. One is the early activation of input mechanisms which allows a user to select any of them at any time, even to use them simultaneously. The other kind of parallellism results from the input syntax, allowing a syntax rule to have more than one simultaneously possible alternative.

An input parser for such a form of input has next been described. Some important properties of the parser are:

1. The possibility to have more than one parse in progress, using inputs from parallel input streams.
2. The possibility to dynamically add and remove syntax rules from the 'currently active grammar'.
3. The ability to remove ambiguities occuring in the current active grammar through (re)assignment of resources to input mechanisms.

Special attention has been paid to user freedom in providing his input. This has been modelled by allowing the user input syntax to be a set of variants over the strict input syntax as used by the parser. The buffer mechanism required for coupling user syntax variants to the input syntax, the input pool, has been introduced and some of its properties are described. This results in a tolerant user interface system which can adequately handle the common situation that production of inputs is done different from accepting it. The input mechanisms organization plays a vital role, they can be hierarchically organised, meaning that complex mechanisms are built from simple ones. Every mechanism is completely described in one unit, called dialogue cell. Every dialogue cell defines the input type and the actual value of that type produced.
By relating the input type to the mechanism used, the parser can maintain a status which only forces it to reject input on the basis of wrong value, never on the basis of wrong type.

The desirable property for a user interface which results from this is that every input the user is capable of producing will be, at first instance, acceptable to the system.

On existing single processor systems, the parallel parsing of input needs to be simulated. For this purpose a scheduler is needed to decide which of the possible input symbols is to be parsed next. The effect of the scheduling algorithms on the user interface has been described.

In future reports a number of further aspects of dialogue cells will be described. Among those are: the interface of the dialogue cell system to an interactive graphics system, the design and implementation of basic dialogue cell libraries, the dialogue value process which maps the input values in internal data structures, automatic error recovery in dialogue cells, picture maintanence, screen management for dialogue cells etc.

Presentational, Syntactic and Semantic Components of Interactive Dialogue Specifications

D.R. Olsen, Jr.

Arizona State University, Tempe, Arizona, AZ 85287,USA

INTRODUCTION

In designing tools for the development of interactive applications, one must deal with the problem of what form of specification should be used to describe the interaction. This paper will address this problem of selecting an appropriate form by defining and describing three kinds of information which must be supplied in defining an interactive dialogue. They are Presentational, Syntactic and Semantic. The presentational specification defines how the interaction is actually bound to the physical interactive resources. This includes logical to physical device bindings as well as allocation of screen space to viewports and selection of virtual devices to be used. The syntactic specification defines the time ordering of inputs so as to map a limited set of interactive resources to a much larger set of semantic actions. The semantic specification defines what the actual operations are that an interactive user can perform and how they are implemented.

This partitioning is instructive because each of these components of an interaction has a radically different medium which most naturally expresses the required information. This partitioning is complicated, however, by some overlap between the components.

It is instructive to note that, depending on the application, either the presentation, syntax or semantics may be the dominant form of specification. For example it may be important to design a set of screen formats with commands that go with them as an early prototype, without paying much attention to the actual syntax. On the other hand, the syntax and presentational aspects may be of trivial importance compared to the computational complexities of the semantics. This leads to a design methodology where any of these forms of specification may serve as the starting point for a design with the other information added later as the design is refined. To support this methodology each form must have a straightforward interface to the others, it must be possible to check the consistency of these interfaces and where possible, one should be able to generate default specifications for one form, given the information in another. For example, given a set of semantic routines, it is possible to generate a simple default syntax and presentation which will allow the interaction to be tested (Olsen 1982). Such defaults can either remain as the actual specification or be refined in later phases of design or implementation.

With this in mind, this paper will proceed by defining each form of specification and describing the kinds of tools which are most suited to them. The impact that each component has on the others will then be reviewed and, finally, the kinds of default specifications that can be generated from a partial specification will be discussed.

PRESENTATIONAL SPECIFICATIONS

As mentioned earlier, the presentational aspect of a dialogue specification defines the appearance of an interactive system to the end user.

This would include the binding of logical to physical devices, the placement and size of viewports as well as the location and appearance of menu items and simulated devices. Note that this also encapsulates most of the device dependent information about an interaction. This specification also contains most of the geometric information about an interaction.

There are two basic sets of information that the presentational specification must deal with. They are contexts and formats. The contexts form the interface between the presentational and the syntactic components and the formats form the interface between the presentational and the semantic components.

A context is a given frame or mode of the interaction which has a specific set of logical/physical bindings associated with it. A context consists of a set of logical input devices and a set of logical viewports. The set of logical devices is assumed to be the set of all devices that are usable in this context. The set of viewports are those viewports that are actually visible in the context. The presentational specification binds logical input devices to specific logical input techniques or devices and binds logical viewports to a physical screen location.

In addition to binding logical to physical resources, the presentational specification also defines the actual appearance of such items on the screen. For example a menu item can be bound to an event device and then the color and shape of the menu item can be defined. Perhaps an icon is drawn for the menu item instead of a textual name. Not only must the presentational specification define the normal appearance of such an item but it must also define any changes to that appearance or other actions that should be taken when the device is enabled (becomes acceptable for input). Similar information must be defined for acknowledgement of an input and feedback of a device's measure (Rosenthal 1982).

In this formulation of a dialogue specification it is assumed that the application desires to present, in the viewports, images of logical objects that are to be manipulated. The presentational specification manipulates a set of object types. Each of these types has a certain number of data fields associated with it. The presentational specification defines what display primitives are to be used to display such an object. These display primitives are defined in terms of the data elements specified for the object. Such a mapping from a data object to a display representation is called a format. A single data object may have multiple formats for the various ways in which the object can be presented. The format chosen may depend on the data values of the object, the current context or viewport, global settings controlled by the interactive user or perhaps the current screen size in which the object is displayed.

There are two primary reasons for factoring out the presentational specification from the rest of the dialogue. The first is the obvious one of preserving device independence. A second and more interesting reason is the kind of tools that can be used to specify a presentation. A major part of the presentational information is geometric. Representation of geometric information in textual form has been a major stumbling block in user interface design. Futrelle has called for an Intrinsically Graphical Language (Futrelle 1978) and Buxton has built the MENULAY system (Buxton 1983) which allows a dialogue specification to be created graphically. Even though not all information is textual, not all information is graphical either. The presentational specification is the logical candidate for a graphical specification tool.

This not only allows for an easy and natural expression of the presentational aspects of a dialogue but also provides a very early external prototype of the system being designed.

SYNTACTIC SPECIFICATIONS

There has been a great deal of discussion about the syntactic specification of a dialogue. Many of the tools that have been created for User Interface Management have been syntactic in nature. The major reasons for this component of an interaction being singled out are 1) the syntax of an interaction is not adequately handled by normal programming languages; 2) there is a large body of well known automated techniques for syntax analysis and 3) the specification of an interaction's syntax goes a long way towards characterizing the interaction itself.

Before exploring syntactic specifications further it is important to note that not all are equally excited about the virtues of syntactic specifications. The main objection being made to such systems is their single threaded nature. Other systems have been proposed, notably SMALLTALK (Gold 1983) and a related proposal by Anson (1982) which models interactions as asynchronous processes or objects which interact with each other. There are three issues in this discussion. First is the importance of a sequenced ordering of inputs, second is the importance of the atomic or independent nature of displayed objects and thirdly the ability to computationally analyze the specification. The work of van den Bos (1983) stands out notably here as being somewhere in between the syntactic and the object oriented approaches.

The heart of the sequencing of inputs issue is one of multiplexing physical devices. Take for example the airplane cockpit. For each logical function or object related to flying the plane there is a control or indicator in the cockpit. For any action that is to be taken the current settings of the controls contain the specification. This approach is not applicable in all settings. Let us take the case of drawing a line. The action is to draw a line, and two operands (the endpoints) are required. If one has a function button and two locator devices, there is no time sequencing required. This is rarely practical and falls apart completely if one is drawing an n-sided polygon. The obvious and even preferable solution is to adopt an ordered sequence in which the points are entered. This solution thus requires a syntax.

The issue of atomic or independent objects or tools arises because most tools for syntax analysis allow only a single thread of dialogue to exist in a given system. This restriction arises because the tools for syntax analysis are so lately sprung from the single threaded world of compiler construction. Van den Bos (1983) has created a system of independent tools, each of which has its own local syntax and can be combined to form more complex tools. This is an important step towards removing the single thread barrier. This still does not address the issue of each object having its own dialogue and control of its own visual presentation. The problem is the basic notion of separation of input and output. This separation of input and output has its source in the early efforts to define graphics packages. This barrier must be bridged if one is to model the interaction as a whole. Some difficulty arises in the presence of such a multiplicity of dialogues as to which object a given physical input is to be sent to.

The issue of having a syntactic specification which can be computationally analyzed is an important one. This allows tools to be written to automatically compute additional information about the dialogue beyond the simple sequencing of inputs. From normal compiler construction we already have obtained checks for conflicts and ambiguity in the grammar. In SYNGRAPH (Olsen 1983a,b) the contexts, which were referred to in the presentational discussion, are automatically computed from the grammar as well as prompting, feedback and rubout capabilities. TIGER (Kasik 1982) provides a unique ability to exploit defaults, canceling or recursive reentry of commands. All of these features are possible because the syntactic specification of the dialogue has been factored out and a specification form such as a grammar, tree or transition network adopted which easily expresses the necessary sequence of inputs and can be easily analyzed.

The purposes of the syntactic specification are: 1) to define a translation between a time sequence of primitive inputs and a sequence of semantic actions; 2) to define what sequences of primitive inputs are acceptable and 3) to specify appropriate actions when incorrect sequences are encountered as well as guiding the user in avoiding incorrect inputs. To accomplish these purposes the syntactic specification has the following interfaces to the other two components. Relative to the presentation specification, the syntactic has a set of logical input devices that are acceptable. It also defines the contexts and what sets of devices belong to them. The syntactic/semantic interface consists of a set of actions that can be performed and a set of object types that they can be performed on. A subset of these object types are those types for which formats exist and can actually be displayed.

SEMANTIC SPECIFICATION

Most systems characterize the semantics of an interactive system by a set of commands, actions or procedures and a set of object types that they can act upon. For each command its operands must be specified and also its dependence upon other commands.

There are three kinds of command operands that must be considered. They are the actual operands, the global operands and the cognitive operands. The actual operands are those that are to be bound to the command by the syntax. About these we must know their type and whether they are read, modified, or both by command. The global operands are those that are implicitly referenced by the command, such as the object currently being edited. We must know whether these are read, modified or both. The cognative operands are those which may not be related to the command because of its implementation but are used by the end user in formulating inputs to such the command. For example, a command for inserting a plumbing fixture may not actually reference the walls of a floor plan. The interactive user however, would want to see those walls to be able to correctly place the fixture. The set of walls, then, is a cognitive operand of the command to place plumbing fixtures.

The dependencies between commands are important because in most systems not all commands are acceptable at any one time. It is not worth the effort to make every command acceptable at all times and in all places if the syntax is going to impose some sequence on them anyway. It is important however that these dependencies be modeled so that they can be checked for correctness and also that cases of highly dependent sets of commands can be flagged as too restrictive. Such dependencies occur as either global dependencies or operand dependencies. Two commands A and B are globally dependent if A reads or modifies a global operand which is read by B. Operand dependencies are much harder to define because they are based on actual object instances which in general are not known until run-time. In essence an operand dependency is where A modifies an object which B also uses as an operand.

Knowing that dependencies between semantic commands exist does not tell us what the restrictions on their sequential ordering might be. They only tell us where such restrictions need consideration. Riddle (1979) has described a software design methodology for modeling such dependencies. An example of a sequential restriction caused by a command dependency would be where a graphical segment must have been opened before any graphical primitive routines can be called. An example of such a restriction imposed by an operand dependency would be where WRITEs cannot be performed on a file until it has been OPENed. In this case the file would be the dependent operand between the WRITE and OPEN commands.

As with the other forms of specification, the semantics have a different form of expression. The semantics of the dialogue are best implemented using a general purpose programming language.

INTERRELATIONSHIPS

This section discusses blurrings of the boundaries between the three forms of specification. Originally they were separated because each had a unique expressive medium that was most appropriate. There are however several tradeoffs between such forms of expression.

Presentational/Syntactic

The interrelationships between the presentational and syntactic aspects of a dialogue revolve around device dependence. Baecker (1979) has argued that simply replacing one physical device with another in a physical/logical device binding is not sufficient when porting an interactive system from one display configuration to another. Frequently the syntax of the dialogue itself must be changed. The organization of the contexts may also require modification. On one hardware configuration there may be limited resources in which case the contexts must all be small. On a different configuration it may be possible to handle large contexts but the slowness with which contexts may be changed might make many small contexts infeasible. This creates a necessity to modify both syntax and presentation when dealing with new devices.

Syntactic/Semantic

A major overlapping between syntactic and semantic specifications occurs in the area of command dependencies. The problem arises as to where it is best to express the sequential restrictions. In the area of command dependencies one can specify a state machine like the one specified in the GKS standard (1982) in which each semantic action is a possible transition of the machine. In the case of operand dependencies such a machine would need to be defined for each object type. Such specifications can greatly clarify the relationships between commands. The specification of these semantic sequences requires a grammar or transition net rather than a general purpose language. This leads one to want to let the syntactic specification define such sequential restrictions. We can possibly infer these restrictions from the syntactic specification that uses the commands, or we may take those restrictions that have been specified in the semantic specification and verify that the syntactic specification is consistent with the sequence restrictions. An interesting side issue is to develop a measure of how many more sequential restrictions are created by the syntactic specification than are actually required semantically. A high value for this measure would indicate a poorly designed dialogue.

A second overlapping area is semantic control of dialogue sequences. In many cases a state machine or a pushdown automaton is not sufficient to characterize the legal sequences for inputs. For this reason systems such as TIGER and that proposed by van den Bos allow for semantic predicates in the dialogue that control which of a set of transitions are acceptable. This seems to answer the need for semantic control of the dialogue.

Semantic/Presentational

The primary question here involves formats. In particular it is the question of what control does the semantics have over what a format looks like. Most of the geometry and display attributes can be semantically controlled by modifying the data in the object. This means that the display management system must be notified each time the semantic actions modify a visible object. Another difficulty lies in deciding how much computational power should be placed in a format. The following categorizes possible levels of computational power in a format.

1) Primitives in the format are defined in terms of constants or object subfields.

2) Primitives are defined in terms of arithmetic and boolean expressions of constants and subfields.

3) Primitives are defined in terms of semantic functions of constants and subfields.

4) Primitives are defined in terms of functions and procedures local to the format.

In general the less powerful the computational abilities in the formats the more subfields must be defined in the objects to provide the values needed to present a format. On the other hand the more extensive the computational information is that is expressed in the format, the less suitable the format is for interactive specification and the more a general purpose programming language becomes appropriate. One can draw the line at level 3 in the list above and still preserve the interactive specification of the format without unduly complicating its computational aspects.

DEFAULT SPECIFICATIONS

As originally discussed, one can design an interactive system beginning with any of the specificational forms depending upon what the dominant aspect of the system is. Because of the inter-relationships between the three forms of specification it is possible to generate automatically some of the information in one form of specification from another. These default specifications are then useful as prototype specifications and may in many cases form the final specification if no more specific tailoring is required. This process would greatly reduce the specificational overhead of producing early prototypes without eliminating the possibility for handcrafted dialogues.

Presentational Defaults

Adequate defaults can be created for contexts from the syntactic specification. From the syntactic specification one can easily determine what the various contexts are. It is also not difficult to determine the set of all logical devices which are used between entering the context and leaving it. This forms the logical device set for the context. Logical events can be mapped to menu items which use the logical device name as the item's image. Bindings of other logical devices can be established arbitrarily to physical devices which match in the types of information that they return. Bindings of logical pick devices will depend on the format mechanism. All of this kind of processing is already done in SYNGRAPH and TIGER.

The creation of default formats is somewhat less satisfactory. The problem lies in automatically providing a default that is at all satisfactory. Many systems are being designed which automatically display data based on its type or structure. All such systems, however, produce an image of the data itself. For example, a line segment would be displayed as a set of four real numbers representing the coordinates of the end-points. What is desired, however, is the image of a line segment. Such defaulted formats are not useless however, because they can be an important tool in debugging an interaction where it is the data itself that the programmer needs access to.

Default Syntax

Given a specification of the semantic actions, it is also possible to generate a default syntax (Olsen 1982). Every semantic action name is mapped to a logical event device. Every unique operand type is mapped to a non-terminal in the syntax. The global or starting context is a non-terminal consisting of the command's logical event followed by the non-terminals for the appropriate operand types. This is followed by some command terminator and a call to the semantic action. Each non-terminal for the operand types has a production for each semantic function which returns a result of that type. In addition, if the type corresponds to an object type, then a logical pick device for that type forms a production. Lastly, if a non-terminal represents a primitive type, then the primitive devices which return such values can form productions for that non-terminal. The example below is an illustration of what can be done.

Semantic actions and functions

```
DRAW(start,end:POINT)
DELETE(l:LINE)

START_POINT(l:LINE):POINT
END_POINT(l:LINE):POINT
```

Default Syntax

```
<command>::=DRAW<point(s)><point(e)>DONE{DRAW(s,e)}
     |DELETE<line(l)>DONE{DELETE(l)}

<line(l)>::=PICK_LINE(l)

<point(p)::=START_POINT<line(l)>DONE{p:=START_POINT(l)}
     |END_POINT<line(l)>DONE{p:=END_POINT(l)}
     |LOCATOR(p)TIP_SWITCH
```

This default syntax can then have a default presentation generated for it. This means that an entire prototype could be generated from semantic specification. This could either be refined or replaced as the design progresses.

Default Command Dependencies

As mentioned earlier, information about the sequential restrictions on commands can be inferred from the syntactic specification. This can be done by creating a FOLLOWS_DEPENDING relation between commands. The relation B FOLLOWS_DEPENDING A holds if A modifies some global variable V which B uses, and there is a path through the syntax specification from some invocation of A to an invocation of B which does not pass through an invocation of an action which modifies V. This FOLLOWS_DEPENDING relation can be used to check modifications to the syntax of a dialogue. Any changes to the FOLLOWS_DEPENDING relation caused by a dialogue modification can be flagged as possible violations of the sequential relationships of the semantic actions. A similar relation can be created to model operand dependencies. Note that the restrictions created by the FOLLOWS_DEPENDING relations are probably stronger than necessary but they do provide additional information to prevent errors in maintenance of dialogue specifications. This is based on the assumption that the initial syntactic specification correctly handles all sequential restrictions on semantic actions.

CONCLUSION

Three aspects of an interactive dialogue have been presented. These aspects are differentiated by the kinds of languages and tools that best represent and manipulate them. The issues related to each aspect have been discussed and the interrelationships between these components identified. Finally, it has been shown how information contained in one component can be used to generate default specifications for another. This facility enhances the verification of consistency in the dialogue as well as reduces the effort required to prototype an interactive system.

REFERENCES

Anson , E (1982) The device model of interaction. Comp Grph 16:3
Baecker R (1979) Towards an effective characterization of graphical interaction. In: Seillac II workshop on man-machine interaction position papers, Mathematisch centrum, Amsterdam
Buxton W, Lamb MR, Sherman D, and Smith KC (1983) Towards a comprehensive user interface management system. Comp Grph 17:3
Futrelle RP, Barta G (1978) Towards the design of an intrinsically graphical language. Comp Grph12:3
Goldberg A, Robson D (1983) SMALLTALK-80: The language and its implementation, Addison-Wesley, Reading, Massachusetts
Graphical Kernal System - Functional description (1982) Draft proposal (ISO/DP 7942)
Hanau PR, Lenorovitz, DR (1980) Prototyping and simulation tools for user/computer dialogue design. Comp Grph 14:3
Jacob RJ (1983) Using formal specifications in the design of a human-computer interface. Comm of ACM 26:4
Kasik DJ (1982) A user interface management system. Comp Grph 16:3
Kamran A, Feldman MB (1983) Graphics programming independent of interaction techniques and styles. Comp Grph 17:1
Olsen DR (1982) A procedure based model for interactive graphics. In: NCGA 82 conference proceedings, vol 2
Olsen DR, Dempsey EP (1983) Syntax directed graphical interaction. In: Proceedings of the SIGPLAN 83 symposium on programming language issues in software systems
Olsen DR, Dempsey EP (1983) SYNGRAPH: A graphical user interface generator. In: Proceedings of SIGGRAPH 83
Riddle WE (1979) An event-based design methodology supported by DREAM. In: Formal models and practical tools for information systems design, North-Holland Publishing Company
Rosenthal DS, Michener JC, Plaff, Gunther, Kessener, Rens, Sabin M (1982) Detailed semantics of graphics input devices. Comp Grph 16:3
van den Bos J, Plasmeijer MJ, Hartel PH (1983) Input-output tools: A language facility for interactive and real-time systems. IEEE transactions on software engineering SE-9:3

Part 4

Interfaces and Implementations of UIMS

UIMS as Part of a CAD System

P. David*, S. Lafont**, and P. Uvietta***

*Ecole Centrale de Lyon, P.P. 163, 69131 Ecully Cedex, France
**RTC La Radiotechnique Compelec, 51 rue Carnot, P.P. 301, 92156 Surennes, France
***Laboratoire Artemis-IMAG, P.P. 68, 38402 St Martin D'Heres Cedex, France

ABSTRACT

This paper describes an architecture of the User Interface Management System as a part of a CAD system. In CAD environment, the multi-media Man Machine Interaction gets more and more desirable. A two-level organisation was choosen to satisfy this requirement:

1. At the first level the Communication Manager takes into account a multi-media work station.

2. At the second level the Dialogue Manager works in a canonical way, i.e. peripheral independent.

A specification language for dialogues is also presented with associated method and tools for interactive program construction.

NOTE

This work has been performed at the laboratoire ARTEMIS-IMAG

1.0 INTRODUCTION

In the C.A.D. context, man-machine communication is a fundamental element. This communication is to be considered both:

- in the design process, where the user expresses how he wishes to act (Design Process User Interface);

- in every design process task (Task User Interface).

Man-machine communication tends to use more and more often multi-media work stations: textual, graphical, vocal input/output... This is very usefull in CAD context because it brings wider communication flexibility. The work station grows gradually around the usual alphanumerical terminal: are added a graphic terminal, a digitiser, a plotter, a hard-copy terminal, a loud speaker, a microphone... We investigated the ways to provide an easy use of such a work station while keeping its actual composition transparent to the interactive program that uses it.

We suggest a two-level structure in order to take into account the peripheral variety without complicating the UIMS (User Interface Management System):

- a Communication Manager for multi-media work station management;

- a Dialogue Manager to handle dialogues and associated actions (algorithms), whatsoever the informations origin and destination are.

Our work aim is to replace progressively the development of interactive programs by specification and automatic programmation of structured dialogues which means a separation between dialogues and algorithms. This organisation requires the introduction of specification techniques for dialogues and automatic production of a skeleton able to handle interactions and to interface efficiently with algorithms.

In this paper, we present this two-level organisation: Communication Manager - Dialogue Manager as well as the structure and treatment of the Dialogue Specification Language. The two managers connected together, constitute the operating structure of the UIMS .

2.0 COMMUNICATION MANAGER

2.1 Its Functionnality

The Communication Manager functions are:

- manage the work station

- prepare the user commands for the Dialogue Manager transforming them into a standard form independent of the operating mode used (free/tutorial, textual/graphic, batch/interactive), translate data from external (user) to internal (system) representation and vice-versa.

It works as a bidirectional translator: on one hand it transforms the users command and data into the standard form already mentioned and on the other hand it gives the system data a format asked by the user.

2.2 The Logical Units Mechanism

We decided to use the logical and physical unit concepts. Each type of information going through the Manager must be allocated a LOGICAL UNIT (LU) which function is to assume a one direction transfer. A PHYSICAL UNIT (PU) is allocated to each terminal belonging to the work station. Thus the communication is performed by attaching a logical unit to a physical unit.

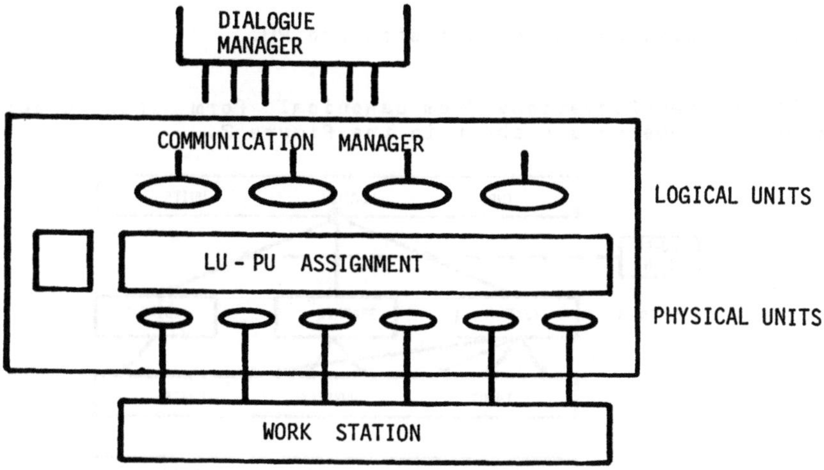

Fig. 1: Logical Unit - Physical Unit

The same physical unit may be attached to several logical units; this corresponds to a reduction of the work station: it is even possible to work with a unique terminal, the alphanumerical one. It would also probably be interesting to attach simultaneously several physical units to one logical unit, especially for ergonomical reasons (for example to send commands simultaneously from the graphic terminal and from a digitiser).

Information interpretation and transformation for transfer between PUs and LUs are done in the following way: the system receives informations through one direction LUs, and it transmits them to the PU connected with the LU.

A more precise study on PUs shows that the choice to use an input canonical form implies a classification into three units groups:

1. alphanumerical input for PUs: typewriter, card, file, tape and graphic terminal in alphanumerical mode;

2. graphic input on graphic terminal;

3. special input on non-standard PU.

There are also three groups for output:

1. alphanumerical output for PUs: typewriter, card, file, tape and graphic terminal in alphanumerical mode;

2. graphic output on graphic terminal;

3. special output on non-standard PU.

These transformations from canonical form into specific form and vice-versa are shown in the figure 2.

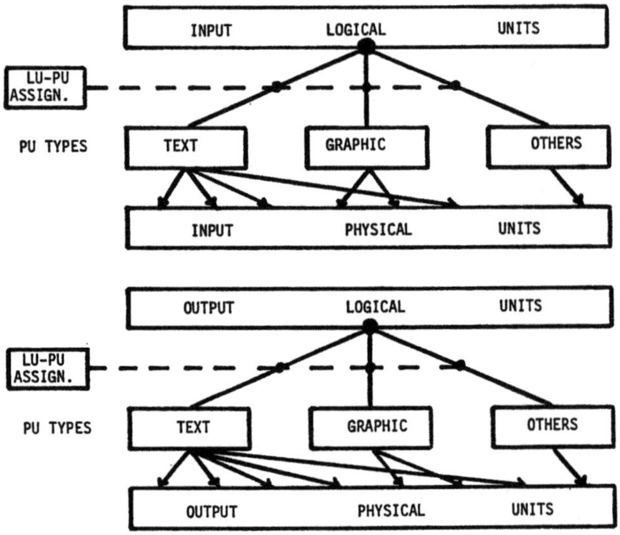

Fig. 2: Transfer between logical units and physical units

A command language is associated with this mechanism; it allows the user to:

- define dynamically the work station composition (conf:)

- know the work station status at a given moment (conf?)

- affect logical units to the physical units (aff:)

- know the units affectations (aff?)

- ask for printing of a trace starting at a certain level (trace:)

- Know the current trace level (trace?)

This set of commands must be available in any environment, i.e. nearly during each operation.

At the beginning of each interactive program, the initial configuration of the work station and the LU - PU assignments are set either to a user specified configuration if any or to a system standard configuration. The user may modify these two characteristics dynamically at any time using the command language above mentionned.

2.3 Lexical Analysis

The lexical analysis function is to determine by analysis of the input string the syntactic units that will be used in the syntactic analysis. The lexical analysis can be done at different levels:

- either it is strictly structural, i.e. it only finds the input string structure (it recognises: an integer or a real number, an identifier or a character string...)
- or it already knows a few informations about semantics of the language and it is able to distinguish a keyword from an identifier, to recognise the type of an identifier, an operator...

We chose to implement both of these analyses one after the other. The first one will be called LEXIC; the second one will be called SEMANT because it performs an analysis that can be classified as semantic even though it is restricted to one syntaxic unit at a time. We decided to take this solution mainly because of the work station utilization. In the work station we may have two types of input - output mechanisms:

1. continuous input - output system, i.e. text lines
2. structured input - output system, i.e. a structured screen with predefined fields.

With a continuous system, we must execute first the lexical one and then the semantic analysis, as with a structured system we need only the semantic analysis because the lexical has already been performed. It is what we call the formated and unformated modes.

The next figure shows how the analysis works. The information comes from the work station. If it is read on an unformated input system, it follows the unformated informations way: the line is cut into single characters, that go through a syntactic unit rebuilding process (CARSUIV) which returns the integer number, real number, special character, text string, or pointed identifier, and has its semantic determined by the semantic analysis (SEMANT). SEMANT uses keywords, identifiers and operators tables and according to the lexical type of the information, it tries to find the syntactic unit semantic type. The syntactic analyser transmits it an information which may give it, for example the type of the identifier it is waiting for. If the information obtained is not sufficient, SEMANT keeps temporarily the identifier as an untyped one, which type it will determine later.

If the information follows the unformated informations way, it goes directly through integer, real number, word, text string... input procedures, and can be transmitted at once to SEMANT for a semantic analysis.

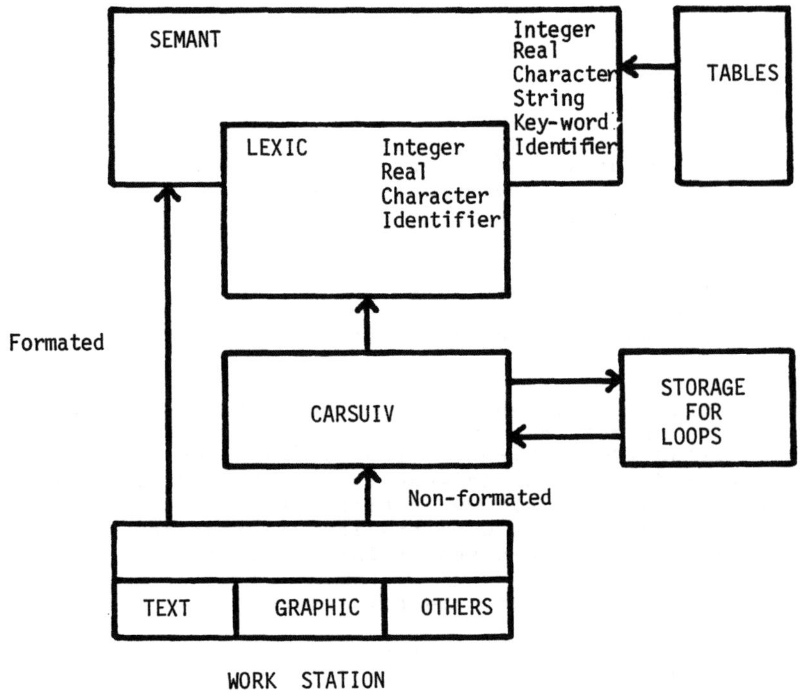

Fig. 2: Organisation of the lexical analysis

2.4 Canonical Form Output

As logical units (LU) and physical units (PU) are separated, the input/output functions available in programming languages cannot be used, for these functions work directly on physical units, the format of which is different for each unit type. This implied for us to develop specific mechanisms in order to address any physical unit type in a unique form.

This mechanism consists in:

- a set of functions notifying the transfer of any information type,
- a standard function for the effective transfer to the physical unit buffer, and the unit activation, if required,
- the management of the buffers associated to the physical units.

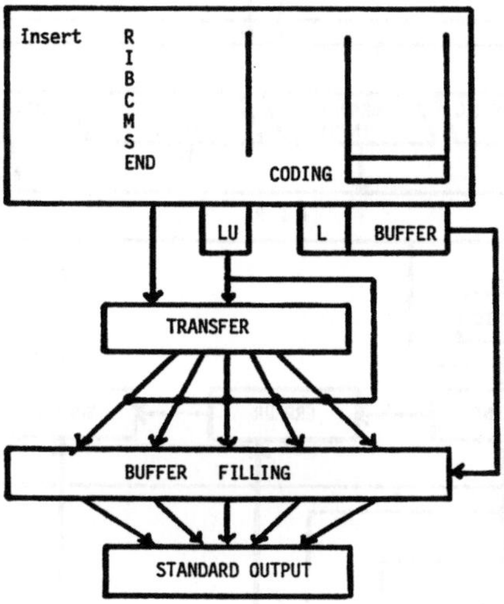

Fig. 4: Principles of the output mechanism

Information transfer functions (insert functions) are available for real, integer, character, logical, 2 characters word, character string and buffer end mark insertions. The TRANSFERT function transfers coded information into the buffer of the physical unit attached to the logical one, and activates the output function, if the buffer is full, or when explicitly required.

Other functions such as tabulations have been added in order to define formated outputs; they are to be used in insert functions.

2.5 Structure Of The Communication Manager

The figure hereafter represents the communication manager structure. The terminals of the work station communicate with the CLP module, which role is to warrant a correspondence betweenlogical and physical units. The information is processed by LEXIC if not formated, then by SEMANT. When in a canonical form (syntactically and semantically correct), the information is transfered to the upper level (dialogue module). For the output phase, informations are transfered to SORTIE module, then to CLP in order to produce effective output on the terminal(s) formerly specified.

The DPT module (definition of the work station) manages the work station definition, specified by means of the COMCOM language, above mentioned.

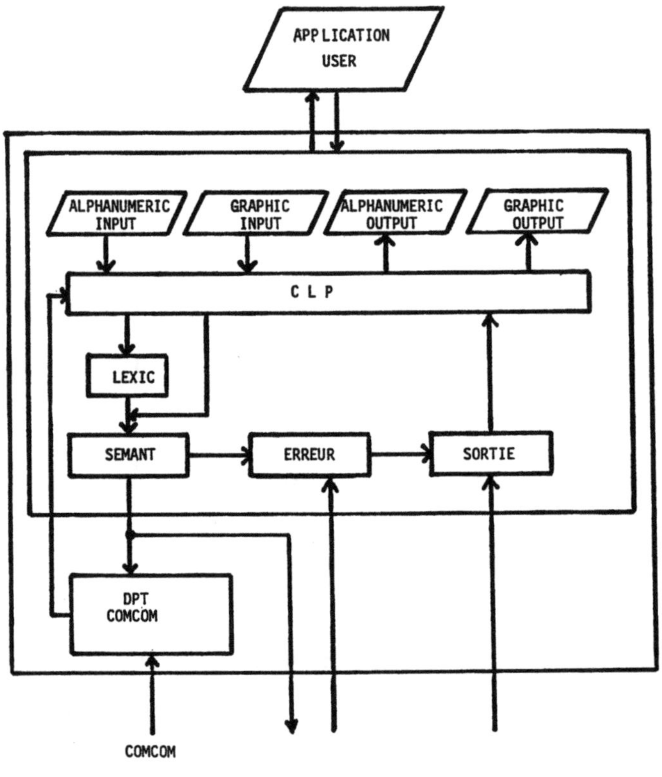

Fig. 5: Communication manager structure

3.0 DIALOGUE MANAGER

The dialogue manager handles interactions, by means of the definition of authorised dialogues, their syntactical structure and the actions to be executed (semantic functions).

Such a dialogue specification may be treated in two different ways:

- direct production of a dialogue manager; the translator compiles the description and construct a directly executable program;

- production of tables to be interpreted by a general dialogue manager.

These two solutions differ basically: the first one is more efficient, but very rigid; the second one processes slowly (interpretation), but is more flexible for modifications.

We chose the second solution, because we intend to improve the application command language possibilities; in addition, the interpreter solution makes it possible to implement the specifications translator and the dialogue manager using a unique program directed by different tables.

According to the syntactic method it uses: top-down or bottom-up, the dialogue manager can either treat deterministic dialogues (top-down), or take into account non-determinism of a natural language sub-set. We chose the top-down method, because it constrains to define more precise dialogues.

The following figure presents the corresponding organisation. Tasks relative to dialogues are expressed as algorithms in semantic functions. The information transfer between the user and the algorithms requires the creation of a data area, interface between the dialogue manager and the algorithms. This zone is used for the storage

- of default values for the optional parameters; these data are handled only by the dialogue manager; a copy of these values is done in the effective parameters area, as many times as required;

- effective values of any parameter; these data may be accessed both by the manager and the algorithms.

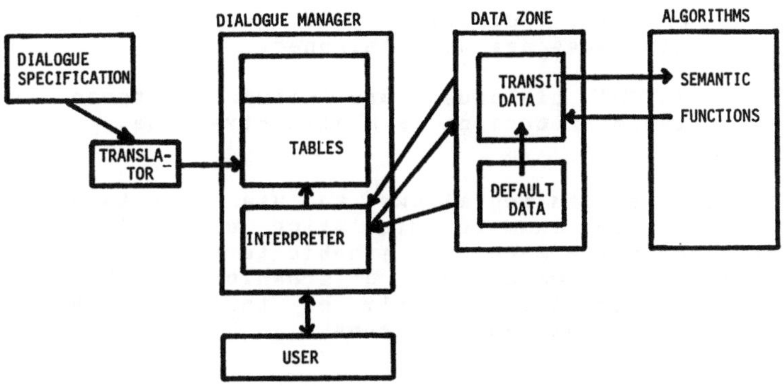

Fig. 6: Structure of the dialogue management

In this context, an interactive program can be defined as: the dialogue manager, specific dialogue definition tables and the semantic functions attached to.

4.0 STRUCTURE OF THE UIMS

The UIMS comprises mainly the communication manager and the dialogue manager. The resulting organisation makes it possible to use various work stations as well as to support both tutorial and free modes. This interaction manager is the crucial component of any interactive program.

For the implementation of an interactive program, informations and specific algorithms (semantic functions) must be provided to communication and dialogue managers, in order to specialise them:

- the communication manager has first to be informed on the characteristics of the work station and initial affectations of logical units. The specification table for semantic analysis and the specific error messages table are to be provided in a second step.

- the description of the application dialogues and the set of semantic functions to be called by the manager are to be provided to the dialogue manager.

Our approach allows to define in a unique specification dialogues that can be run in different modes; these modes are:

- FREE: the user manages freely directs completely the dialogue; help messages (related to the knowledge level the user chose) are provided by the system on the user's request.

- TUTORIAL: the system directs the dialogues, displaying menu-type information on the current available possibilities.

- GRAPHIC: dialogues use graphic tools; these dialogues are tutorial ones.

- BATCH: dialogues are formerly stored in a file; their processing is a batch-type one.

This organisation allows to use simultaneously several terminals, for example displaying all help messages on a control screen, a menu on a graphic terminal or use a keypad terminal. The management of graphic or alphanumeric screens may be realised independently of the specific application, specifying the interaction areas.

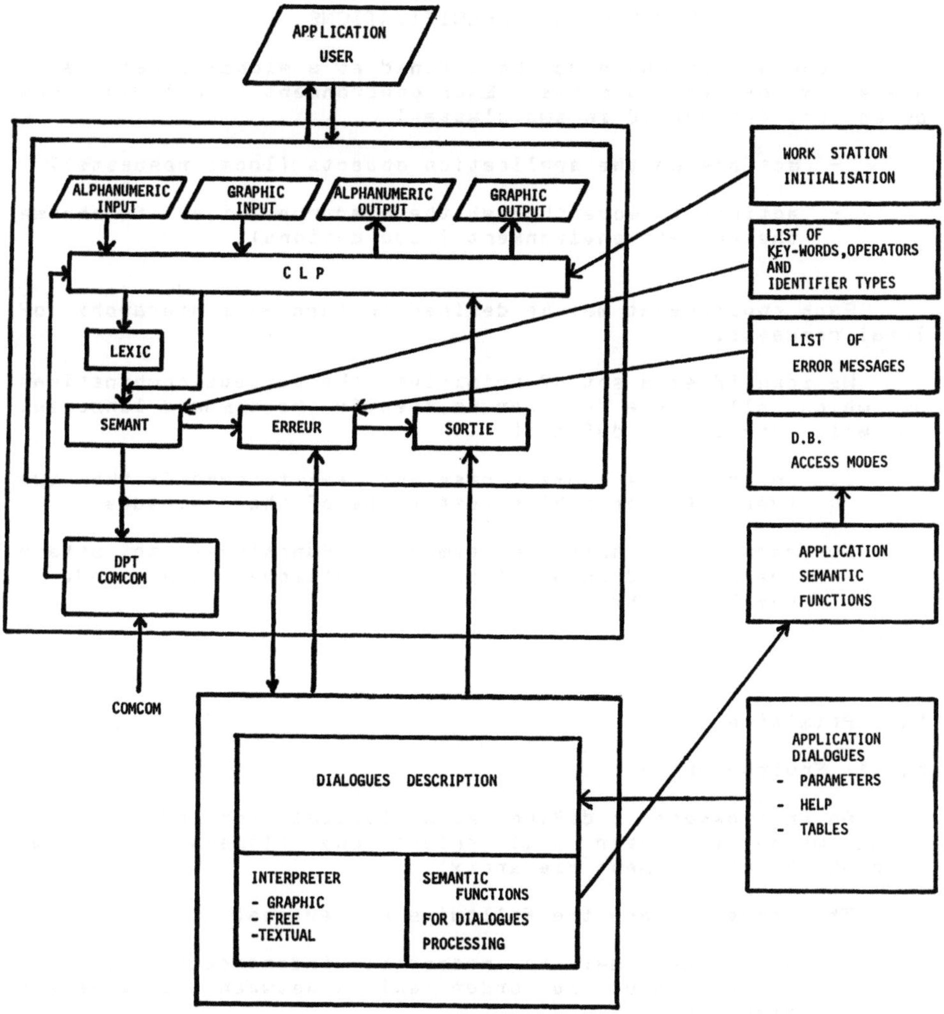

Fig. 7: UIMS structure and interactive program implementation

An application with graphic mode utilization, based on the GRIGRI graphic software, has been already implemented, using GRIGRI primitives instead of free format commands:

- RVAL, NVAL, CVAL for alphanumeric data inputs (real, integer, string);
- POSITION for coordinates collection;
- IDENTIFICATION for graphic objects identification;
- MENU for the selection of an alternative in a menu.

The same approach can be used for GKS integration.

5.0 A LANGUAGE FOR DIALOGUE SPECIFICATIONS

A command language may be defined at a global level as a hierarchy of environments. Each environment is a logical set of actions decomposed in two classes:

- actions on the application objects (local requests);
- actions to move through the hierarchy, i.e. to change the current environment (move actions).

Each environment may be defined in turn as a hierarchy of local requests.

We identified a set of primitives the various combinations of which allow the designer to specify the command language. Two main groups were defined:

1. environment, command case and leaf to specify the two types of hierarchies (structure of the dialogues)
2. parameters, helps and semantic functions, to attach the required information to be attached to any node of any hierarchy.

5.1 Primitives

5.1.1 Environment -

An environment is defined as a logical set of actions, among which the user will select one element (up or down through the environment hierarchy).

The requests have the following properties:

- any request may be processed independently of the others, thus no order exists between the different requests
- any local request is repeatable as many times as necessary
- no move action is repeatable, by definition (e.g. quit request)

5.1.2 Command -

A command is a sequence of actions. The main properties are the following:

- the required informations concerning each action are provided by the user in a pre-detedetermined order by the application designer,

- the execution of a command does not produce a move in the environment hierarchy.

5.1.3 Case -

A case is a set of pre-defined requests among which the user selects one and only one element. A case node may be specified as a component of a command node; a selection without repetition may be defined in such a way.

5.1.4 Leaf -

A leaf is a terminal action.

5.2 Informations Attached To The Nodes

5.2.1 Parameters -

Two types of informations have to be distinguished:

1. Key-words, i.e. information specified by the application designer
2. parameters, i.e. information depending on the application context, to be provided by the user. Two sub-sets have been here defined:
   - the parameters the value of which is dynamically provided by the user, e.g. a file-name
   - the parameters chosen by the final user among a finite set of elements, pre-defined by the application designer.

Each parameter may be specified with a default value.

5.2.2 Messages -

Two classes of messagesto be provided to the user, if required, have been defined:

1. HELP MESSAGES: a set of such messages can be attached to any node; each message is associated to an information on the user's knowledge level. These messages are provided on the user's request.
2. PROMPT MESSAGES: prompt facilities can also be specified, if the provided information is incomplete. Prompts are available for key-words and parameters.

5.2.3 Semantic Functions -

A set of algorithms is attached to each node, executing the specified treatments (semantic verifications, processing of the informations provided by the user, etc.).

5.3 A Specification Language For Command Languages

For a flexible and more efficient specification of all the command languages, the so-called LSLDC (Specification Language for Command Languages) has been implemented. The application designer has to specify:

- the organisation and the functionalities of the dialogue structure,
- the organisation of the relative data management, i.e. the type of parameters memorisation (immediate or stored information)
- the organisation of semantic functions

6.0 INTERACTIVE PROGRAM IMPLEMENTATION PROCESS

The DDG (Dialogue Description Grammar) is transformed into the DDG table by the grammar transformer. The DDG table plus the associated semantic functions and the general grammar interpreter constitute the translator PPTRAD. This work is done by the LDC System Designer.

```
        DIALOGUE
        DESCRIPTION
        GRAMMAR    ____________
         (GDD)   ! GRAMMAR      !
           --->! TRANSFORMER !
                 ____________
                       !
                       V  PPTRAD Translator
             ________________________
            !   ____________           !
            ! ! D D G TABLE !          !
APPLICATION !   ____________           !  APPLICATION
DIALOGUES   !        !                 !  DIALOGUES
DESCRIPTION !        V                 !  GRAMMAR   ____________
  (AiDD)    !  ____________     _____  !   (AiDG) ! GRAMMAR      !
 O      --->!! INTERPRETER !<->! S.F.!!--------->! TRANSFORMER !
/!\         !  ____________     _____  !            ____________
/ \          ________________________                    !
Interactive                                               !
Program                !-----------------------------------
Designer               V PPLDC Interaction Program
             ________________________
            !   _____________          !
            ! ! Ai D G TABLE !         !
            !   _____________          !
APPLICATION !         !                !
DIALOGUES   !         V          _____ !
  (AiD)     !  ____________     ! Ai !!
 O    ------>!! INTERPRETER !<->! S.F.!!
/!\         !  ____________     _____ !
/ \          ________________________
Interactive
Program
User
```

Fig. 8: Interactive program implementation process

For an application the Interaction Program Designer specifies the AiDD (Application Dialogues Description). The translator receives as input data AiDD, the Ai Application Dialogue Description. It verifies these specifications (syntax and semantic) and generates AiDG, the Application Dialogue Grammar. From AiDG, the grammar transformer builds the AiDG table.

The Interactive Program Designer must also develop the application semantic functions.

The Ai application is now ready to be used: the application dialogues are given as input data to the PPLDC interactive program made of the AiDG table plus the Ai application semantic functions and the general grammar interpreter.

The activation of PPLDC will start the interactive program execution. Now Interactive Program User can work with this program.

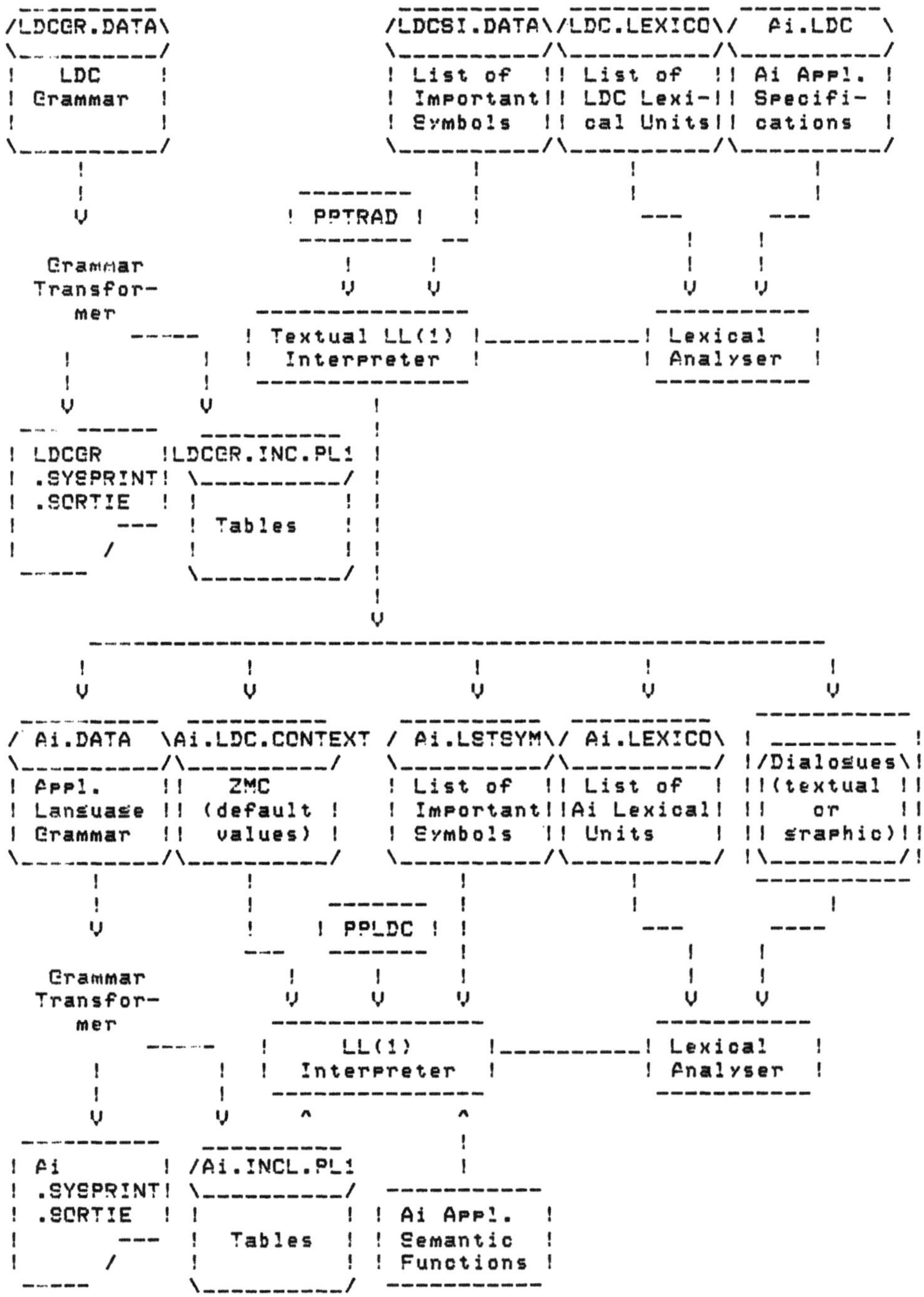

Fig. 9: General organisation

To start, the user must give the name of the application he wants to dialogue with. This produces the initialisation of the dialogue which consists mainly in a work station initialisation. The initialisation to be performed is specified for each application in the specification header. However, at any moment during the communication, the user may modify or ask informations about the work station composition through COMCOM.

CONCLUSION

We presented in this paper a possible architecture of a multi-media UIMS, a dialogue specification language and associated methods and tools for interaction program construction.

This approach was implemented and a prototype is working. The next step in the developpment is the introduction of some new facilities, mainly the possibility to create new commands or to modify them, and to be able to take into account new user's or application requirements.

BIBLIOGRAPHY

A. LEDUC-LEBALLEUR, M. LUCAS, F. MARTINEZ
Conception et realisation d'un logiciel graphique interactif independant du contexte d'utilisation: le logiciel de base GRIGRI
RAIRO Computer Science, vol. 12, no 2, pp. 147-173, 1978

B. DAVID
Man-machine communication in the specification, implementation and use of an integrated CAD/CAM system
IFIP W.G. 5.2-W.G. 5.3 Working conference on man-machine communication in CAD/CAM, Tokyo, oct. 1980

M. DELAUNAY, J.F. GRABOWIECKI
Note technique d'utilisation du transformateur de grammaire LL(1)
Rapport de recherche no 234, IMAG, sep. 1981

J.J. THOMAS, G. MOULIN
Graphical input interaction technique
Computer graphics, Jan. 1983

The Unification of a Dialogue Manager and a Graphics System

E. Edmonds and S. Guest

Human-Computer Interface Research Unit, Leicester Polytechnic, United Kingdom

1. INTRODUCTION.

1.1. SYNICS/DDL.

SYNICS/DDL is a software tool for the construction of user interfaces to interactive systems, and for the prototyping of interactive systems (Edmonds, 1981, 1982; Guest, 1982).

The underlying philosophy of SYNICS/DDL assumes that it is both possible and desirable to construct interactive systems with the user interface being an explicit and separable component. The size, or "depth", of the interface will inevitably vary from system to system.

SYNICS/DDL provides a design language and a corresponding construction tool for user interfaces. It does not assume any particular analogies for modes of interaction, such as the Xerox work (Kay & Goldberg, 1977) or the Carnegie-Mellon COUSIN system (Hayes & Szekley, 1983). However, the SCHEMA facility of SYNICS/DDL, described below, allows the implementer to construct interfaces which exhibit and embody standard styles of interaction. Graphics facilities are being incorporated at the moment. Work is currently being done from the opposite direction, on adding dialogue design tools to GKS, in Darmstadt (Hanusa, 1983).

Whilst table-based syntax-driven parsers are well known (Feldman and Gries, 1968), their consistent application in the provision of 'front-ends' to interactive systems has received relatively little detailed study. Two main reviews have been written, by Edmonds (1981) and by Jacob (1983a). The latter has appeared in an abbreviated form in Jacob (1983b). Neither of these reviews, however, paid very much attention to graphics.

1.2. DIALOGUE EVENTS.

Interactive dialogues are seen by the system as sets of events, each of which involves either a user input or some output from the background (applications) program that influences the direction of the dialogue. The implementer of a user interface describes, in SYNICS/DDL, each potential event. In broad terms the description of a dialogue event includes the following items:-

a display, or modification of a display, to be output (e.g. a menu).

a classification of possible inputs from the user or background (e.g. each menu selection plus "any other input").

A background action for relevant input classifications (e.g. the selected task).

The appropriate next dialogue event (e.g. a "help" event for a meaningless selection).

A dialogue event is called a NODE of the dialogue description. The total set of dialogue events can be viewed as a recursive transition network. This view provides a simple diagrammatic form in which the interface can be represented.

1.3. SCHEMATA.

SYNICS/DDL allows dialogue events, or related sets of dialogue events, to be specified in outline forms, called schemata. A schema may contain parameters (unspecified elements) in any of its components. A dialogue event is able to invoke a schema with specified parameters. This facility enables repetitive or standardised interface activities to be defined in outline once only and then used at will.

1.4 INPUT CLASSIFICATION.

The action to be taken at a dialogue event may depend in quite a complex way on the user input. If, for example, the interface were to an interactive programming language, the dialogue action could depend strongly on whether or not the input string was a legal command in that language.

SYNICS/DDL incorporates a parser so that the implementer can, where necessary, specify input classification on the basis of chosen syntactic descriptions. In addition, integral semantic descriptions are allowed. In this way complex transformations of the input string can be passed to the background.

1.5. EXCEPTIONS AND HOOKS.

Dialogue event specification is achieved using comprehensive facilities but even assembler level programming does not always provide the freedom that a programmer requires, as the popularity of a microcoding demonstrates. Consequently SYNICS/DDL provides its users with the facility for incorporating their own routines, in conventional languages, into the decision-making process at any dialogue event. Specifically, the input classifications may be realised by user supplied routines. Alternatively the parsing process may, in full or in part, be driven by user supplied routines, as may the semantic transformations. These facilities are not normally required but have proved invaluable in one advanced project in which SYNICS/DDL was used to parse and transform English into certain standard underlying forms. One way in which the facility was used was to incorporate an efficient look up routine to decide whether or not a given word belonged to a specific set of known nouns.

2. SYNICS/DDL + GKS = SYNICS2.

2.1. GRAPHICAL VERSION OF SYNICS INCORPORATING GRAPHICS.

SYNICS2 will be different to the current system in the way it is initially specified. Context editing of the source is proposed as the way that the designer will see each node description. Each node will be checked before it is accepted and any error in structure reported. The dialogue will only be checked as a whole when requested by the designer.

In SYNICS2, as currently proposed, GKS output (GKS, 1982) will be available in the display part of the description of a node. Any values that are required are expected to be supplied by the background task or applications program. These values include end-points of lines and cell arrays, which the system will request from a programmer provided routine or through, for example, a common Fortran block. This obviously requires that the program sets up the appropriate data before the dialogue can continue.

There are occasions when this data may be constant, e.g. cell arrays of forms. These will be stored in data files which SYNICS2 will open and access. Thus a standard format for a cell array parameter list, for example, would be a set of three records in a formatted variable length file. Other parameters could also be presented to the interface in this way. The background task then builds these files at run-time as required.

In an intelligent single user workstation a single output device will normally be supported. With the current trend in computer systems this may be able to support multiple windows where each could be a GKS workstation. Care must be taken to ensure that control of these pseudo-devices can at least be monitored by GKS if it cannot be in total control. Note that some systems provide the user with a method of overriding current workstation or window selection.

2.2. GRAPHICAL INPUT IN SYNICS2.

Inputs from GKS can be seen initially as mainly made up of <u>inquires</u> of the system. Most will be used by the SYNICS2 as user input and scanned in the normal way. This process should be capable of being overridden and the GKS values returned via the common block or file. If no other response is expected then the interface will normally look at the keyboard or main input device. The option to look at the background task and use data provided by it to control the dialogue will continue to be supported.

As with SYNICS/DDL, SYNICS2 will have a simple link with the background. The system will treat all data as ASCII strings, even for GKS <u>inquires</u>. Thus if numeric values are to be passed back through the interface after being scanned, then the background will have to convert the value itself, even though SYNICS2 may have validated it in some sense.

The ESCAPE function may be utilized to switch the communication link of workstation and background task from SYNICS2 to a bypass. Future GKS uses of this feature may affect our decision on this aspect of the proposed revised system.

3. THE FIRST STEPS TOWARDS SYNICS2.

The SYNICS/DDL system provides a sound basis for the new facility. Initial development (see fig. 1) will be GKS level Øa based and implemented on a workstation which provides no transformation and has a raster graphics display. Therefore there will be a direct one to one relationship between world co-ordinates and device co-ordinates. Initially cell arrays will be held on disk with the filename specified. Inquires of pixel and pixel array will return data in the same way. Most of the other inquires will result in static responses. All of these can be scanned and returned via the interface software in ASCII format. All references to the GKS Meta-file will be disregarded. Graphical output will be to one master workstation so that workstation definition is avoided. This single workstation driver will not allow for device dependent calls such as the generalized drawing primitives and escape. Normal style interaction will exist initially, but on encountering GKS commands the system will automatically open GKS and the workstation if not already so done. Closing GKS will return to normal text mode.

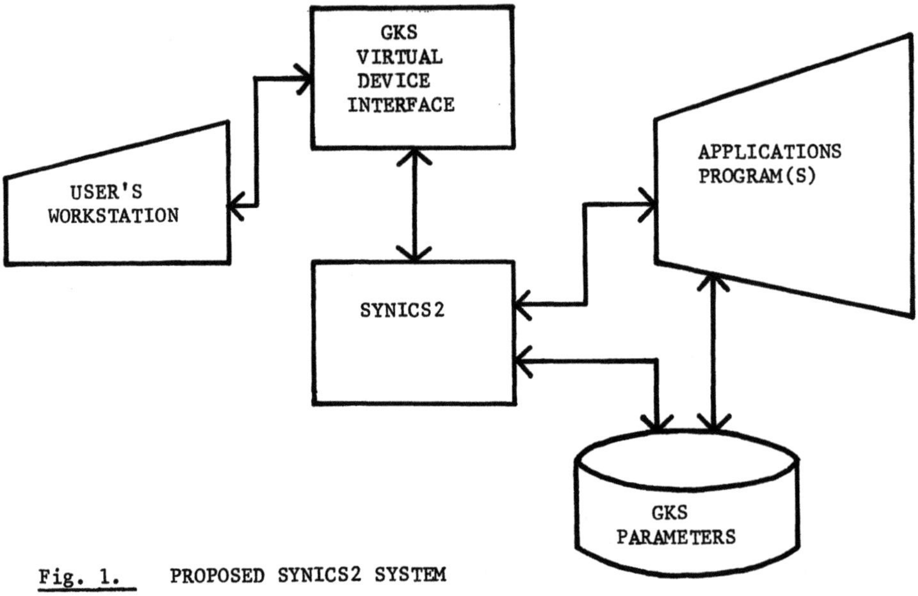

Fig. 1. PROPOSED SYNICS2 SYSTEM

SYNICS/DDL is available on a range of machines including the ICL PERQ under PNX. This implementation will shortly be available, as SYNICS1.5, incorporating certain extra facilities. These will include the editing facilities outlined above and an optional dialogue monitor which keeps a complete, time-stamped, log of user interactions through the interface. The monitor is being implemented in such a way as to provide a play-through facility to enable the user to review their earlier actions and decisions. Other machines on which SYNICS/DDL has been mounted include VAX, B6800, GEC 4090 and Harris. A simplified version, SSYNICS, is being developed for small machines. The initial work on SYNICS2 will concentrate on the ICL PERQ and PNX.

ACKNOWLEDGEMENT.

The work described in this paper has been partly supported by the Science and Engineering Research Council. Thanks are also due to Richard Hammond and Steve Scrivener.

REFERENCES.

EDMONDS, E.A. Adaptive man-computer interfaces in Computing Skills and the User Interface. Coombs and Alty (eds.) AP. 1981.

EDMONDS, E.A. The man-computer interface - a note on concepts and design. IJMMS, 16, 1982.

FELDMAN, J. & GRIES, D. Translator writing systems, CACM, 11, 1968.

GKS. Draft International Standard. ISO TC97/SC5/WG2 N163, 1982.

GUEST, S.P. The use of software tools for dialogue design. IJMMS, 16, 1982.

JACOB, R.J.K. Survey and examples of specification techniques for user-computer interfaces. Naval Research Laboratory Report, Washington, D.C. 1983a.

JACOB, R.J.K. Using formal specifications in the design of a human-computer interface. CACM, 26, 1983b.

HAYES, P.J. & SZEKLEY. Graceful interaction through the COUSIN command interface. IJMMS, Vol. 19, 1983. p.p. 285-306.

HANUSA, H. Tools and techniques for the monitoring of interactive graphics dialogues. IJMMS, Vol. 19, 1983. p.p. 163-180.

KAY, A. & GOLDBERG, A. Personal dynamic media computer, March 1977, p.p. 31-41.

The Flexible Configuration of Interaction Environments using GKS and Workspaces

G. Enderle

SEL AG, Helmuth-Hirth-Strasse 42, 7000 Stuttgart 40, Federal Republic of Germany

INTRODUCTION

The design of a graphically supported dialogue between an operator and an application program can be greatly facilitated by the new standard for Computer Graphics, the Graphical Kernel System GKS (GKS 1983). However, using GKS will not lead automatically to a pleasant user dialogue. The application program must exploit the functions of GKS in a carefully planned way to adapt the communication process both to the actual workstations present in an installation and to the specific needs of the application and of different users.

For creating interaction environments, an interaction processor has been designed that uses GKS functions for addressing the graphical workstations. The interaction environment can be modelled according to workstation capabilities, to application program needs, and to operator requirements. In a configuration process, this modelling of the interaction process is performed. The results of the configuration process are stored in tables on files called "interaction workspaces". When an operator starts a specific interactive application, he selects the interaction workspace he wants to use. A modification of the interaction workspace is also possible during the application session. In this way, any user can have a number of interaction workspaces that are adapted to specific applications and to different workstations he uses.

During an application session, the dialogue is controlled by an interaction monitor. It obtains input data from the operator and passes the relevant information to an application subroutine. All the information on how the input data is obtained from the operator is taken from the interaction workspace, the interaction process is controlled by the interaction monitor without interfering with the application program. Only the actual input data is passed to the application program in a standardized way.

The main module of the interaction monitor is a command processor that reads commands from various sources and analyses them. The command syntax is defined in a command definition table that is part of the interaction workspace. The command syntax and the terminal elements of the syntax definition also define the structure of the data passed to the application subroutines. Every command has an associated application subroutine that receives the data entered by this command. Series of commands can be associated with functions keys, or with menue items, they can be grouped in parametrized macros, or they can be obtained from external files. The definition of macros, function key definitions, and menue definitions are part of the interaction workspace. The operator can define macros, function keys and menues during an application session. Even with the basic part of the interaction monitor being a command processor, it is possible to define dialogues without actual operator commands by using function key and menue definitions.

The definition of a command indicates where in the commands what type of input data has to be supplied by the operator. Together with the type, the name of an interaction variable is given in the command definition. Interaction variables are part of the interaction workspace, they specify how an input value can be specified by the user: By which input devices, with what kind of prompts and echos, or if there are default values.

The interaction monitor has been set up in a first version as part of the presentation graphics editor E82. The monitor handles all the the interactions for a graphical editor with additional presentation graphics capabilities. A raster graphics workstation and a storage tube workstation are used for this application with two different interaction workspaces adapted to these devices. Experience shows that GKS is a very flexible means for configurating interactive environments. The workspace approach allows the management of many different such environments.

OVERVIEW

An interactive application system is built up from an interaction processor and an application program consisting of modules working on an application database. The kernel of the interaction processor is a command processor. The system has an "external control" system structure. A monitor calls an input module for obtaining a command. Then the command is analyzed using a command syntax description. After the command has been successfully parsed, an appropriate application routine is called that is supplied with the relevant information from the commend by the monitor.

The command processor includes facilities for the definition and invocation of parametrized macros, and for the inclusion of batch files. Alphanumeric values in the commands can be specified as constants or variables. Such variables are important in macros and batch files.

If the command syntax description indicates to the parser that required information on the command is missing, it will be obtained from the user by means of input functions.

All input will be handled by using the interactive functionality of the Graphical Kernel System, GKS. The type of the values to be obtained, the physical input device used for getting the logical values, echo and prompt characteristics are described by interaction variables defined in the command definition. Independent from the way how the input is obtained, the application program module will always be supplied with a standardized, consistent, and complete set of input parameters.

A macro can be associated with a choice alternative of a choice input device. In this way function keys and tablet menues can be used to work with the interactive application system. Function keys or menu item selections can be used to drive the system. Although the kernel of the interaction processor is a command processor, the user can operate the system without typing commands.

The command definition, the interaction variable definition, macro-definitions and association of macros to choice alternatives are stored in workspaces. These workspaces are stored on external files and read into internal work areas of the interaction processor at the beginning of the session. They can be changed by used commands and saved on external storage on user request, and retrieved from there. In this way the command environment can be adjusted to device characteristics, application requirements and user needs. Every user can have an arbitrary number of workspaces.

The graphical output from the application program is currently done by the application modules directly by calling GKS output functions. However, for all information on output attributes and the output transformation pipeline will be taken from a GKS output workspace. The output workspace can be considered a generalization of the GKS bundle concept. By using output workspaces, the output environment can also be tailored to different output devices, application requirements and user needs.

More workspaces exist within the application layer of the system. These workspaces contain specific application-related values that can be adjusted by the user, and saved on and retrieved from external files. The interaction processor supplies utility functions for these application workspaces, the values themselves will solely be under the control of the application. E.g., for a module creating piecharts on a graphical workstation, all structure information (how many pies, how many explanatory texts, etc.), geometrical information (center of pies, radius, etc.) and attribute information (text fonts, text sizes, colours, etc.) are contained in an application workspace.

STRUCTURE OF THE INTERACTIVE SYSTEM

Figure 1 shows the system structure. Basically it is an "external control" structure in the terms defined by the Seattle Workshop on Interactive Techniques (Thomas et al. 1982).

The main parts of the system are:

- The monitor calling the interaction processor to obtain command information and then calling an application module. Then the next command is obtained, etc.

- An application program consisting of different modules. Every module is associated with a command. All application modules work on the same application data structure. A module consists of an entry subroutine called from the monitor and a number of other subroutines.

- The interaction processor with a command processor as major part that handles all input from the user.

- The Graphical Kernel System used for graphical output and for user interactions.

- The graphical workstation.

- A set of workspaces: interaction workspaces, GKS output workspaces and application workspaces.

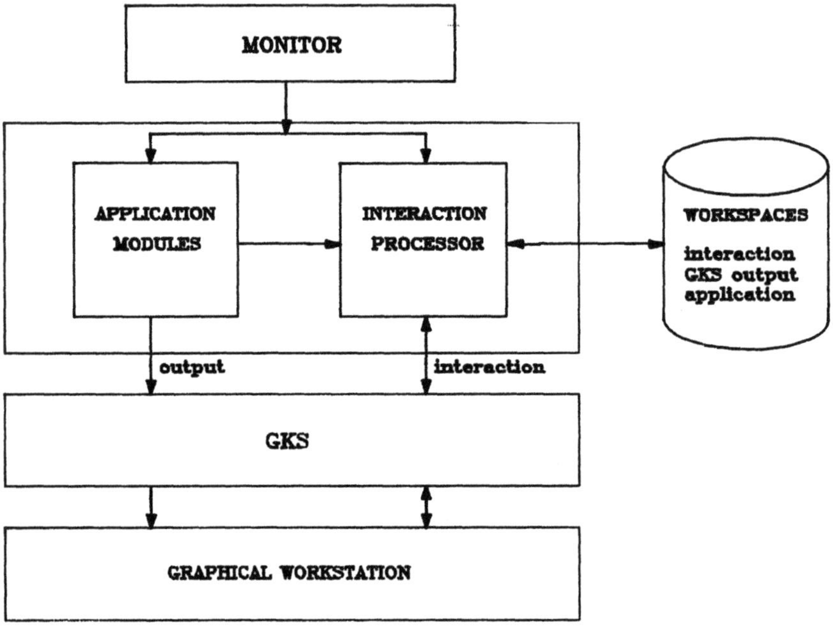

Fig. 1. Structure of the interactive system

The UIMS parts of the system are the monitor and the interaction processor with its workspaces. The application modules are called by the monitor, however, experience has shown that in a number of cases the application modules need services of the interaction processor while processing an application task. This leads to elements of "internal control" present in the system.

Two examples for such services follow: The application module, after semantic checking of the values, can decide that a value is invalid. Then the application program can ask the interaction processor to supply a better value. The interaction processor will obtain the desired value from the operator and pass it to the application. The interaction processor will use device-, prompt- and echo- information defined by an interaction variable whose name is passed to the interaction processor by the application module.

Another reason for an application module to call the interaction processor directly is to dynamically change initial values of interaction variables. E.g., the locator value will be set such that on the next reference of the interaction variable the locator echo (crosshair) will appear at the desired place.

THE COMMAND PROCESSOR

The command processor does not offer new or unusual facilities (except, maybe, that he is completely built on GKS and thus ensures portability and device independence). In order to supply a framework for the following sections, an outline of the functionality of the command processor is given here.

Command syntax definition

The syntax definition of the commands is contained in a command workspace. Commands are defined in the following way:

```
commandname ptr_to_application commandsyntax ;

commandname: name of the command, identifier with up to 32
   characters

ptr_to_application: pointer associating an application module with
   the command

commandsyntax: description of the syntax of the command. It uses
   the following symbols:
   IDENTIFIERS          identifiers have to appear in the command as
                        written in the syntax definition.
   { a1 | a2 | a3 ... } alternatives. One must be present in the
                        command.
   [ ....   ]           optional part of the command.
   [* ....  ]*          this part can appear zero or any number of
                        times.
   !I !R !S !C !L !B    at these positions in the command, an
                        integer-, real-, segment-, character-,
                        locator-value or identifier, respectively,
                        has to appear.
   ( ) = ...            other characters must appear in the command
                        as written in the syntax description.

    end of syntax definition
```

Integer or real values are coded on the commands in the usual way, e.g., "4", "55", or "1.2", "-7.4e-28". Characters are included in apostrophes, e.g., 'ABc' 'don''t feed'. Identifiers obey usual programming language rules, e.g., ABC123 lower_case MY$$$. Lower case identifiers are equivalent to their upper case counterparts. Segments are coded in the commands by S%, followed by a segment number, e.g., "S%5", "S%8". (Normally the operator will identify segments by picking, however). Locators are coded by including a pair of real or integer numbers, separated by commas, in a pair of brackets, e.g., "(1,2)", "(5.7e-2, 3.8e-2)".

Example for a command syntax definition:

```
   ROTATE %333 [* !S ]* !R [ !L ] ;
```

The ROTATE command is associated with application module 333. It will expect a number of segment names and a real number representing the angle. If the locator is present, it will represent the center of rotation, otherwise the segments will be rotated around the origin.

With this definition, the following examples would represent valid commands:

```
ROTATE S%1 S%5 S%7 30.0 ;
ROTATE S%10 15.0 (10,10);
```

Variables

Anywhere in a command where a constant value is expected, a variable may be used instead. Variables are declared and set using special commands.

Example:

```
%DECLARE %L1 LOCATOR INIT(10,10);
%DECLARE %A REAL;
%SET %A = 30;
```

Now following ROTATE-command can be used:

```
ROTATE S%1 S%5 S%7 %A %L1;
```

The segments 1, 5 and 7 will be rotated 30 degrees around point (10,10).

Macros

The command processor contains a macro definition and calling facility. Macros can have parameters. Macro definitions are saved in interaction processor workspaces.

Example:

```
%MACRO MAC1;
%DECLARE %M1 %M2 REAL MPARM;
%DECLARE %I1 %I2 INTEGER MPARM INIT(0);
   command
   command
   command
   ....
%ENDMACRO;
```

Commands within macros can be commands or macro calls. Macro parameters are declared within the macro definition as MPARM. When the macro is called, the values of the macro parameters are substituted in sequential order by the actual parameters given on the macro call. Uninitialized macro parameters have to be supplied with the macro call.

Valid calls in the example:

```
MAC1 0.3 0.5 3 5;
(%M1=0.3, %M2=0.5, %I1=3, %I2=5)
MAC1 10 20;
(%M1=10.0, %M2=20.0, %I1=%I2=0, initial value)
```

Batch files

Batch files containing commands and macro calls can be executed using the %INCLUDE command:

```
%INCLUDE filename;
```

This will read and execute input from the file referred to as "filename" and will then return to primary input.

Choice associations

The command processor allows the association of a macro or command with the choice alternative of a choice input device. This will normally be a function keyboard or a menue on a screen or on a tablet. For the choice devices, either a GKS-supplied choice device or a choice device modelled by the interaction processor can be used. (E.g., choice selection for the tablet can be handled via a GKS locator input from that tablet).

Missing values and parsing

An important feature of the interaction processor is the comparison of command input against the command definition during parsing. If there is a mismatch, it is assumed that the value required by the command definition is missing. It will be obtained from the operator using prescribed prompting and echoing techniques from an appropriate device (see section on interaction variables). In this way, a user needs only to specify the command name, he will be prompted for the required values of the command.

The application module will always be supplied by the interaction processor with a complete set of input values. They are passed in a standard parameter list. The data structure of the values passed from the command input reflects the command syntax definition.

Other interaction processor functions

There are a number of additional support functions that are handled by the interaction processor without bothering the application modules, e.g., allocating, opening, rewinding and closing of files, saving and retrieving workspaces, and help-, inquire-, trace- and dump-functions.

INTERACTION VARIABLES

With every value in the command definition (i.e., !I, !R, etc.), a variable name can be associated that refers to information on characteristics of that value and how the value shall be obtained from the operator if it is not present in alphanumeric form on the command. We call such variables interaction variables. They are associated with the following information:

- input data type (String, Identifier, Segment, Locator, Real, Integer);

- initial value;

- input device (GKS workstation, input device class, device number). If the value is not given directly in the command, the operator will be prompted and the value will be obtained from this input device. An Integer type value can, e.g., be supplied by STRING input (typing a number), by CHOICE input (function keys or menue) or by PICK input (picking a primitive of a menue segment).

- input requirement class. It determines whether the value is required or optional. If it is optional, the initial value is used as the default value. For a required value, the input can be requested as part of the command string or from the specified input device. If the value is not given in the command string, the interaction monitor will get it from the input device.

- echo and prompt type. The possible echo and prompt types depend on the input data type and on the input device. Prompt information is included, e.g., prompt strings or prompt segments for menues. Besides the echo types offered by the GKS implementation, additional echo types are realized by using an interaction loop over the monitor and GKS output functions. E.g., displaying a segment, using pick input, and interpreting the pick identifier as an Integer type value for the application program.

For our previous example with the ROTATE command, we could change the command definition to:

```
ROTATE %333 [* !S/pickrseg/ ]* !R/angle/ !L/rcenter/ ;
with the interaction variables pickrseg, angle and rcenter:
pickrseg: type=SEGMENT,
          prompt='PICK SEGMENTS TO BE ROTATED, QUIT BY BREAK',
          requirement=REQUIRED, deviceclass=PICK, deviceno=1,
          echo=STANDARD.
angle:    type=REAL,
          prompt='ENTER ANGLE',
          requirement=REQUIRED, deviceclass=KEYBOARD, deviceno=1,
          echo=STANDARD.
rcenter:  type=LOCATOR,
          requirement=OPTIONAL,
          default value=(0,0).
```

The command: ROTATE;
will then first prompt for the segments and then for the angle using the prompt strings, the input devices and the echos defined by the interaction variables. Since the locator is optional, it will not be prompted for.

WORKSPACES

Three types of workspaces contain all relevant information that makes up the interaction environment:

- the interaction processor workspaces, containing macro definitions, command syntax definitions, interaction variables, choice associations, and additional information such as external file names and status.

- the GKS output workspace, containing all information related to standard attributes and transformations for graphical output, and

- the application workspace, containing information relevant for the graphical aspects of that application.

All these workspaces can be saved and retrieved under user control. At the beginning of a session, they are read into internal work areas by the interaction processor. By commands, workspace values can be changed. The changed workspaces can be saved on external files. In this way every user can have a number of workspaces that are adapted to specific devices or applications and to his personal taste.

IMPLEMENTATION

The ideas lined out here have been implemented in an application system that allows creating, changing, storing and retrieving pictures and the presentation of data in standard formats (pie charts, histograms, diagrams, reliefs, black-and-white and coloured contour charts, etc.) (Enderle et al. 1983). It could be shown that by interaction variables, macros and choice associations, together with the workspace approach, interaction environments can be created in an easy and flexible way. They can be adapted to various user needs, to different devices and to the application. This all is done while at the same the portability of the whole system and the device independence is maintained. The system is implemented in FORTRAN77 on IBM and VAX computers with Tektronix 401x, AED512 colour raster, and IBM3277-GA workstations (pictures can also be transferred to plotters). The interaction processor is the basis of the interactive application projects we plan in the near future.

PROBLEMS

Even if there is the possibility to create different interaction environments in an easy way, the question remains: Which such environment is optimal (or at least very good) for the user and for the application task he has to achieve using interactive techniques? Both the questions:

- what is a good interaction environment?
- how can it be created?

need to be answered. In the first area, every interactive computer user has made various experiences which not always were positive. But it is difficult to precisely specify what makes a good user interface. In the second area, the outlined approach using GKS and interaction workspaces is a promising attempt that can be expanded and refined. The results of the Seeheim workshop provide important guidelines for the further work.

REFERENCES

Thomas J.J., Hamlin G.H., et al. (1983) Graphical Input Interaction Workshop Summary, Computer Graphics 17(1)

ISO (1983) International Organization for Standardization: Information Processing - Graphical Kernel System (GKS) - Functional Description, ISO DIS 7942

Enderle G., Bechler, K.-H., Fischer, C., Marek, U., Olbrich, W. (1983) Der Graphische Editor E82 - Benutzungsanleitung, KfK 3558

Recent Experiences with Input Handling at PMA

J. Matthys

Philips and MBLE Associated, Tweestationsstraat 80, 1070 Brussel, Belgium

1.0 INTRODUCTION.

1.1 Historical Context.

Since 1979 the software development group at PMA has been involved in a major CAD project for electronics within Philips. This activity aims at unifying the multiplicity of approaches to electronics CAD and integrating the diversity of application programs involved.

From the outset, graphics were recognized as an essential vehicle for the description and handling of electronic networks.

To start with, a hierarchical data structure was defined, covering, to the best of our ability, the requirements for the graphical handling of layered networks. A number of tools were planned around this data structure:

1. an interactive graphical type and menu editor;

2. a digitizing program for manual lay-out and routing;

3. a full interactive network editor, combining the functionality of 1 and 2;

4. algorithmic additions to 3.

Moreover, a number of fundamental decisions were taken, in particular the decision to base the programs on a device independent package. Since this happened in a pre-GKS age, the a CORE-based package was chosen, i.e. DI-3000 (TM) (1). However, to keep all possibilities open, we worked in such a way, that the effort of replacing DI-3000 by a GKS based package would be minimal.

Another decision was to apply Plasmeijer's (1981) Input Tool Model, in order to achieve maximal flexibility with respect to the definition of the user dialog. This attempt was premature and not very successful.

The type editor was submitted to pilot users, and subsequently updated to incorporate a number of improvements they suggested.

---

(1) DI-3000 is a product of Precision Vision Inc., Boulder, Colorado.

The digitizing program has no direct attachments to a graphical package (except for hardcopy generation), but was nevertheless an interesting exercise in input management. The same procedure was followed with respect to pilot users and updates according to their suggestions.

For the other parts it is too early to draw conclusions.

1.2 Aim and Scope of the Programs.

1.2.1 The Interactive Graphical Type Editor.

The primary aim of this editor is the generation of graphical types to be used in logical or electrical schemas, although it is our intention to keep it as universal as possible for two-and-a-half dimensional applications. User interaction amounts essentially to picks for selection of commands and items, locator and string input for the definition of the primitives.

It was written and tested on a configuration consisting of a Megatek 7000 with a secondary alphanumerical terminal, normally a VT100. Transfer to other configurations with comparable characteristics offered no noteworthy problems.

1.2.2 The Schematic Input Program.

The schematic input program uses a large digitizer for the manual placement and routing of networks. User interaction is again reduced to menu picks, locator input for positioning and routing, and an occasional string input.

2.0 INTERFACE MANAGEMENT

2.1 Program Structure.

The general program architecture is, in both cases, a hierarchical tree of states. In a given state a number of interactions are legal. Some of them result in a transition to a lower state, others return to a higher level in the hierarchy (in general, but not always the parent state), still others do not affect the state (e.g. help, default settings, etc.). As a rule only menu picks can affect the state of the program.

The original idea was to use the Input Tool Model (ITM), to uncouple as much as possible the logical structure from the actual coding.

2.2 User Interface Management Using ITM.

2.2.1 Introduction.

Attracted by the simplicity of the Input Tool Model (Plasmeijer 1981), and by the availability of an implementation (in C), we decided to use it for the definition of the user dialog.

To avoid any misunderstanding, it should be clear that the ITM we used was an early version of what was recently published as Input-Output Tools (IOT) (Van den Bos et al. 1983). At least one fundamental error of the original version was corrected, but a number of claims made by the authors should be subjected to careful examination. In the following, only the subset we used is briefly reviewed.

2.2.2 The Model.

The Input Tool Model is based on a hierarchical notion of input tool. Each tool is expressed in terms of lower level tools, using a very simple syntax. At the lowest level we have basic tools, that cannot be decomposed any further; at the highest level we have the application.

Each tool essentially consists of:

- an input rule;
- local declarations, including internal tools;
- an initialization section;
- a tool body.

The latter two parts consist of executable statements, executed respectively on activating the tool and when the tool is completely matched.

A tool can, in principle, have return parameters and instance parameters.

A distinction is made between internal and external tools. Internal tools are defined inside a parent tool and have no impact outside the latter; external tools can be applied everywhere (with the exclusion of recursivity).

Provision was made for a special ESCAPE tool, but this feature was not included in the implementation we used, and we felt we could live (at least temporarily) without such a facility.

The input rule contains tools (A, B in the following rules), tests (T) and the following operators, given in increasing order of priority:

A + B = A or B

A & B = A and B

A ; B	=	A followed by B
|T|:A	=	if T then A else empty
A:|T|	=	A; if T then matched, else failed
A *	=	zero or more A's
A $	=	while A not empty do A

2.2.3 The Architecture.

The ITM set-up is the following.

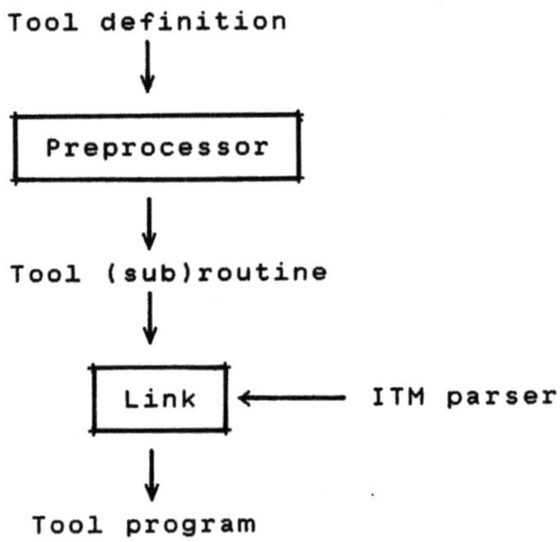

At run time, the parser builds a parse tree according to the input rules. This parse tree looks like a binary tree, but multiple instances of a tool appear as one node.

Once the tree is set up, the actual parsing starts by moving down the tree and activating the necessary tools, according to the operators. This includes the execution of the respective init sections.

Then the user has to make some input, i.e. trigger some basic tool. In general, more than one instance of the triggered tool is active. So the parser now moves upwards, from all active instances of the basic tool, to check the complete or partial match of all the higher active tools. The bodies of all completely matched tools are executed, and failed tools are released.

Then the cycle starts all over again. When the main tool is completely matched, the program exits.

2.2.4 Our Experience.

Our problems were essentially of two kinds, on one hand performance, on the other ease of use.

Performance was the reason why we finally abandoned ITM. The parser as it was conceived, introduced a lot of overhead. Nevertheless it took us some time to realize the extent of the problem, since the response times were, at the beginning, quite satisfactory.

However, it soon appeared that performance degraded dramatically with over-all complexity of the parsing tree. Some local updates in the parser improved the response time with a factor ten. But eventually we had to resign, when an overhead of about one second CPU time per interaction was measured on VAX, for a tree of 250 nodes.

A complete redesign of the parser could probably have brought the response time within acceptable limits. However, planning constraints did not allow for such an additional effort, and on the other hand we became aware of the fact that combining ITM with a request-only package such as DI-3000 does not make much sense. In such circumstances ITM hardly offers any advantage over straightforward structured programming. The preprocessor remains valuable in view of an easier dialog definition, but the parser becomes, in any case, a mere overhead generator.

The second problem, if not directly related, was nevertheless aggravated to a large extent by the poor performance.

In spite of the appearances, the model is not easy to work with. Side effects often occurred when least expected. The fact that it was vital to find the most economical, instead of the most natural expression, did nothing to relieve this situation.

Furthermore, executable statements can only occur in init and body sections, which leads to a disturbing inflation of the number of tools involved. Since the init section is executed whenever a tool is activated, care must be taken that no problems occur, due to a repeated execution if a tool is active more than once at a given moment. Similarly, since the body was only executed for matched tools, there was no way to undo something done in the init section of a failed tool. This problem has meanwhile been solved by the introduction of an additional "clean-up" section (at the price of new overhead of course).

2.2.5 Conclusions.

To conclude, I would say that the Input Tool Model certainly is intellectually appealing as a model. However, at least in the state we used it, at the end of 1982, it still had a long way to go before it could be used in a real application with an acceptable performance.

When the authors of the model recently (Van den Bos et al. 1983) claimed that

> "The model has been used in demonstration-oriented projects with very satisfactory results. Ease of

> programming is accompanied by efficient execution. So far no degradation with respect to traditional interactive programming parameters, such as response time, has been observed."

this should be interpreted very carefully and very literally. I believe the statement is essentially true, as long as the complexity of "demonstration-oriented projects" is not exceeded; at the low end of the complexity spectrum we did not complain on response times either. I am very sceptical as to the general validity of the statement. If the industrial implementation called Ftool, mentioned in the paper, is indeed the version we worked with, it is absolutely wrong to infer that the criteria for efficient execution are satisfied.

2.3 Actual Implementation of the Input Handling.

2.3.1 Physical Device Handling.

Both programs use similar physical input devices, a tablet and a keyboard.

In the type editor the DI-3000 interface is used to access the devices. This means, in particular, REQUEST type input from logical device classes. However the VT100 keyboard remains accessible for normal Fortran READs from the application.

A graphics package is not directly required for the schematic input program (the hardcopies are generated in a detached process). The important feature here is that the digitizer is physically connected on the same line as the VT100; all possible input therefore comes via the same channel which results, in fact, in an event sequence.

2.3.2 The Type Editor: Use Of Logical Input Devices.

The availability of logical input devices is undoubtedly beneficial in developing, maintaining and transporting programs. Nevertheless, they do not solve all input problems, even some fairly common ones.

This is especially true if, as in CORE (and hence in DI-3000), only REQUEST input is provided. The problem with request mode is that it must be known at all moments exactly what input is expected. Obviously this is not always the case; a number of alternatives are, in general, possible.

At our request, PVI implemented a "software pick" function in DI-3000; this function takes virtual device coordinates as input and returns segment number and pick identifier of any primitive at the given position. This way it became possible to build PICK on top of LOCATOR (at the price of performance - when applying software pick, any possibility of fast hardware pick the device may offer is forsaken). So, in practice, only LOCATOR input is used and wherever necessary, software pick is applied to find the selected item. Note that for menu picks the LOCATOR input is used directly to identify the entry (see section 2.4.2).

This "merging" of logical input classes was not possible with STRING or KEYBOARD input, since a different physical input channel is involved. Here we restricted keyboard input to specific points in the dialog. However, as soon as a full GKS implementation can replace DI-3000, EVENT input mode will allow us to get rid of these limitations.

On the other hand, DI-3000 allows the combination of any input class with an additional button selection. On an installation with multi-button devices, the possibility therefore exists to differentiate between otherwise identical inputs on the basis of the trigger button used. Unfortunately, this is only a differentiation within a given input class; since the latter is determined by the subroutine call, it is not possible for the operator to generate an input of a different class simply by using another button.

2.3.3 The Schematic Input Program: Single Channel Input Handling.

The advantage of a single input channel is that it behaves like an event queue. Since the range of possible events in this case is small, a relatively simple input analyzer is sufficient to differentiate between the following alternatives:

- keyboard and digitizer input;
- (in the case of digitizer input) menu picks and points in a data page.

In the case of keyboard input, the input analyzer is also able to recognize textual input of the menu commands.

The first distinction - between keyboard and digitizer - is trivial; the format produced by the digitizer is very characteristic.

In the second place the analyzer knows what is where on the digitizer, menus on one hand, data pages on the other. This way it is able to transform input from a page to the corresponding world coordinates, and input from a menu to whatever command or item selection is required.

Currently the semantic interpretation of the input is left to the calling routine.

2.4 Menu Handling.

2.4.1 Introduction.

Both programs are largely menu driven. However, the exploitation techniques used differ in this fundamental point, that on an input-output device such as the Megatek, menus are generated at run time, whereas on an input-only device, menu output and menu input are uncoupled in time. As a result, in the former case, the input management is mainly done by a dynamical control of the menu entries displayed, so as to guarantee that no irrelevant selections can occur. Since this is impossible on a digitizer, the input handler in this case concentrates on the interpretation of the given commands.

The uncoupling of menu input and output in the case of input-only devices, and, in general, the impossibility to handle menus in a completely device independent way, led us to the definition of a specific data type for menus, called polychoice.

Due to time constraints, this feature was not yet implemented in the graphical editor, where an ad hoc menu generating routine is used. It provides fixed as well as dynamic menus, and the exploitation technique used anticipates on the availability of polychoice primitives. Meanwhile some progress has been made and menu handling using polychoice primitives will be introduced shortly.

2.4.2 The Polychoice Primitive.

A first underlying idea was that menus as a whole, and the individual entries in particular, must be identifiable logically as well as geometrically, i.e. the set up should be such that the selection can be made indifferently using pick or locator input. The first goal is achieved by generating the menus as segments, with the individual entries as distinct pick_ids. The second by having, as first and essential part of each menu and each entry, their geometrical limits; on activating a menu, its limits are determined with respect to the device viewspace, whereas the entry limits are always defined relative to the menu; this allows an efficient two-stage search to identify a selected menu entry.

The next point is, what do we need menus for ? In general they are used to select an item, a command or both. Therefore, the polychoice primitive contains an item identifier, a command identifier or both. Having the multi-button set-up in mind, instead of a single command identifier, the possibilty to define any number of (button number, command) pairs is provided (hence the prefix poly-).

Finally, we need a description of what we want to see in a given menu entry, and how we want to see it. In general this is some representation of the item to be selected, or a text string expressing the action we want to execute. The last element in the polychoice primitive is therefore a pointer to the representation to be used, according to the visualization attribute of the primitive.

Selection and representation data can coincide, e.g. in the case of a type selection menu, where both refer to the same type, which is represented in the menu, depending on the visualization attribute, as a simple text giving the type name, or as a full graphical view. On the other hand, in a colour selection menu, the item to be selected is a colour index, whereas its representation is e.g. a rectangle with the given colour.

Currently a proto-implementation of a menu editor is available. It allows to define a command menu, and also to derive selection menus from a given data structure. Update facilities in this experimental version are very restricted. Hardcopies of the menus can be made for use on the digitizer.

For applications on an input-output device, the visualization of any menu is associated with a given state of the program. Since menus are, in general, generated as a whole, it was often necessary to reduce a menu to a single entry to achieve sufficient flexibility.

3.0 CONCLUDING REMARKS

I would like to emphasize two focal points with respect to user interface management: first, and of prime importance, user feedback, second, the problem of device independence.

3.1 User Feedback.

Notwithstanding the theoretical advances that can and will be made in the field of user interaction, we should remain conscious of the fact that the user is and always will be the ultimate judge; therefore, there is no substitute for de facto user experience. Incidentally, the same applies, mutatis mutandis, to a UIMS, the user here being the dialog designer.

Ideally, the program, and in particular the user interface, should grow in a continuous collaboration between user, designer and implementor. However, for a lot of more or less justified reasons this never quite works out. At best, one or two potential users (or, more often, their boss) are involved in a preliminary requirement analysis and later on in the specification review. Unfortunately, more often than not, the communication breaks down at this stage, and the program is implemented on the basis of the "accepted" specifications. However, since no specification is ever complete, a lot of gaps remain to be filled, especially with respect to such down-to-earth practical aspects as the user interface. The universal law of the least resistance then results in the implementor, left on his own, taking decisions that make life easier for himself, but not for the user.

Swartout and Balzer (1982) already drew the attention to the inherent dangers of such an approach.

It is therefore important to have continuous contact between users, designers and implementors, and to adopt a development strategy based on "fast prototyping". This approach requires an effort of everyone involved, and a willingness to listen to each other. The accent should be on short, frequent contacts, rather than on long, formal meetings. The fast prototyping gives the users something to try their hands on, at a stage that otherwise irreversible design decisions can still be rectified. It certainly must be applied whenever the implementor is in doubt about the correct solution of a practical problem; but even if he is fairly confident that he made the right choice, no harm is done and unpleasant surprises are avoided.

3.2 Device Independence.

Device independence is a worthy goal, but very difficult to achieve. A typical example is the contents and the layout of menus, which depend on the screen dimension and resolution. As long as the only concern is to facilitate the transfer of an existing application to a new hardware, there is hardly a problem. However, if a given application must run simultaneously on installations that are not identical (and often trivial differences are the worst), one is easily tempted to apply some "greatest common denominator" philosophy, which at best maximizes the mediocrity of the result.

Logical input classes are not always adapted to the practical needs, especially not if only request mode is available. A very common example of a problem situation occurs when the input of a single physical device should be interpreted as a different class, depending on the viewport it came from.

Without underestimating the importance of a device independent level of abstraction, a higher, problem oriented level is certainly worthwhile, especially in CAD where the device independent level can be unacceptable for performance reasons.

4.0 POST SCRIPTUM: REACTIONS ON THE WORKSHOP.

Central in the study of User Interface Management Systems, we have the twin relations between interface and application on one hand, between user and interface on the other.

It seems logical that application and interface should be made, as much as possible, independent from each other. However, how often can this really be achieved ? Separating a chess program interface from the actual playing algorithms, so as to be able to use it for a checker program, is one thing, designing a sophisticated CAD interface independently from the application quite another. In general, such a separation involves a more or less important simplification in the designer's model of the application M(d,a), and there is, a priori, no reason why this should coincide with the user's model M(u,a).

As concerns the relation between the user and the interface, we have the problem of the designer's model of the user M(d,u). This subject is studied in a recent paper (Dagwell, Weber 1983), where the complexity of such a model is emphasized, as well as its inherently dynamical nature. The results are qualitative rather than quantitative, but two conclusions stand out.

1. Such a model is not single but multiple valued: it cannot be determined independently of the design context.

2. Moreover it changes in time, due to education and/or experience.

In Mac an Airchinnigh's notation this means that M(d,u) depends on a, and that it has a nonzero time derivative. This seems a very interesting point for further investigation.

There is a striking parallelism between the problems related to the designer's model of the user and those related to the terminology of interaction. Here also there seems to be a context and time dependency, making it very difficult to come to an agreement on the interpretation of even the most common and fundamental terms. Just what is an interaction, a user interface, a user interface management system ? Obviously the answer is not simple, and the opening made in working group omega, to tackle the problem from a conceptual angle, may well be a significant one.

5.0 ACKNOWLEDGEMENT.

The author wishes to thank Guy Marechal for his constant help and encouragement. Many ideas included in this paper are due to him.

6.0 REFERENCES.

Dagwell R, Weber R (1983) System designers' user models: a comparative study and methodological critique. Comm. ACM 26: 987-997.

Plasmeijer MJ (1981) Input tools - a language model for interaction and process communication. PhD thesis, University of Nijmegen.

Swartout W, Balzer R (1982) An inevitable intertwining of specification and implementation. Comm. ACM 25: 438-440

Van den Bos J, Plasmeijer MJ, Hartel PH (1983) Input-output tools: a language facility for interactive and real-time systems. IEEE Trans. on Softw. Eng. SE-9: 247-259

Some Thoughts on the Interface Between User Interface Management Systems and Application Software

J. Sibert, R. Belliardi, and A. Kamran

The George Washington University, Department of Electrical Engineering and Computer Science, Washington, DC, USA

INTRODUCTION

This paper summarizes the keynote presentation in the topical area of the relationship between user interface management systems (UIMS) and application software. We were asked to prepare this presentation because of our implementation experiences in a UIMS environment. Accordingly we will focus on our experiences during our implementation effort. But first, we will begin by establishing a working definition of a user interface management system. We will then discuss some desirable capabilities of UIMSs in general, and, finally, the interface to application software in the context of a sample application.

Working Definition of a User Interface Management System (UIMS)

Before we can discuss our main topic, we must begin by accepting a working definition of a UIMS. We feel that a UIMS represents a higher level of abstraction than, for example, a graphics subroutine package. The end user of an application does not see the UIMS, but only the user interface. The UIMS manages all aspects of this user interface. By this, we mean not only the interactive dialog between the user and the computer, but also all of the output, including application specific output. This last assumption is somewhat radical, but we consider output, including semantic output, to be inseparable, from the user's point of view, from the interface. Therefore, a true user interface management system must manage the output as well as the interactive dialog. Another aspect of a UIMS is that it should be possible to change the user's view of the application without changing any application code. In fact, the user interface should be reconfigurable and variable without resort to coding at all. Finally, we feel that a user interface management system is an integrated software tool. This implies integration between the dialog specification tools and the run time support environment. A library of subroutines cannot be a UIMS.

Some Desirable Characteristics of a UIMS

As a result of our experience with user interface management systems (Kamran and Feldman (82)) and in the design and implementation of user interfaces, (Sibert (83)) as well as the experience of others as reported in the literature, we feel that a good UIMS should exhibit certain characteristics. The characteristics are summarized in Table 1 with special emphasis given to those for which the interface with application software is an important issue.

A UIMS should support a sufficiently robust set of data types to allow the specification of at least the following generic operations: (1) The user should be able to specify a position either absolutely or relatively, and (2) He should be able to specify quantities either as integers or real numbers and be able to specify a character string.

The user interface management system should also support a variety of selection options including objects from a display and selecting items from a menu. These selection types become particularly troublesome in two situations. The first occurs when it is necessary to select multiple items from the same set without knowing in advance how many items must be selected. The second is when the contents and size of the set are not known until run time. We call this run time enumeration. In terms of data types, the only issue which involves application software in a significant way is that of run time ennumeration of selection items.

A UIMS should be capable of providing immediate feedback at all three levels of the dialog: lexical, syntactic, and semantic. Of these, only the semantic level implies a direct connection with the application software. However, it is important to note that under certain circumstances all three levels of feedback can be represented simultaneously. For example, consider disposing of a document in the Apple Lisa user desktop environment. The document is selected and an icon representing the document is dragged to a garbage can. The action of putting the icon in the garbage can represents lexical feedback by constantly showing a cursor location representing mouse movements, syntactic feedback by changing an object's position on the screen, and semantic feedback by inserting the object in the garbage can indicating that the object has been deleted.

A good UIMS should be able to support a wide variety of interaction styles, depending upon physical device availability and characteristics of the user such as relative level of sophistication for the task, left or right handedness, etc. This, of course, is one of the major motivations for developing the UIMS concept in the first place. The UIMS should be able to produce context-sensitive messages. Specific examples of these messages are error or help messages. Good user interface design principles tell us that an error message or a help message that is not context-sensitive will frequently give either too much or too little information to the user, only furthering his confusion. Obviously, for messages to be context-sensitive, the UIMS must communicate in some way with the application software. We also feel that the UIMS should support the simultaneous availability of input devices. This implies that it should be possible to configure a user interface in such a way that the user can at his option use a mouse graphics tablet, keyboard, or programmed function key to generate the same semantically and syntactically correct command.

Our experiences have led us to believe that under certain circumstances, the application should influence the flow of control, although we feel that the main responsibility for flow of control should rest with the interactive dialog. An example of application influence over flow of control is a situation dependent on calculations carried out within the application module. Given the results of these calculations, certain paths in the dialog may cause errors and should therefore be avoided. In this situation, the UIMS should make it impossible for the user to select those paths.

Finally, the UIMS should encourage the design of good user interfaces. For example, it should be possible to change the syntax of a given command from operator-operand to operand-operator and allow that change to apply consistently throughout the dialog without any rewriting. We call this semantic invariance.

The UIMS Environment at The George Washington University

We have developed a partial implementation of a UIMS which we call the Abstraction Interaction Handler (AIH). The AIH is described in detail elsewhere (Kamran and Feldman (82)), so only a brief discussion of it is given here. The AIH is a tool for handling all of the interactions in the dialog. Its name derives from the fact that, from the point of view of the application programmer, the AIH presents an abstraction of interaction--which is similar to logical input-output devices but at a higher level of abstraction. The AIH consists of an interaction language which is represented as an Augmented Transition Network (ATN). The nodes in the ATN are of seven different types as shown in Table 2. The dialog once specified in the interaction language, is interpreted as a finite state machine.

The AIH does not include a tool for interactive dialog specification nor does it manage output for the application software. In fact, a decision was made early in its design that there would be only one way communication between the AIH and the application. Therefore, no mechanism was specified for passing information from the application to the AIH.

In order to test the effectiveness of this concept, we developed a non-trivial application which we will now describe.

The Augmented Transition Network Editor

As part of an ongoing study of the human factors of human-computer interfaces we have been focusing on methodologies for designing human-computer dialogs. One aspect of this focus is the development of software tools for dialog designers. Since we do not wish to restrict the population of dialog designers to include only computer programmers, we searched for a highly interactive, non-linguistic, design methodology. With our background in graphics, the idea of specifying the dialog graphically was especially attractive. Furthermore, in our experience for designing and analyzing user interfaces, we have relied extensively on augmented transition networks (ATNs) as a tool for specifying the syntax of the user interface. Accordingly, we set out to design an interactive graphic ATN editor.

Following our top-down methodology, (Foley and van Dam, (82)) we designed the ATN editor from the user's point of view. The resulting design included standard operations on directed graphics such as adding and deleting nodes, adding and removing arcs, etc. In addition, we included operations to annotate both nodes and arcs, a facility for defining subdialogs, and standard graphics capabilities such as zooming. The interaction style was designed to be highly graphic, using a locator such as a tablet or mouse for both node placement and selection of nodes to be annotated or deleted. For commands, we planned to use primarily a menu and graphics oriented style with text input used only for annotation purposes.

Upon completion of the user level design, we began considering implementation strategies. It was our intention almost from the beginning to use the ATN editor as a tool for generating interaction language (IL) specifications for the abstract interaction handler (AIH). Our original strategy was to implement the ATN editor as a straightforward interactive graphics editor. We would then write a translator to convert the data structure generated by the ATN editor into the IL. However, coincident with the completion of the user level design, the current implementation of the AIH was being finished. A non-trivial application was required to test the AIH, so we decided to implement the ATN editor as an application of the AIH. The decision, of course, was not based merely on temporal coincidence. Since the ATN editor is a graphics application it enabled us to test not only the AIH but also our growing library of interaction techniques. Furthermore, the AIH is itself based on the concept of an ATN, so we felt that by using the AIH data structure directly for the ATN editor, no translator would be necessary. Naturally, reality proved not to be so simple.

Some Problems We Encountered

As we began implementation of our application, it became apparent that the very simplicity and elegance of the AIH design which made it appealing theoretically, produced an array of problems in using it for a real application. Briefly, some of the more important problems areas are:

1. The selection of an arbitrary number of items from a set becomes a problem when, for example, an indeterminant number of operands must be selected. If the interface design provides default values for a set of attributes, the user should have the option of overriding any arbitrary subsets of these defaults without re-specifying the entire set.

2. The selection of items from a set of dynamically changing size is a problem when the number of possible choices is determined by the application semantics at run time.

3. In some cases, a computation carried out within the application software may result in values which will generate a semantic error later in the dialog if certain paths are followed. These paths, therefore, should be

closed to the user. This becomes a problem when the UIMS is unaware of the results of such a computation and is therefore unable to redirect the dialog.

4. The AIH splits the responsibility for semantic error recovery between the user and the application but takes none upon itself, making it impossible to handle semantic errors properly. There are really two different kinds of semantic errors. In the first case, the user specifies a syntactically correct statement, but the statement is semantically meaningless (e.g., the man ate the house). In the second case, the statement is semantically correct but was not, in fact, what the user intended. Obviously, in the latter case the system can do nothing to handle the error since it cannot detect it. In the former case, the application module can frequently recognize the error and issue a message. But, when it becomes necessary to backup or to undo the changes that may have occurred, the application is helpless since dialog control flow rests entirely with the AIH.

5. In general, the process of backing out of a dialog and undoing any changes that have occurred in the application domain is extremely difficult. The basic problem is that the dialog proceeds by state transitions where every state represents an interaction task. It is frequently necessary to pass through an arbitrary number of such states before a complete statement is formed. It is therefore necessary to know how many states to backup in order to undo changes.

The proceeding examples are illustrative of the range of problems associated with our implementation of an ATN editor. Some of them resulted from characteristics of the AIH implementation, while others relate directly to the application software.

The problem of selecting an arbitrary number of items was caused by a simple oversight in the original design and has been corrected by adding a new node type definition to the AIH. Problems 2 and 3 were more difficult to solve since they involved communication with the application program. It became clear to us that some aspects of the original AIH design, primarily the one-way communication with the application and the finite state grammar, would prove too restrictive for this application. In fact, one of our purposes in pursuing this application was to determine just where these restrictions would become critical. In particular, the solution of problem 2, the selection of items from a dynamically changing set, clearly requires two-way communication with the application software. In order to provide this communication, it was necessary not only to define a new interaction node type but also to provide message buffers accessible to both the AIH and the application, along with a protocol for message passing between them. This in turn implied that the interpreter must be more complex in order to handle these messages. Accordingly, we have adopted a more complex grammar based on a push-down automation (PDA) and which we describe more fully elsewhere (Belliardi (84)).

In addition, this more robust model solved the problems of application influenced flow of control and semantic error recovery, leaving only the problems of backing-out and undoing changes. A PDA-based grammar is normally defined to be a recursive transition network with the stack providing the mechanism for recursion. In order to handle the backing-out problem satisfactorily for the user interface, we have adopted a slightly different model. Although it is reasonable for the interpreter to back up one step at a time, it is not always desirable for a user to specify each step. For example, if a user has performed a sequence of interactions which ultimately results in a semantic action at the end of the sequence but then wants to undo the results of that action, he should not be forced to backout of the whole sequence one step at a time. More importantly, from the point of view of implementing the dialog, it is impossible to determine the user's intent at an arbitrary interaction node. The user "chunks" a series of actions together to form a closed semantic action. For example, the command "copy file 1 to file 2" requires three actions on the user's part, but represents one closed semantic action. If this command fails, the user may wish to respecify all or part of it or he may simply wish to forget it. The UIMS can provide this range of capabilities to the user only at certain points in the dialog; the points where the semantic action is closed. Accordingly, we use the concept of a sentence in the dialog as a natural way to represent this semantic closure. Beginnings and endings of such sentences are defined at dialog specification time. The interpreter recognizes the beginning of a sentence and begins stacking transitions. If a backout is requested, it is then possible to specify--once again at dialog definition time--whether to backup one step at a time or one sentence at a time. The decision can also be left to the user at run time.

The only remaining problem is the classic one of undoing the result of semantic actions. There are basically three approaches to this problem. The first is to provide an inverse for each semantic routine. This approach clearly increases the amount of application code and may not be feasible for all applications. A second approach keeps complete state information at appropriate points in the dialog. Undoing is merely a restoration of a former state. This method clearly becomes space inefficient for applications with large data structures, especially when multiple levels of backout with undo are allowed. It does, however, have the advantage of simplicity. The third, and probably most popular method, is to defer application state changes temporarily and only make them permanent after a given number of subsequent changes. This has the advantage of avoiding space inefficiency but is somewhat more complex to implement. We are currently employing the strategy of saving states, primarily because of the difficulty of implementing the deferred change strategy within our current model. Ultimately, we will most likely use some form of deferred change.

Concluding Thoughts

Our experiences building an application on top of the AIH have led us to revise our overall model of a user dialog specification to allow more robust communication with the application domain and to include a more intelligent interpreter. These revisions really represent extensions to the previous model rather than development of an entirely new model. Ultimately, such a new model may well be necessary despite the fact that our revisions are able to handle all of the problems we encountered with our application. We feel this way because dialog management is only part of a UIMS. In addition, the UIMS should be capable of influencing the external representation of all output, including semantic output, if it is to manage the user interface. This implies that some form of representational techniques library, analagous to our interaction techniques library is necessary. These techniques could be developed by experts in graphic design and visual communication and would be available to all applications. Ultimately, this approach could lead to inclusion of a knowledge based subsystem to produce an appropriate graphic (or non-graphic) user representation of information from the application domain. In fact, we find ourselves going even further into the knowledge engineering area in search of more intelligent user interface management.

ACKNOWLEDGEMENTS

The work reported on in this paper was partly supported by the United States National Aeronautics and Space Administration under contract NAS5-27585 and the United States Department of Energy under grant DOE E-A S05-83ER13122.

Table 1.

SOME DESIRABLE CHARACTERISTICS OF A UIMS

- o Robust Set of Input Date Types
  - Selection from a Set (Multiple Selections, run time enumeration*)
  - Position
  - Quantity
  - Character String
- o Immediate Feedback (Dynamic)
  - Lexical
  - Syntactic
  - Semantic*
- o Multiple Interaction Styles
- o Context Sensitive Messages*
  - Error*
  - Help*
- o Simultaneous Availability and Usability of Multiple Input Devices for One or More Tasks
- o Under Certain Circumstances the Application may influence Flow of Control*
- o Encourages Good User Interface Design
  - Syntactic Invariance
  - Semantic Insurance
- o Support Multiple Levels of Backout (undo)
- o Multiple Simultaneous (and visible) Tasks
- o Adaptability (including dynamic, during execution) of User Interface
- o Provide a Complete Ensemble of Interface Design Tools
  - Graphics Editor
  - Menu, Command Specification, Forms Specification
  - Tools for Linking to Syntax (dialog flow) and Semantics (application routines)

Table 2.

NODE TYPES OF THE ABSTRACT INTERACTION HANDLER

Select Category

Select Operation

Select Entity

Position

Quantify Integer

Quantify Real

Text

REFERENCES

Belliardi, Rodolfo and John L. Sibert (1984) A Simple Model for a Comprehensive User Interface Management System. George Washington University, Institute for Information Science and Technology Report Number GWU-IIST-84-25

Bleser, Teresa, and James D. Foley (1982) Towards Specifying and Evaluating the Human Factors of User-Computer Interfaces. Proc. Conf. on Human Factors in Computer Systems, Gaithersburg, MD. p. 309-314

Foley, James D., and Victor L. Wallace (1974) The Art of Natural Graphic Man-Machine Conversation. Proc. of the IEEE, 63, 4. p 462-471

Foley, James D., and A. van Dam (1982) Fundamentals of Interactive Computer Graphics. Addison-Wesley Publishing, Reading.

Graphic Input Interaction Technique Workshop Summary, Computer Graphics. 17, 1 (1983) p 5-30

Green, Mark (1981) A Methodology for the Specification of Graphical User Interfaces. Computer Graphics, 15, 3

Jacob, R.J.K. (1983) Using Formal Specifications in the Design of the Human-Computer Interface. CACM, 26 4

Kamran, Abid, and Michael B. Feldman (1983) Graphics Programming Independent of Interaction Techniques and Styles. Computer Graphics. 17, 1. p 58-66

Kasik, David J. (1982) A User Interface Management System. Computer Graphics, 16, 3

Olsen, D.R., Jr. (1983) Automatic Generation of Interactive Systems. Computer Graphics, 17, 1 p 53-57

Rubel, Andrew (1982) Graphic Based Application-Tools to Fill the Software Gap. Digital Design

Sibert, John L., and James D. Foley (1983) User-Computer Interface Design for a Presentation Graphics System

Wong, Peter C. S., and Eric R. Reid (1982) FLAIR--User Interface Dialog Design Tool. Computer Graphics, 16, 3 p 87-98

Part 5

User's Conceptual Model

The Role of a User's System Model, and its Relevance to User Interface Management

M. Apperley* and R. Spence**

*University of Waikato, New Zealand
**Imperial College, London, United Kingdom

INTRODUCTION

Of the major attributes of an interactive computer system - examples of which range from cash dispensers to engineering design workstations - the command dialogue is recognized as being particularly vital. A good command dialogue is not only easily learned, but is then essentially instinctive to the user, so that conscious thought can be directed instead to the real problem at hand. In contrast, a poor command language is difficult to learn, intrudes - by reason of the need for conscious thought - upon the main task, and may well be unsympathetic in the sense that command errors will often have catastrophic consequences.

USER'S MODEL OF THE SYSTEM

For interaction with a computer system to be fruitful at all, the user must have some conceptual model of the system. Such a model characterizes the system's response to command inputs. Initially, during the learning phase, the user will discover that a particular action leads to a corresponding reaction. However, as "analysis based" learning proceeds via system use, the model will be transformed into a "synthesis-based" one, enabling a needed reaction quickly and instinctively to be mapped into the required command action.[1] The need for such "inverse" relations to be easily discriminable seems clear.

The nature of the user's system model can vary widely, not only from one interactive computer system to another, but during the course of use of a single system by a single user. Models may be visual, aural, tactile or motor, or a combination of these: and any of these aspects of the model may have a static or dynamic[2] dimension. The most appropriate at any one moment in the learning or use period is not easy to establish.

The nature of the dialogue determines the model which the user ultimately acquires. Moreover, the definition/specification of a dialogue by a dialogue designer has a great deal in common with the process used by the user to construct his model of the system.

THE FORM OF THE USER'S MODEL

The concept of system state and its perception by the user is import-

1 A good example is the driving of an automobile: initially one discovers the action of the accelerator and clutch: much later, the need to avoid an obstacle will (instinctively) lead to the necessary action involving accelerator and clutch.

ant to the construction of a user's model. Commands cause an alteration of state. Thus, commands are related to system states in the same way as the navigational actions of a ship are related to the seaways of the world. It is important to realize that two related models may be constructed by the user. One concerns the domain of system states, another the commands which cause movement from one state to another. Just as it is not necessary to have visited all seaways of the world to become a good mariner, but rather the techniques of seamanship, so also is it not necessary to have visited all possible states of a system to become proficient in the command language.

To select an analogy from written dialogue, we should emphasize that what the user is principally seeking and (correctly or incorrectly) forming as he uses the system is a syntactic model of the dialogue: he is not attempting to learn the complete vocabulary. Thus, the learning of the command language should be fast and aim for completeness (Fig. 1). Familiarity with possible states can be acquired much more slowly, and need only be adequate to deal with the problem at hand.

SYNTHESIS OF THE USER'S MODEL

How does a user construct his model of the system? Via the learning process, based on reference to instructions and, importantly, perhaps also through exploration. One can explore via "perturbation", i.e. by changing the system's state, though such exploration is only encouraged or successful if some degree of symmetry is present in the command language, allowing easy return to the original state. Exploration will not be encouraged if the user knows that an incorrect command will be expensive in time, money, or the mental effort involved in recovery. It is for this reason that, in the illustrative example described later, only one action causes an "expensive" computation to be initiated.

ATTRIBUTES OF THE USER

In order to propose, for implementation, a user's system model, certain attributes of the user must be borne in mind as being relevant to effective conceptual model building. On the basis of what is known of the human being's memory, it seems safe to assume, first, that the rules of the command language should be simple and few. Only in this way can learning be quick and easy. If confusion arising from rule exception and doubtful application is to be avoided, the rules should furthermore be applied consistently and crisply[3]. Since learning is a cumulative process, it is probably helpful if the different actions comprising a command dialogue, as well as the different states that may be of interest, can be orthogonal in some sense, and therefore clearly differentiated.

If the object of commands is to establish a particular state, then certain requirements must be met. First, the user should be aware of his current state: it may, for example, be identical to or minimally removed from the desired state, or the commands required will depend upon the current state. It may also help if the transition from the

---

2 For example, a student of dance may easily recall a long and complicated sequence of steps, perhaps because they are associated with a dynamic sequence of body motor actions.

3 Crisp is the opposite of fuzzy. What we're saying is that there should be no cases where a rule is modified by a small degree.

current state to a new state is "continuous" in some sense, since humans are familiar with continuous movement.[4] In particular, continuity would assist the building of the user's model of the vocabulary.

Fig. 1

Learning requirements for command language and possible states

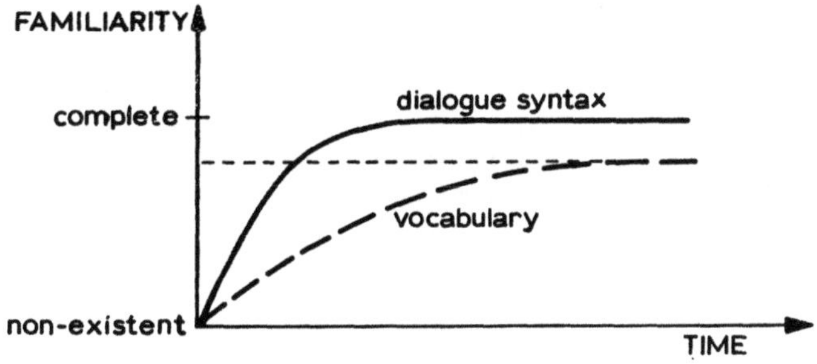

EXAMPLE

An example will serve to illustrate the foregoing discussion. The command language described (Spence and Apperley 1983) refers to an interactive-graphic electronic circuit design system called MINNIE (Spence and Apperley 1977).

A typical system can exist in a multitude of states but, to allow effective human perception and cognition, a basis for representation must be found which is essentially simple. The representation chosen for MINNIE is based on a directed graph, such as that shown in Fig. 2.

Fig. 2

A directed graph representation of a typical hierarchical command structure

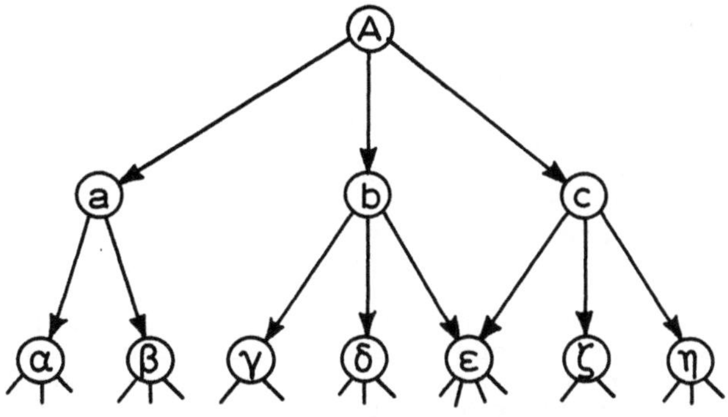

A permissible state of the system can be defined by a set of nodes, including the root node, connected by a set of similarly directed branches. For example, Ab represents a state in which either γ, δ or ε may be chosen from a menu. Although, in some trivial cases, the menu of choices offered at any time may be sufficient to define the current state, in general this implies learning on the part of the user, and as demonstrated by node ε in Fig. 2, ambiguities or uncertainties can arise. The menu presented at ε will be the same regardless of whether ε was chosen from b or c, yet clearly these alternatives represent two different states - Abε and Acε. In other words

---

4 One would learn more about the geography of London by moving from place to place by helicopter than by using the Underground.

the complete specification of the current state requires a knowledge of all choices leading to this state, a corollary of the definition given above.

An historical record of the commands which led to the current state, and thus a complete definition of the current state, can readily be provided by dividing the menu into two areas; one area displaying the choices selected to arrive at the current state, and the other comprising the menu of possible choices from this state. For the command structure represented in Fig. 2, Fig.3(a) shows the menu presented at A; the summary of the current state (A) and, beneath it, the menu of choices possible from this state (a,b,c). If b is selected, then the resulting menu (Fig. 3(b)) shows the current state as Ab and the choices from this state as γ δ and ε.

Fig. 3 Menus presented at states A and Ab respectively in the structure of Fig. 1. ◀ indicates the choice in (a) leading to (b).

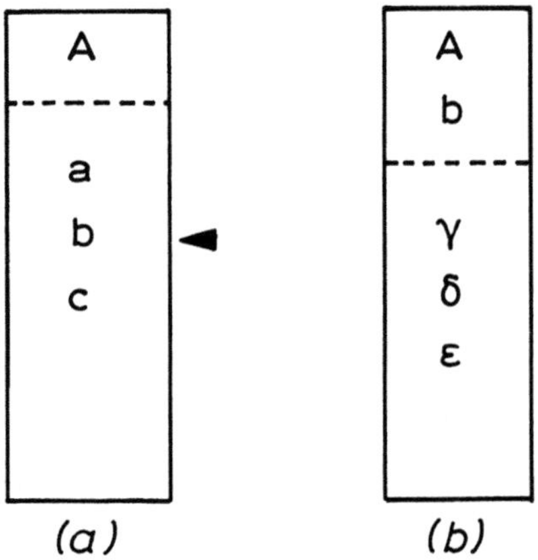

Bistable Menu Items

Menu items have two possible states - active and inactive or, more simply, chosen and not chosen: they can be described as bistable. Under normal circumstances, those items describing the current state (i.e. above the dotted lines in Fig. 3) are active. These two states can be represented on the display screen by differing intensities - bright for active and dim for inactive.

There are two major benefits of this bistable concept. The first, more obvious, benefit is that of feedback or confirmation. If computation or file-access is necessary to satisfy a menu choice, so that the menu representing the new state cannot be presented immediately, it is sufficient to have the chosen item brighten as confirmation of its selection. The second benefit is that as an item has just two possible states, the same action that is used to select an inactive item (to render it active) can also be used to cancel or deselect an active one (to render it inactive). The state of a menu item, and thus the consequence of its selection is obvious from its intensity, and normally also from its position in the menu.

Selective retreat

The ability to both select and cancel menu items, combined with the summary of state display described above, provides a very powerful method for navigation through hierarchical command structures. Suppose the user has arrived at the state Abε in Fig. 2. The displayed menu will appear as in Fig. 4(a). If the user now wishes to move to some other state, say Acη, this can be achieved in a straightforward manner. First it is necessary to cancel b, as c is an alternative to b. This produces the menu shown in Fig. 4(b) corresponding to state A, the one from which b was originally selected. Then the new state is chosen by selecting c, producing the menu shown in Fig. 4(c), followed by η, producing the state Acη shown in Fig. 4(d).

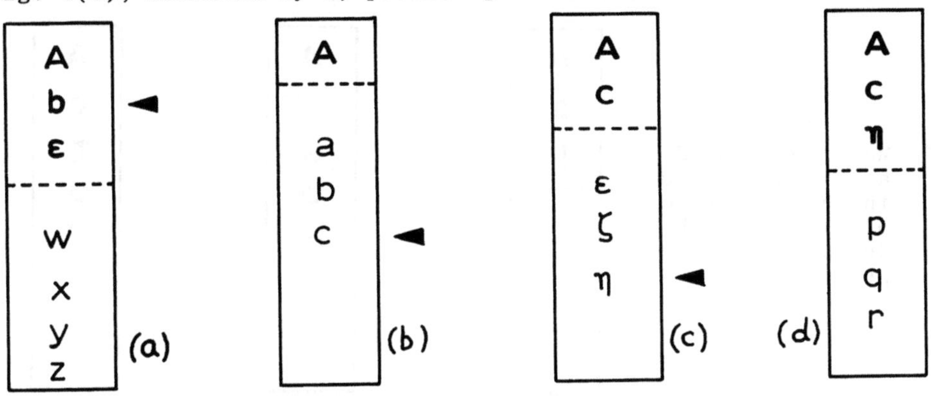

Fig. 4 The use of bistable menu items and the "summary of state" display to provide for selective retreat and navigation through the command structure. ◀ indicates the choice leading to the next menu in sequence.

By this means the dialogue is made stable, in that any command can be simply reversed using the same action by which it was selected (incremental retreat), and at the same time provision is made for selective retreat, in that the user can return immediately to any state along the path leading to the current state.

Default choices

Certain default selections can usually be assumed in an interactive dialogue. Provided that it is relatively easy for the user to alter these choices if necessary, the default selections can save a considerable amount of time and effort. Such a facility can readily be implemented by providing for a single default path from each node in the directed graph representation of the command structure, as shown for example in Fig. 5, where the bold arrows represent default options.

Fig. 5

A directed graph representation of the command structure showing default paths

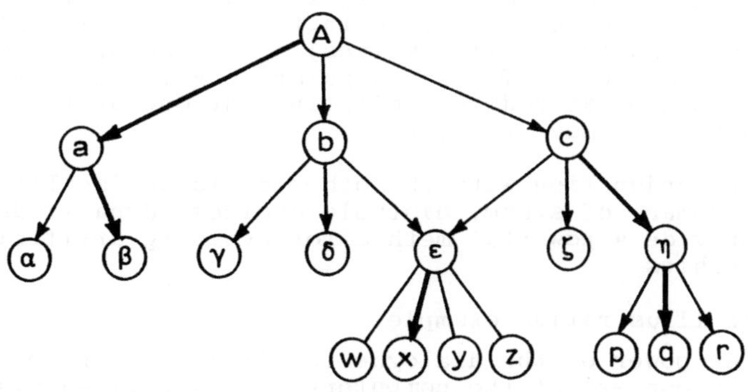

Because of the default path A-a-β, the initial menu displayed for this structure would be that shown in Fig. 6(a), representing the state Aaβ. If some other state is required, for example Ac???, then a can be cancelled leading to the menu of Fig. 6(b). When c is chosen from this menu, the system moves to state Acηq, as shown in Fig. 6(c), because of the default path c-η-q. If this is not the

Fig. 6 Menus presented at various states in the structure of Fig. 4, with default choices present

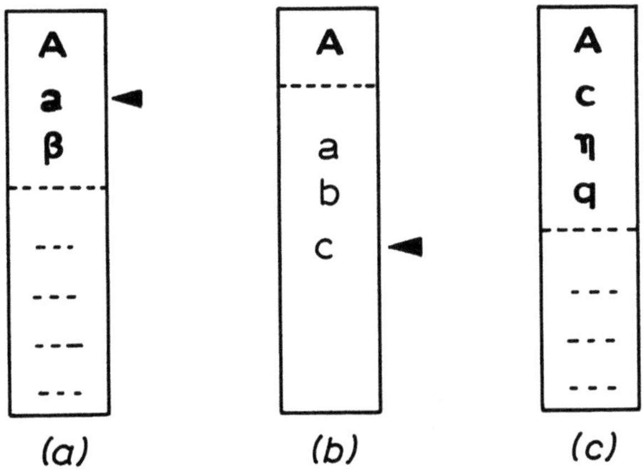

required state then η or q can be cancelled as appropriate, and an alternative selection made.

These default paths need not be fixed; in addition to having pre-defined default paths where appropriate, the system can be made to adapt the default path from any node to be the most recent choice from that node. In practice, this scheme reduces remarkably the number of selections necessary to achieve a desired state.

Parameter nodes

There are many instances in interactive dialogues where the choices offered in a particular state are merely parameter definitions, and all lead to the same subsequent node. Such a choice is illustrated by the command structure of Fig. 7(a). In the initial state A, the user is offered a choice of colour (perhaps for a later graph plot). Whichever one is selected, the resulting state will be A?B, where? represents the chosen colour, and the user will be offered a choice between p, q and r. A more convenient representation of such a parameter choice, particularly in cases where the number of alternatives is large (e.g. in the definition of numeric values where there are an infinity of alternatives) is by use of a parameter node as shown in Fig. 7(b). The rectangular box represents a range of options presented at node A; selecting any one of the options causes the system to move to node B.

In conjunction with the other dialogue facilities so far described (summary of state, bistable choices, dynamic default), parameter nodes provide a powerful method for avoiding artificially imposed hierarchies.

An illustrative example

The power of the dialogue facilities described can be illustrated in the context of the computer-aided circuit-design system previously mentioned. Fig. 8 shows a portion of the dialogue structure of this

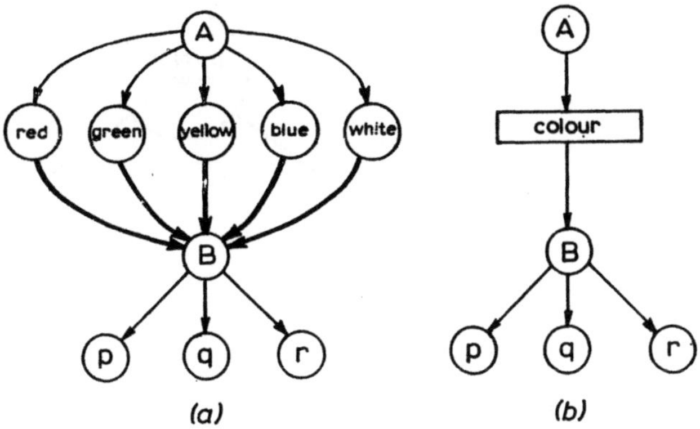

Fig. 7

(a) A structure for the choice of a parameter "colour", and (b) a more convenient representation of such parameter nodes.

system. Suppose that the user has drawn a circuit diagram using the light-pen, in state Aa. By a series of selections the user then signifies an intention to examine circuit properties (B; selected after cancelling A) in the frequency domain between certain frequency limits (default values are provided; other values can be entered using a light-pen) in particular a large-change sensitivity analysis (β; a selection from the menu at f) with a particular component designated as being variable (a single selection from the circuit diagram). If, after observing the results of these actions, the user decides that some detail of the circuit requires alteration, the dynamic default facility ensures that only the selection of A (by cancelling B) is needed to cause transfer to the state Aa wherein the alteration can be effected. Subsequently, reselecting B causes a transfer back to the previous analysis state Befβp when the user wishes to continue with the analysis. Further default paths may be established from nodes c,d,γ,δ etc. during the course of use, providing a means for rapid transfer between commonly used sections of the structure.

COMMENT

The preceding section described a number of techniques to aid in the management of a hierarchical menu dialogue. These techniques enhance the user's ability to navigate through the system state space, and yet the rules associated with the techniques are few, simple, and consistently applied.

A state diagram notation has been used to provide a complete description of the menu dialogue. Such notation could form the basis of both the dialogue designer's original description, and the user's model. Indeed, a pocket guide using the notation would enhance the user's modelling process and, at the same time, provide a useful reference.

REFERENCES

Spence R, Apperley M D (1977) The interactive-graphic man-computer dialogue in computer-aided circuit design. Transactions IEEE on Circuits and Systems CAS-24: 49-61.

Spence R, Apperley M D (1983) Hierarchical Dialogue Structures in Interactive Computer Systems. Software-Practice and Experience 13: 777-790.

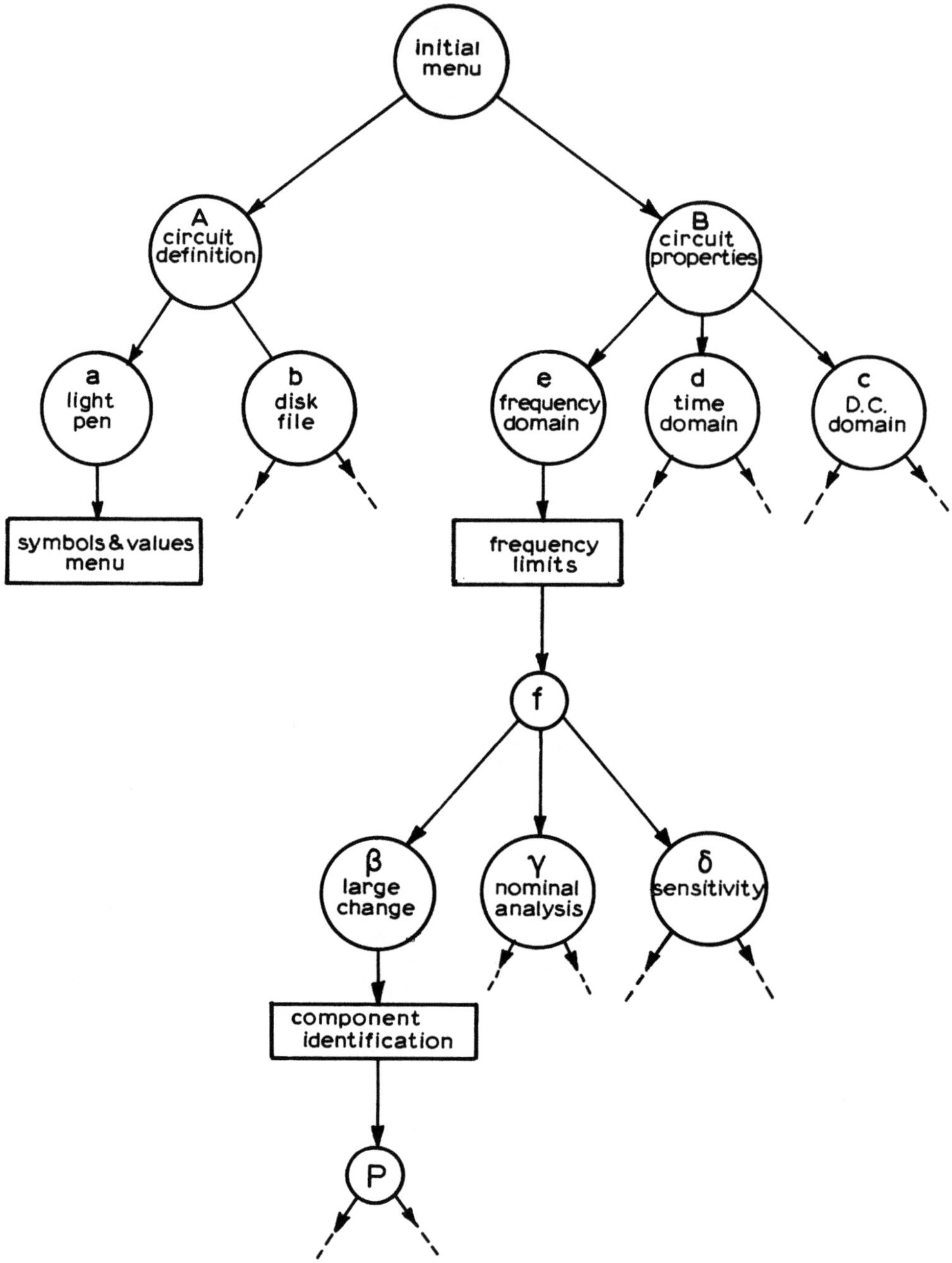

Fig. 8 Dialogue structure of the MINNIE system for electronic circuit design

A Model of a User's Conceptual Model of...

M. Mac an Airchinnigh

Department of Computer Science, University of Dublin, Trinity College, Dublin, Ireland

ABSTRACT

The so-called "User's Conceptual Model" (UCM) now occupies a place of importance in the design of the user interface of interactive (computer graphics) systems. At the computer side of the interface there has been much excellent research done on (graphical) input tools, culminating in the ideas that now form the basis for the Graphical Kernel System (GKS) Version 7.2 input functions. On the user's side of the interface there is still much to be done. It is envisaged that models of UCMs will form the basis of an Information/Knowledge/Data Base that is accessed by a "User Interface Management System" (UIMS), an integrated collection of software tools whose function it is to enable the specification, implementation and maintenance of a user-computer interface that is "user-oriented" and (self-)adaptive. The formal specification of such UCMs is a natural prerequisite for that of the user-computer dialogue. A formalism based on Minsky's frame theory and an extension of the Vienna Development Method (VDM) is outlined in this paper. Taking "user" to mean "application programmer", I present examples taken from a model of a UCM of GKS Version 7.2. Canonical encodings are presented in Ada [1] and canonical semantics in Anna, a language for annotating Ada programs.

KEY WORDS

canonical encoding, canonical semantics, native semantics, universe of discourse, usager, user's conceptual model, user interface management system, utilisateur

INTRODUCTION

> "The first principle is KNOW THE USER" -
> Wilfred J. Hansen (1971) p. 527.

The set of human-computer interfaces is a small but growing fuzzy[2] subset of the set of so-called man-machine interfaces. That the subset is fuzzy may be inferred by considering the man-machine interfaces of, say, an embedded system. For example, the pilot of a modern aircraft with a computer-controlled navigation system is a human being who must interface with a very complex machine, the aircraft. Usually, the interface is considered to be a man-machine interface and not a human-computer interface. However, viewing the pilot's interaction with the

---

1 Ada is a registered trademark of the U.S. Government, ALO

2 A formal definition of fuzzy sets is given in appendix A. Since the class of fuzzy sets properly contains the class of "ordinary" sets, then it is not necessary to use the qualification "fuzzy" unless to describe those sets which are definitely not "ordinary".

navigational system in isolation allows room to consider it as human-computer interface. It is customary to speak about user-computer interfaces (or just user interfaces) rather than human-computer interfaces. Not only is the human seen in the role of operator or manipulator of the computer system and, hence, is a user, but also the meaning of the term user may be widened to include an (intelligent and non-human) agent such as another computer, or a robot, or whatever. Taking user to have this more general meaning, it is possible to develop formal specifications related to the user-computer dialogue and then to tailor these specifications, if necessary, in the particular case where the user is a human being. Such is the approach taken by the IFIP WG 2.7 in its construction of a Reference Model for Command and Response Languages (Beech and Kugler) and is adopted in this paper. This is not as broad a generalization as it might at first appear to be. Since we wish to consider formal methods, then the ultimate objects of interest are mathematical models - a model of the user, a model of the computer system, a model of the application domain, etc. A theory of interaction is then a matter of expressing the relationships that ought to exist between the different models. Such a theory provides the framework for user-computer dialogue specification tools.

Without loss of generality, we will consider the user, whom we wish to model, to be a human being. Naturally, such a model can only be a crude approximation of the reality. There are many different ways in which users may be classified (Schneider et al. 1979; Mac an Airchinnigh 1982). They may be considered to be programmers or non-programmers. They may be naive programmers, expert programmers or master programmers (Schneider 1982). One also has end-users, mid-users and system support-users (Smith 1980). Part of the problem in user classification is due to the fact that one is trying to discretize that which is essentially a continuum. The nomenclature is varied. As a first step in formulating a model of the user, it seems necessary to take a close look at current terminology.

Consider the term user. It is heavily "overloaded". To come to an understanding of what exactly "user" meant I looked to the French language. Instead of "user" I introduced the terms "usager" and "utilisateur". (For French speakers, read user and utilizer, respectively. The degree of confusion over the meaning and use of the term user is highlighted by the fact that the usual translation of user in French is utilisateur!).

- A usager is one who avails of the facility of some service (say, the "canned" package). It corresponds closely to the concept of "end-user".

- A utilisateur is one who is actively engaged in using (utilizing) some tool (say, a general-purpose programming language).

Admittedly, the distinction between usager and utilisateur is subtle (as it is in the French language). Naturally, such a classification is relative and dynamic. The usager of a "canned" package may be the utilisateur of some programming language and vice versa. Where the "canned" package is an Ada package (ALRM 1983), then there are at least three distinct classes of user:

- the package designer who constructs the package

specification for each object abstracted from the application domain and defined in terms of a set of canonical semantics such as Anna (Krieg-Brueckner et al. 1982).

- the package implementor (i.e. utilisateur) who builds the package body and supplies the semantics for the formal verification of the implementation.
- the package user (i.e. usager) who employs the package in his/her own program.

Note that a single Ada programmer may subsume these logically distinct roles. Although this may be the usual situation at present, it is envisaged that there will be an actual separation of roles with the arrival of standard Ada packages and "off-the-shelf" software (Mac an Airchinnigh 1984). The GKS application programmer whom I consider in detail in this paper, is assumed to be "au fait" with Ada. Furthermore, it is envisaged that he/she will have access to an Ada binding of GKS (still in the future!) that is solidly based on the principles of data abstraction (and thus consisting largely of well-defined Ada packages).

FRAMES, VDM, AFFIRM, and FUZZY SET THEORY

> "Notation suited as a tool of thought in any topic should permit easy introduction in the context of that topic" - Kenneth E. Iverson (1980) p. 445.

In 1975, Marvin Minsky (1975) proposed a frame theory for the representation of knowledge. Essentially, a frame was to be thought of as a data structure for representing a stereotyped situation. The actual structure itself was like a network of nodes and relations (as in a semantic net). A frame was supposed to consist of a two level hierarchy of information. At the top level, the knowledge represented was always true (i.e. absolute knowledge). On the other level, the knowledge represented was only relative to a particular situation. Since each frame presented only one viewpoint of a particular thing, then a collection of related frames (a frame-cluster) was required for a complete knowledge representation of the object in question.

Although Minsky did not propose any specific notation for the representation of knowledge via frames, artificial intelligence researchers quickly developed frame-based language systems - FRL-0 at M.I.T. (Goldstein and Roberts 1979) and KRL at Xerox PARC (Bobrow and Winograd 1977), among others - for that purpose. A notation akin to that of FRL-0 was used as a first attempt in specifying a user classification and user's conceptual model in (Mac an Airchinnigh 1982). Thus, a specific user (USER-581) who was considered "expert" in FORTRAN (dialect unspecified) and a "novice" in SPSS, was defined by the (partial) frame:

```
USER-581

A-KIND-OF       $VALUE   FORTRAN-USER
                         SPSS-USER
                $DEFAULT DCL-USER
...
EXPERTISE-LEVEL $VALUE    (FORTRAN (EXPERT 0.9)
                          (SPSS (NOVICE 0.15))
                $DEFAULT  (DCL (EXPERT 0.92))
...
```

DCL denotes Digital Corporation's command and response language for the VAX 11/780 (VAX 1980). The numerical values express the degree of expertise of USER-581 in terms of elementary Fuzzy Set Theory and were arbitrarily chosen for illustrative purposes only! "USER-581" is the name of the frame and "A-KIND-OF", "EXPERTISE-LEVEL", are the names of the slots. The frame is essentially an extended property list (à la Lisp). Each property consists of three parts:

(1) the property name - e.g. A-KIND-OF, EXPERTISE-LEVEL, ...;

(2) the property class - e.g. $VALUE, $DEFAULT, ...;

(3) the property value - e.g. FORTRAN-USER, ...;

It is the property class that tells us how to interpret the property value. Property classes currently in use are:

(a) $VALUE - the value field is the value of the property;

(b) $DEFAULT - the value field is the default value of the property;

(c) $IF-NEEDED - the value field contains a function to compute the required value of the property;

(d) $IF-ADDED - similar to (c);

(e) $IF-DELETED - similar to (c);

Using Lisp, one is able to experiment with the frame approach to knowledge representation. Ultimately, one must ask oneself, what is a frame? In other words, it is of interest to have a formal specification of frames, frame-clusters, etc.

In a recent paper, Reimer and Hahn (1983) outline a formal specification of a frame data model, using the VDM language (Bjoerner and Jones 1978). Their model is similar to the Data Base models proposed by Bjoerner (1980). The adoption of this formalism (or a similar one) implies that:

(1) one is committed to a particular model for the representation of knowledge.

(2) one has the possibility of integrating concepts from different fields, such as Data Bases and Artificial Intelligence.

(3) one can build the knowledge base using Ada as easily as using Lisp.

Rather than spend a large amount of time developing a completely new formal specification language, it seemed reasonable to explore the possibility of extending and adapting existing formalisms. Certainly, as noted in (Mac an Airchinnigh 1984), the above frame notation is neither concise nor precise. It is just Lisp, after all! This paper introduces an extension to an existing formal language used by IFIP WG 2.7 (see appendix B) which is a blend of VDM and the AFFIRM specification language (Thompson and Ericson 1981). Using this notation, it is easy to reformulate the frame model developed in (Reimer and Hahn 1983):

```
OBJECT TYPE Frame = Fname → Slot
NEEDS OBJECT TYPES Fname, Slot, ...
DECLARE f: Frame, fn: Fname, s: Slot, ...
OPERATIONS
    create-frame(): Frame,
    add-Slot(f,s): Frame,
    delete-Slot(f,x): Frame,
    ...
...
END Frame;
```

The use of ellipsis in the notation serves several purposes:

(1) The omitted material should be clear from the context - i.e. the reader can supply the missing details.

(2) The example is already too big and the rest is omitted.

(3) The omitted material is of no concern at this point.

(4) The omitted material has already appeared before this - i.e., I want to avoid unnecessary repetition.

(5) Frankly, I don't know what should go here - the usual case when developing a new object type.

(6) ...

It is left to the reader, as a challenge, to discover which meaning is implied by the ellipsis hereafter!

USER INTERFACE MANAGEMENT SYSTEM (UIMS)

> "The UIMS approach is not new; many instances of similar systems were described at Seillac II. However, much more experience is now available, both about the details of working with a UIMS, and about the problems encountered when working without one." (GITT 1983) p. 16.

What is a User Interface Management System? It has been likened to a Data Base Management System (DBMS) (GITT 1983; Buxton et al. 1983).

Such an analogy is helpful if one already has a good conceptual model of what a DBMS is (Fry and Sibley 1976; Jardine 1977). Assuming that such a comparison is valid, then research and development in this area ought to be of considerable benefit towards the specification and implementation of a UIMS (i.e. transfer of knowledge by analogy). Such has apparently been the case with the TIGER UIMS. Its Interactive Command and Control Language (TICCL) is processed similarly to a schema definition language in a DBMS (Kasik 1982).

The field of Data Base research is not the only domain towards which one ought to look for guidance in developing a good conceptual model of what a typical UIMS ought to be. Springing from an interactive computer graphics background, the future UIMS will provide a vast variety of interactive techniques and (physical) devices. The obvious starting point here is the Draft ISO Graphical Kernel System (GKS) for 2-D graphics (GKS 1982) with particular emphasis on its presentation of input functions (Rosenthal et al. 1982) which form the basis for the implementation of the user's side of the dialogue. Accepting this as the foundation on which to build, the UIMS researcher is free to concentrate on other aspects of user-computer interaction, in particular those related to modelling and formal specification.

The Workshop on Data Abstraction, Data Bases and Conceptual Modelling, held in Pingree Park, Colorado, June 1980, has resulted in a cross-fertilisation of ideas from researchers in the fields of Data Bases, Artificial Intelligence and Programming Languages (WDDC 1981). There are many respects in which their deliberations and findings are relevant for the theoretical development of the UIMS (since the user pops up everywhere!). Perhaps, E.F. Codd's remark about casual users is indicative of this significance:

> "Both in the DB and AI worlds there are subcultures concerned with intelligent interfaces for use by the casual user. I feel there should be more support not only for translation of natural language, but more generally interactive communication ..." (ibid.) p. 89.

On notations and formalisms, Sowa (1981) asserts that no matter which one is used, it must represent aspects of seven basic kinds of knowledge: Generalization hierarchy, functional dependencies, domain roles, definitional mechanisms, conventional schemata, procedural attachment, and inference mechanisms.

> "Enter the cognitive psychologist, the software psychologist, and the cognitive modeller from Artificial Intelligence (AI), all breathing heavily!"

Specification of, and experimentation with, models of the human mind has involved the energies of (cognitive) psychologists and AI researchers alike (Schank and Abelson 1977). The exchange of ideas has been an enriching experience for all concerned. However, it must not be thought that harmony and agreement prevail (Dreyfus 1979). The issue of the representation of Knowledge has been mentioned above. But the significance of AI work for the development of a UIMS does not rest there. The whole experimental programming philosophy which underpins AI (Sandewall 1978) has carried over into the realm of rapid prototyping. Such is the complexity of dialogue design that experimentation and prototyping are absolutely essential! The "feel" of a good interactive system has been likened to the impressions generated by a piece of music. Both can only be experienced over a period of time (Hansen 1971)!

At Seillac II (Guedj et al. 1980), the importance of an integrated programming support environment (PSE) for the programmers of user-interfaces was recognised. The classical instance of a PSE is, of course, INTERLISP (Teitelman and Masinter 1981). Although not widely used (relative to the "usual" sort of programming languages), its influence on the programming community has been profound and immense. It comes in for special mention, for instance, in the "Stoneman" document where it is to be regarded as a model for what an Ada Programming Support Environment (APSE) should look (feel?) like (STONEMAN 1980). The central feature of the APSE is the data base which is the repository for all information associated with each software project for the entire life cycle of same (ibid.). I argue that one of the key software tools of an APSE will be a UIMS (Mac an Airchinnigh 1984) to manage the different kinds of Ada programmers. Conversely, work done in this area will impinge directly on the research into UIMS, in general. The APSE has become a focal point of computer science research in the United States and Europe. However, there are at least two other major research thrusts that are of key concern - the so-called Fifth Generation Project of Japan (Shapiro 1983) and the ESPRIT project of the European Community (ESPRIT 1983). Both of these envisage user-interfaces of marvellous richness. Thus the UIMS must be considered in the context of all three massive undertakings.

So, what is a UIMS? Literally, a UIMS is a system for the management of user-interfaces. That a system is necessary, is due to the innate complexity of user-computer interactions. There are three parts to such interfaces:

(1) The user

(2) The computer

(3) The application domain

It is convenient to let u denote a user, c a computer and a an application domain. Let $M[u,a]$ denote the conceptual model that user u has of application domain a. To be useful for the purpose of building a UIMS one must be able to encode this conceptual model on some computer c. Such an encoding is represented by $M[c,M[u,a]]$. In general, $M[x,y]$ denotes a model M of an object y possessed by an object x. Of course, users have other conceptual models such as $M[u,u]$ and $M[u,c]$. Although this is a very elementary (and almost trivial) notation, it does have its uses (Mac an Airchinnigh 1983). A formal specification of the user-computer dialogue is then a matter of formally specifying the relationship between the models $M[c,M[u,u]]$, $M[c,M[u,c]]$, and $M[c,M[u,a]]$.

The model of the user which will be available to the UIMS, will cover three principal aspects:

(1) physical;

(2) cultural;
(3) cognitive.

That part of the model which deals with the physical properties of a user has been the subject of "classical" ergonomics. For truly (self-) adaptive interfaces, it is trivial to take into account items such as:

- user is human?
- user is blind?, colour-blind?
- user is ambidextrous?, left-handed?, right-handed?, ...
- ...

Cultural properties are rarely considered in human-computer dialogue specification. But they are very important. What is the user's preferred (natural) language? That the user knows English may not be enough! Are there icons which may be offensive (appealing)? For example, what would a Buddhist programmer think of a certain well-known smiling Buddha icon (Singh et al. 1983)? A gentle introduction to the use of iconic representation may be found in (Lodding 1983).

Finally, the user has a cognitive side. I do not want to propose new theories of human cognition. Rather, I want to identify and represent significant concepts pertinent to a specific application domain. It is this which is the subject of this paper.

USER'S CONCEPTUAL MODEL (UCM)

> "These utterances are to be interpreted (recursively) as international English utterances: Any meaningful exchange of utterances depends on the prior existence of an agreed set of semantic and syntactic rules. The recipients of the utterances must use only these rules to interpret the received utterances, if it is to mean the same as that which was meant by the utterer" - the Helsinki Principle (van Griethuysen 1982).

The user's (conceptual) model plays a central role in the design of interactive (computer graphics) command and response languages (Newman and Sproull 1979; Guedj et al. 1980; Green 1981; Moran 1981; Foley and van Dam 1982; GITT 1983). There are many facets to such UCMs. To each UCM there corresponds a universe of discourse (Mac an Airchinnigh 1983) which is essentially the set of all concept bindings (representations) relevant to a specific application domain (the so-called task domain). All concepts must be made manifest to the external world in some form. To indicate the fact that I wish to discuss a concept as distinct from its binding I use a tagged woolly diagram. A discussion of such diagrams and inherent problems associated with them may be found in (Mac an Airchinnigh 1983). Although the diagrams have been used solely for illustrative purposes so far (and have had many related precursors - and contemporaries-- in the literature), they will be brought into the UIMS knowledge base as iconic representations of concept bindings (for display on a graphics workstation, for example). Consider the GKS application programmer who has the concept of colour. What does this mean? Colour (and colour naming) is a very complex subject (Foley and van Dam 1982). There is the physical aspect, the physiognomic aspect, the perceptual aspect and the theoretical aspect. As reasoning human beings, we work with colour models and these are manifold. Different groups of people have their own conceptual models of colour - the artist, the physicist, the psychologist, the computer graphics application programmer, etc. Even within a group, there may be many different colour models. For example, in the Graphical Kernel System (GKS), the colour model is the so-called RGB colour model (GKS 1982) - a "hardware-oriented" model that is used in colour monitors. Therefore, the GKS application programmer would be expected to know this model and to provide the "end user" with a suitable "person-oriented" colour model such as, say, the HSV colour model (Foley and van Dam 1982).

A woolly diagram to represent the concept of RGB colour might look like:

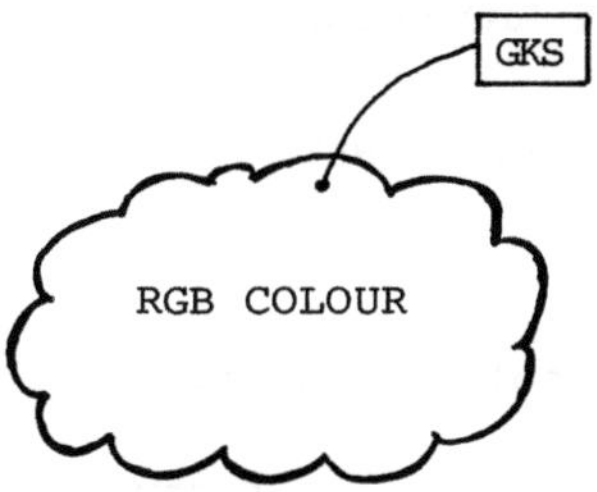

Fig. 1

Here the tag is "GKS". By convention, tagging is done using an appropriate English word, phrase, acronym, abbreviation, etc. (To get into really deep water, one may consider the tag itself to be a woolly diagram and follow through with the consequences). A related woolly diagram which "refines" the previous concept is

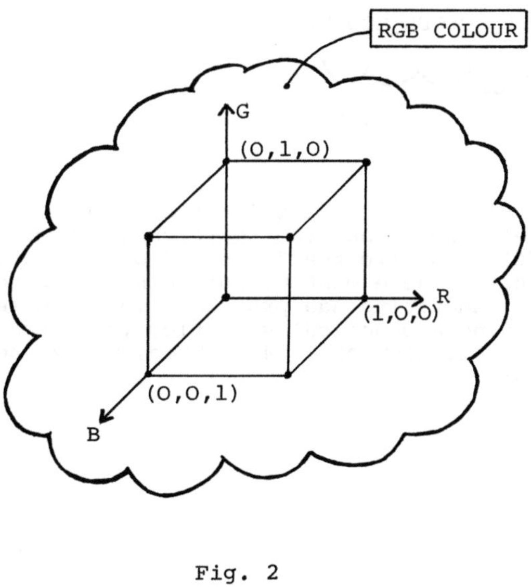

Fig. 2

Suppose now that the same programmer also possessed a canonical encoding (in Ada) of an implementation of the RGB colour model, such as the following:

```
package RGB_COLOUR_MODEL is
     type RGB_COLOUR is private;
     BLACK: constant RGB_COLOUR;
     ...
     YELLOW: constant RGB_COLOUR;
     WHITE: constant RGB_COLOUR;
     function MAKE(R,G,B: FLOAT) return RGB_COLOUR;
     function SELECT_R(C: RGB_COLOUR) return FLOAT;
     function SELECT_G(C: RGB_COLOUR) return FLOAT;
     function SELECT_B(C: RGB_COLOUR) return FLOAT;
     -- ...
private
     -- FOR IMPLEMENTOR'S EYES ONLY!
     -- ...
end RGB_COLOUR_MODEL;
```

We may represent this by the woolly diagram:

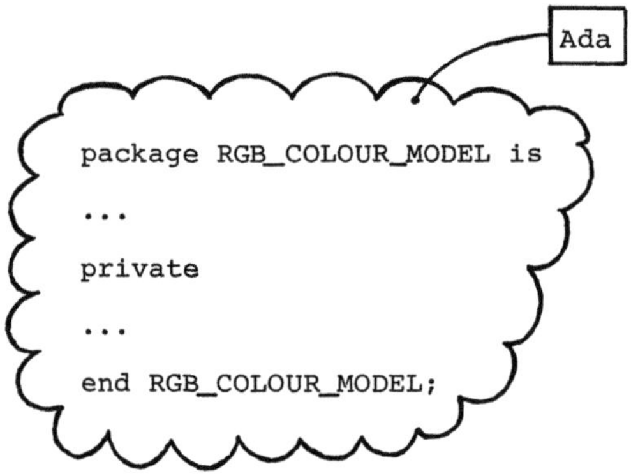

Fig. 3

However, this particular Ada encoding for the RGB_COLOUR_MODEL is deficient! It is well known that the Ada package specification does not, of itself, suffice to give the "meaning" of the package (Krieg-Brueckner et al. 1982). There must be something extra to augment it. Anna, a language for annotating Ada programs (ibid.) offers the possibility of providing a canonical semantics for the Ada package specification (Mac an Airchinnigh 1984). Thus, we extend the RGB_COLOUR_MODEL to read:

```
package RGB_COLOUR_MODEL is
     type RGB_COLOUR is private;
     BLACK: constant RGB_COLOUR;
     ...
     YELLOW: constant RGB_COLOUR;
     WHITE: constant RGB_COLOUR;
     function MAKE(R,G,B: FLOAT) return RGB_COLOUR;
     function SELECT_R(C: RGB_COLOUR) return FLOAT;
     -- ...
     --| axiom
     --|      for all R,G,B: FLOAT, C: RGB_COLOUR =>
     --|           C = MAKE(SELECT_R(C) SELECT_G(C),SELECT_B(C)),
     --|           R = SELECT_R(MAKE(R,G,B)),
     --|           G = SELECT_G(MAKE(R,G,B)),
     --|           B = SELECT_B(MAKE(R,G,B)),
     --|           ...
     --|           BLACK = MAKE(0.0,0.0,0.0),
     --|           BLUE = MAKE(0.0,0.0,1.0),
     --|           ...,
     --|           BLACK /= BLUE,
     --| ...
     private
     -- FOR IMPLEMENTOR'S EYES ONLY!
        -- ...
     end RGB_COLOUR_MODEL;
```

where the vertical bar introduces the Anna annotation. Now, writing the tag as "Ada with Anna" renders the woolly diagram to be a "self-sufficient" concept binding!

Apart from this canonical semantics, it is expected that the "average" GKS application programmer will have his/her own native semantics that may be different from Anna. For instance, the particular extended object-oriented VDM of this paper is one such possible native semantics. Using this notation, the RGB_COLOUR_MODEL may be formally specified by

```
OBJECT TYPE
     RGB_colour :: s-R : Rvalue s-G : Gvalue s-B : Bvalue
...

OPERATIONS
     make_colour(r,g,b) : RGB colour,
     select_R(c) : Rvalue,
     select_G(c) : Gvalue,
     select_B(c) : Bvalue,
     ...
END RGB_colour
```

(Full details are provided in appendix B).

There are, of course, other possible candidates for the role of native (and, indeed, canonical) semantics. Consider, for example, the specification techniques presented in (Carson 1983).

To each concept we expect a collection of bindings (much like the frame-cluster idea). Among these bindings, I have identified as significant, the iconic representation set, the canonical language encoding set, the canonical semantics, and the native semantics. Let us now look at the kinds of concepts that our "typical" GKS application programmer ought to have.

THE GKS APPLICATION PROGRAMMER (GKSAP)

> "Kann man sich nicht denken, dass Menschen eine andere Farbengeometrie haetten als wir? - D.h. doch: Kann man sich nicht Menschen mit andern Farbbegriffen denken als den unsern; und das heisst wieder: Kann man sich nicht vorstellen, dass Menschen unsre Farbbegriffe nicht haben, und dass sie Begriffe haben, die mit unsern Farbbegriffen in solcher Weise verwandt sind, dass wir sie auch 'Farbbegriffe' nennen moechten?" - Ludwig Wittgenstein[3] (1977).

The GKSAP is the mediator between the "end-user" of an application program (AP-USAGER) and the GKS system. Currently, the GKSAP also fills the role of dialogue designer and to the extent that he/she is working with an Ada binding of GKS, then one can expect the GKSAP to be a package designer, probably knowledgeable in Anna.

As the subject area matures, we will see the function of dialogue designer becoming the principal role with that of GKSAP becoming subservient. This service of interactive computer graphics to the needs of the computing community is akin to that of mathematics in relation to the Sciences. Presently, the GKSAP must master two (non-disjoint) universes of discourse for application programming:

- domain of 2-D graphics à la GKS;
- domain of dialogue specification.

What are the big concepts of GKS? The concept of RGB colour has already been discussed in detail above. That of HSV colour merely mentioned. Certainly, at the very least, a GKSAP will be familiar with a canonical Ada encoding such as

```
package RGB_COLOUR_MODEL is
...
end RGB_COLOUR_MODEL;

package HSV_COLOUR_MODEL is
...
end HSV_COLOUR_MODEL;

with RGB_COLOUR_MODEL; use RGB_COLOUR_MODEL;
with HSV_COLOUR_MODEL; use HSV_COLOUR_MODEL;
package ON_COLOUR_MODELS is
    ...
```

3 "Can't we imagine people having a different geometry of colour than we do? That, of course, means: Can't we imagine people who have colour concepts which are other than ours; and that in turn means: Can't we imagine that people do not have our colour concepts and that they have concepts which are related to ours in such a way that we would also want to call them 'colour concepts'?"

```
        function RGB_TO_HSV(C: RGB_COLOUR) return HSV_COLOUR;
        function HSV_TO_RGB(C: HSV_COLOUR) return RGB_COLOUR;
        ...
    end ON_COLOUR_MODELS;
```

Browsing through the GKS functional specification document (GKS 1982), one can easily identify other concepts such as "workstation", "transformation", "coordinate system", "abstract input", "abstract output", ... In a GKSAP's UCM of GKS, all of these concepts must have their iconic representations, canonical Ada encodings, canonical and native semantics, etc. This work is currently being undertaken at the Department of Computer Science, Trinity College, Dublin.

What about the dialogue specification? What tools are available? This is the subject matter of this workshop. At least one can point to the concept of dialogue cells (Borufka et al. 1982) as one possible approach. I have already argued for the formalisation of the task domain, about which one can conduct a dialogue. The conceptual model approach can also be addressed to the domain of the dialogue itself. What are the significant concepts in dialogue? I would like to present just one concept which I believe is fundamental to any user-interface that aspires to be called "friendly" - the history concept, inspired by the history list mechanism of Interlisp. (For example, the concept of "trails" in (Nievergelt and Weydert 1980) is essentially a history concept à l'Interlisp!). The basic philosophy behind the user interface of the Interlisp programming environment is that the user addresses the system through an active intermediary agent known (affectionately) as the programmer's assistant (Teitelman 1972). This programmer's assistant has the job of collecting and saving information about the activities of the user and his/her programs and to utilize this information to assist the user and his/her programs in those activities. In order to carry out its job, the programmer's assistant records in a history list, the user's input, a description of the side effects of the operation and the result of that operation. In other words, a history of the user's interaction with the system is kept. Such a history list is, in a sense, the memory of the programmer's assistant that records the information associated with the individual events that have occurred in the system, each event corresponding to one user input (Teitelman 1978).

Associated with each event is an event number which may be utilized by the user in later interactions. Although not the only means by which events may be referenced, it is the most convenient for illustration of the Interlisp History commands. A user may manipulate (past) events in many different ways and for different reasons. Events may be undone, redone or fixed; events may be saved and retrieved. Such is the importance of the history concept in interactive computing that it has been incorporated into the IFIP WG 2.7 Reference Model for Command and Response Languages (Beech and Kugler).

Essentially, a History is just a sequence of events:

```
OBJECT TYPE
    History = Event*

NEEDS OBJECT TYPES
    Event, N1;

A-KIND-OF OBJECT TYPE
    Sequence

HAS-INSTANCES
    User_History, Session_History, Context_History,
    Activity_History

DECLARE
    h: History;
    e: Event;
    i: N1;

OPERATIONS
    Create_History(): History;
    Append_Event(h,e) : History;
    Fetch_Event(h,i): Event;
    Delete_Event(h,e): History;

ERROR OPERATIONS
    History_Error(h): History;
    History_Error_Event(h,e): History;
    History_Error_Index(h,i): History;
END History
```

The A-KIND-OF field indicates that the History object is really "a kind of" Sequence object. In other words, the semantics pertaining to sequences carries over to histories. (Note that the sequence in VDM has the attributes of both sequential and random access!). The HAS-INSTANCES field indicates the instantiations that might be expected in a given implementation. Although it is not stated in the above small example, there are relationships between the different kinds of histories. For example, a typical event in a context_history would be an activity_history.

EXPERTISE

> "Simple, user-friendly, adaptive command languages will be developed. They will make it possible to adapt the guidance, the commands and the error handling to the individual user's experience, skill and habits." (Warman et al. 1979).

Human beings are fallible. They learn, they regress, they remember, they recall, they forget, and they make mistakes. Their knowledge of themselves and the world about them is often incomplete, inexact, approximate, or even erroneous. In modelling (human) users and their conceptual models one must try to capture these attributes. Expertise level (degree of skill) is one aspect of the user that I have considered (Mac an Airchinnigh 1982).

Using only the primitive notions of Fuzzy Set Theory (see appendix A), one defines U to be the set of all "users". Then, let E by a fuzzy subset of U which denotes "experienced" users. We have immediately

$$E \triangleq \{\mu_E(x)/x \mid x \varepsilon \text{support}(E)\} \qquad [1]$$

Clearly, this piece of mathematics is not very illuminating by itself. It simply states that expertise-level is a real number in the closed interval [0,1]. To map this into some sort of expertise category, I used a value mapping of the form

$$V : [0,1] \rightarrow \{\text{NOVICE}, \text{INTERMEDIATE}, \text{ADVANCED}, \text{EXPERT}\} \qquad [2]$$

where

$$V(y) \hat{=} \begin{cases} \text{NOVICE} & , \text{ if } y \varepsilon [0.0, 0.3) \\ \text{INTERMEDIATE}, & \text{ if } y \varepsilon [0.3, 0.5) \\ \text{ADVANCED} & , \text{ if } y \varepsilon [0.5, 0.8) \\ \text{EXPERT} & , \text{ if } y \varepsilon [0.8, 1.0] \end{cases} \qquad [3]$$

A full discussion of this approach to expertise level may be found in (ibid.). An alternative approach is to consider the expertise-level as a (partial) function E from the cartesian product of the set of users X and the set of objects Y onto the closed interval [0,1] of the real number line.

$$E : X \times Y \rightarrow [0,1] \qquad [4]$$

Let u_i be a user of the FORTRAN-66 programming language (denoted by o_j, say) and who has an expertise value of 0.3. Then, one might write

$$E(u_i, o_j) = 0.3 \qquad [5]$$

From this starting point one can construct the fuzzy subset

$$\{\ldots, 0.3/(u_i, o_j), \ldots\} \qquad [6]$$

where the ordered pair (u_i, o_j) has the grade of membership value 0.3. (For further details on the (elementary) theory of Fuzzy Sets, the reader is referred to (Kaufmann 1975).

My use of expertise level as a modelling aid is similar to the certainty factor of EMYCIN (van Melle et al. 1981), an expert system-building tool of AI, and the scales in Conceptual Dependency Theory (Schank and Abelson 1977). Unlike these latter two which use a value domain that is symmetric about the origin, I adhere to the simple [0,1] range.

How does one actually determine such expertise levels? My own (convenient) solution, which is a classical one, is to propose some theories as to how it may be accomplished and to suggest how these theories may be tested via experimentation. In the light of results, the theories may be amended, refined or discarded! In other words, I propose a hypothetical grade of membership function. As a starting point, I consider one of the standard functions $S(u;\alpha,\beta,\gamma)$ of Fuzzy Set Theory (Zadeh 1975):

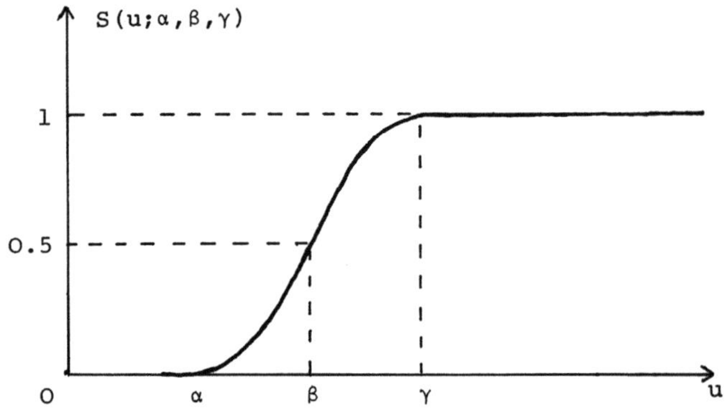

Fig. 4

(See appendix A for the formal definition).

However, I don't yet know how to automatically determine a particular user's increase (decrease) in level of expertise. I hypothesise that, given a basic set of commands for manipulating objects in an application domain, one might be able to assert the level of expertise based on the use (misuse) of same. (Once again, the Interlisp PSE, which has statistics gathering facilities automatically built in, functions as the test bed for experimentation and experience.)

CONCLUSIONS

A User Interface Management System will provide the necessary tools for the specification, implementation and maintenance of the user-computer dialogue. In order to be able to do this effectively, it must have access to a knowledge base that contains, among other things, a model of the class of user and a corresponding model of that class of user's conceptual model of some specific application domain. There are differing kinds of formalisms and languages involved in these models. An object-oriented extended VDM is proposed as both a tool for the formal specification of concepts and as an instance of a particular user's native semantics. The programming language Ada and the associated annotation language Anna are proposed for canonical encodings of concepts and the corresponding canonical semantics, respectively. (This does not rule out the possibility of other GKS language bindings being used in a given GKSAP's UCM of GKS). Finally, an interactive prototyping language, such as Interlisp, is essential, both for the encoding of knowledge in the knowledge base and for conducting experiments in interactive techniques.

However, it is important to keep in mind that this paper preceded the deliberations of the various working groups at the Seeheim Workshop.

It ought to be reread in the light of their findings reported in this volume. Particularly relevant to the present work are the results of working group Omega on the User's Conceptual Model. The M-notation presented in this paper has been superseded by the more refined M-R-C notation of that group. For example, rather than write $M[c,M[u,a]]$, one would use $C(R(M(u,a),F),P,S)$ where C denotes the encoding of some representation R of the conceptual model M possessed by the user u of application domain a. F denotes a knowledge representation formalism and P denotes a programming language with its associated set of semantics S. In other words, the M-notation is confined to conceptual models and is not applicable to models in general. Furthermore, it seems that the notation that I have used based on Minsky's frame theory could be improved by incorporating the conceptual graph notation considered by that group. A possible direction of research in the formal specification of the user's conceptual model would be to apply the theory of fuzzy sets to this conceptual graph notation and bind the result together in the context of the frame theory.

ACKNOWLEDGEMENTS

I often wonder is there really anything I can call my own! The references in the next section were a great source of inspiration. In particular, I would like to acknowledge (Beech 1980; GITT 1983; Green 1981; Guedj et al. 1980; Minsky 1975; Moran 1981; Newman and Sproull 1979; Sandewall 1978; Teitelman and Masinter 1981). A debt of gratitude is owed to my colleague Hans-Juergen Kugler who was responsible for introducinq me to IFIP WG 2.7 and to the members of that group who have assisted me in the object-oriented approach. The extended VDM is theirs. Finally, I am grateful to the various members of Ada-Europe with whom I have come in contact. They helped me to see the "real" significance of Ada. I wish to acknowledge the advice given by my supervisor, Professor J.G. Byrne and the discussions held with members of the workshop which together led to an improvement on the original draft. Needless to remark, any errors contained herein are my own.

APPENDIX A

> "... concepts are represented by fuzzy sets"
> (Goguen Jr. 1981)

A fuzzy set may be considered to be a generalization of the concept of set. Let upper case letters denote (fuzzy) sets and lower case letters (suitably decorated with subscripts, perhaps) denote the elements of (fuzzy) sets. The letter U will denote, as is customary, the specific universe of discourse.

A fuzzy subset A of a universe of discourse U is characterized by a membership function $\mu_A : U \rightarrow [0,1]$ which associates with each element x of U, a number $\mu_A(x)$ in the interval $[0,1]$, which represents the grade of membership of x in A (Chang 1975).

The support of A, denoted by support(A), is the subset of U defined by

$$\text{support}(A) \hat{=} \{x \mid x \in U \text{ and } \mu_A(x) > 0\} \qquad [7]$$

The definition of A may now be conveniently given in terms of the support of A:

$$A \hat{=} \{\mu_A(x)/x \mid x \varepsilon \text{support } (A)\} \quad [8]$$

For example, suppose that

$$U = \{1,2,3,\ldots,10\} \quad [9]$$

Then,

$$A = \{0.5/3, 0.7/4, 1.0/5, 0.5/8\} \quad [10]$$

is a fuzzy subset of U, where

$$\text{support}(A) = \{3,4,5,8\} \quad [11]$$

Note the use of "/" to separate the grade of membership value $\mu_A(x)$ from the member x of U.

Standard grade of membership functions are available for theoretical work (Zadeh 1975). Two such functions, S and Π, are:

$$S(u;\alpha,\beta,\gamma) \hat{=} \begin{cases} 0 & \text{, for } u \leqslant \alpha \\ 2\left(\frac{u-\alpha}{\gamma-\alpha}\right)^2 & \text{, for } \alpha \leqslant u \leqslant \beta \\ 1-2\left(\frac{u-\gamma}{\gamma-\alpha}\right)^2 & \text{, for } \beta \leqslant u \leqslant \gamma \\ 1 & \text{, for } u \geqslant \gamma \end{cases} \quad [12]$$

and

$$\Pi(u;\beta,\gamma) \hat{=} \begin{cases} S(u;\gamma-\beta,\gamma-\frac{\beta}{2},\gamma) & \text{, for } u \leqslant \gamma \\ 1-S(u;\gamma,\gamma+\frac{\beta}{2},\gamma+\beta) & \text{, for } u \geqslant \gamma \end{cases} \quad [13]$$

APPENDIX B

The formal notation is based on a blend of the Vienna Development Method (Bjoerner and Oest 1980) and the Affirm specification language (Thompson and Ericson 1981). I have renamed the key words of (Beech and Kugler) to suit my own taste and introduced some extra notation to augment the original model. A similar notation has appeared recently in the literature (Efe et al. 1983).

An object type specification contains the following sections:

(1) OBJECT TYPE - defines the name of the new type and the structure of the new type in terms of other types.

(2) NEEDS OBJECT TYPE - contains a list of other object types that are used in the specification of the new type.

(3) A-KIND-OF OBJECT TYPE -- gives the generalization hierarchy for this type.

(4) HAS-INSTANCES - gives the instantiations of this new type.

(5) DECLARE - identifiers denoting instances of objects used as arguments in the OPERATIONS and ERROR-OPERATIONS sections are conveniently grouped in a special declaration section.

(6) OPERATIONS - operations on the new type are listed here.

(7) ERROR-OPERATIONS - operations on the new type that handle the raising of exceptions.

(N.B. (3) and (4) are optional!)

Example:

```
OBJECT TYPE
     RGB_colour :: s-R : Rvalue s-G : Gvalue s-B : Bvalue

NEEDS OBJECT TYPES
     Rvalue, Gvalue, Bvalue

DECLARE
     c : RGB_colour,
     r : Rvalue,
     g : Gvalue,
     b : Bvalue

OPERATIONS
     make_colour(r,g,b) : RGB_colour,
     select_R(c) : Rvalue,
     select_G(c) : Gvalue,
     select_B(c) : Bvalue,
     ...

ERROR-OPERATIONS
     RGB_colour_error(c) : RGB_colour,
     RGB_colour_error_Rvalue(r) : RGB_colour,
     RGB_colour_error_Gvalue(g) : RGB_colour,
     RGB_colour_error_Bvalue(b) : RGB_colour,
     ...

END RGB_colour
```

where the detailed semantics of the operations are:

Operation make_colour:

```
make_colour(r,g,b) =
     (is-error-Rvalue(r) -> RGB_colour_error_Rvalue(r);
     is-error-Gvalue(g) -> RGB_colour_error_Gvalue(g);
     is-error-Bvalue(b) -> RGB_colour_error_Bvalue(b);
     T -> mk-RGB_colour(r,g,b))

TYPE: Rvalue Gvalue Bvalue → RGB_colour
```

```
Operation Select_R:

     Select_R(c) =
          (is-error-RGB_colour(c) -> RGB_colour_error(c);
          T -> s-R(c))

     Type: RGB_colour -> Rvalue

Operation Select_G:

     Select_G(c) =
          (is-error-RGB_colour(c) -> RGB_colour_error(c);
          T -> s-G(c))

     TYPE: RGB_colour -> Gvalue

Operation Select_B:

     Select_B(c) =
          (is-error-RGB_colour(c) -> RGB_colour_error(c);
          T -> s-B(c))

     TYPE: RGB_colour -> Bvalue
```

REFERENCES

ALRM (1983) Reference Manual for the Ada Programming Language, ANSI/MIL-STD 1815A. Alsys, La-Celle-Saint-Cloud, France
Beech D (ed) (1980) Command Language Directions. North-Holland Publishing Company, Amsterdam
Beech D, Kugler H-J (to be published) The IFIP WG2.7 Reference Model for Command and Response Languages
Bjoerner D (1980) Formalization of Data Base Models. In: Bjoerner D (ed) Abstract Software Specifications. Springer-Verlag, Berlin Heidelberg New York, p 144
Bjoerner D, Jones CB (1978) The Vienna Development Method: The Meta-Language. Springer-Verlag, Berlin Heidelberg New York
Bjoerner D, Oest O (1980) Towards a Formal Description of Ada. Springer-Verlag, Berlin Heidelberg New York
Bobrow DG, Winograd T (1977) An Overview of KRL, a Knowledge Representation Language. Cognitive Science 1: 3-46
Borufka HG, Kuhlmann HW, ten Hagen PJW (1982) Dialogue Cells: A Method for Defining Interactions. IEEE Computer Graphics and Applications vol 2 no 5 25-33
Buxton W, Lamb MR, Sherman D, Smith KC (1983) Towards a Comprehensive User Interface Management System. In: SIGGRAPH'83 Conf. Proc. ACM SIGGRAPH Computer Graphics vol 17 no 3 35-42
Carson GS (1983) The Specification of Computer Graphics Systems. IEEE Computer Graphics and Applications vol 3 no 6 27-41
Chang CL (1975) Interpretation and Execution of Fuzzy Programs. In: Zadeh LA, Fu K-S, Tanaka K, Shimura M (eds) Fuzzy Sets and their Applications to Cognitive and Decision Processes. Academic Press, Inc., New York San Francisco London, p 191
Dreyfus HL (1979) A Framework for Misrepresenting Knowledge. In: Ringle M (ed) Philosophical Perspectives in Artificial Intelligence. The Harvester Press, Brighton, England, p 124
Efe K, Miller C, Hopper K (1983) The Kiwinet-Nicola Approach: Response Generation in a User-Friendly Interface. IEEE Computer vol 16 no 9 66-78

ESPRIT (1983) Proposal for a Council Decision adopting the first European Strategic Programme for Research and Development in Information Technologies (ESPRIT). Commission of the European Communities COM(83) 258 final, Brussels

Foley JD, van Dam A (1982) Fundamentals of Interactive Computer Graphics. Addison-Wesley Publishing Company, Reading, Massachusetts

Fry JP, Sibley EH (1976) Evolution of Data-Base Management Systems. ACM Computing Surveys 8: 17-42

GKS (1982) Graphical Kernel System - Functional Description, Draft Proposal ISO/DP 7942. ANSI USA

Goguen Jr. JA (1981) Concept Representation in Natural and Artificial Languages: Axioms, Extensions and Applications for Fuzzy Sets. In: Mamdani EH, Gaines BR (eds) Fuzzy Reasoning and its Applications. Academic Press, London, p 67

Goldstein IP, Roberts B (1979) Using Frames in Scheduling. In: Winston PH, Brown RH (eds) Artificial Intelligence: an MIT Perspective vol 1. The MIT Press, Cambridge, Massachusetts, p 253.

GITT (1983) Proc. of the Workshop on Graphical Input Interaction Techniques. ACM SIGGRAPH Computer Graphics vol 17 no 1 5-66

Green M (1981) A Methodology for the Specification of Graphical User Interfaces. In: SIGGRAPH'81 Conf. Proc. ACM SIGGRAPH Computer Graphics vol 15 no 3 99-108

Guedj RA, ten Hagen PJW, Hopgood FRA, Tucker HA, Duce DA (eds) (1980) Methodology of Interaction. North-Holland Publishing Company, Amsterdam

Hansen WJ (1971) User Engineering Principles for Interactive Systems. In: Proc. of the Fall Joint Comp. Conf. AFIPS Press 39: 523-532

Iverson KE (1980) Notation as a Tool of Thought. Comm. of the ACM 23: 444-465

Jardine DA (ed) (1977) The ANSI/SPARC DBMS Model. Proc. of the Second SHARE Working Conf. on Data Base Management Systems. North-Holland Publishing Company, Amsterdam

Kasik DJ (1982) A User Interface Management System. In: SIGGRAPH'82 Conf. Proc. ACM SIGGRAPH Computer Graphics vol 16 no 3 99-106

Kaufmann A (1975) Introduction to the Theory of Fuzzy Subsets, vol 1, Fundamental Theoretical Elements. Academic Press, London

Krieg-Brueckner B, Luckham DC, von Henke FW, Owe O (1982) Draft Reference Manual for ANNA - A Language for Annotating Ada Programs. Universitaet Bremen and Stanford University

Lodding KN (1983) Iconic Interfacing. IEEE Computer Graphics and Applications vol 3 no 2 11-20

Mac an Airchinnigh M (1982) Classifying the User. ACM SIGCHI Bulletin vol 14 no 2 3-8

Mac an Airchinnigh M (1983) The $\sum$-concept. ACM SIGCHI Bulletin vol 4 no 4 8-15

Mac an Airchinnigh M (1984) Ada Packages and the User's Conceptual Model. ACM SIGPLAN AdaTEC Ada Letters vol III no 4 III-4.70--III-4.77

Minsky M (1975) A Framework for Representing Knowledge. In: Winston PH (ed) The Psychology of Computer Vision. McGraw-Hill Book Company, New York, p 211

Moran T (1981) The Command Language Grammar: a representation for the user interface of Interactive computer systems. Int. J. Man-Machine Studies 15: 3-50

Newman WF, Sproull RF (1979) Principles of Interactive Computer Graphics. 2nd edn. McGraw-Hill Book Company, New York

Nievergelt J, Weydert J (1980) Sites, Modes, and Trails: Telling the User of an Interactive System Where he is, What he can do, and How to get to places. In: Guedj RA, ten Hagen PJW, Hopgood FRA, Tucker HA, Duce DA (eds) Methodology of Interaction. North-Holland Publishing Company, Amsterdam, p 327

Reimer U, Hahn U (1983) A Formal Approach to the Semantics of a Frame Data Model. In: Proc. of the Eighth Int. Joint Conf. on Artificial Intelligence, Karlsruhe vol 1 337-339
Rosenthal DSH, Michener JC, Pfaff G, Kessener R, Sabin M (1982) The Detailed Semantics of Graphics Input Devices. In: SIGGRAPH'82 Conf. Proc. ACM SIGGRAPH Computer Graphics vol 16 no 3 33-38
Sandewall E (1978) Programming in an Interactive Environment: the LISP Experience. ACM Computing Surveys 10: 33-71
Schank RC, Abelson RP (1977) Scripts, Plans, Goals and Understanding, An Inquiry into Human Knowledge Understanding. Lawrence Erlbaum Associates, Publishers, Hilsdale, New Jersey
Schneider ML (1982) Models for the Design of Static Software User Assistance. In: Badre A, Shneiderman B (eds) Directions in Human/ Computer Interaction. Ablex Publishing Corporation, Norwood, New Jersey, p 137
Schneider ML, Wexelblat RL, Jende MS (1980) Designing Control Languages from the User's Perspective. In: Beech D (ed) Command Language Directions. North-Holland Publishing Company, Amsterdam, p 181
Shapiro EY (1983) The Fifth Generation Project - A Trip Report. Comm. of the ACM 26: 637-641
Singh B, Beatty JS, Booth KS, Ryman R (1983) A Graphics Editor for Benesh Movement Notation. In: SIGGRAPH'83 Conf. Proc. ACM SIGGRAPH Computer Graphics vol 17 no 3 51-62
Smith H (1980) Human-Computer Communication. In: Smith HT, Green TRG (eds) Human Interaction with Computers. Academic Press, London, p 5
Sowa JF (1981) A Conceptual Schema for Knowledge-Based Systems. In: Proc. of the Workshop on Data Abstraction, Databases and Conceptual Modelling. ACM SIGPLAN Notices vol 16 no 1 193-195
STONEMAN (1980) Requirements for Ada Programming Support Environments. US Department of Defense
Teitelman W (1972) Automated Programmering - The Programmer's Assistant. In: Conf. Proc. of the Fall Joint Comp. Conf. AFIPS Press 41: 917-921
Teitelman W (1978) Interlisp Reference Manual. Xerox PARC, Palo Alto, California
Teitelman W, Masinter L (1981) The INTERLISP Programming Environment. IEEE Computer vol 14 no 4 25-33
Thompson DH, Ericson RW (eds) (1981) AFFIRM Reference Manual. USC/Information Sciences Institute, California
van Griethuysen JJ (ed) (1982) Concepts and Terminology for the Conceptual Schema and the Information base. ISO/TC 97/SC 5 - N695, ANSI USA
van Melle W, Carlisle Scott A, Bennett JS, Peairs MAS (1981) The EMYCIN Manual. Report no STAN-CS-81-885, Stanford University
VAX (1980) Vax Software Handbook. Digital Equipment Corporation
Warman EA, Hermans E, Bo K (1979) Computer Graphics - A Projection for the Future. In: Guedj RA, Tucker HA (eds) Methodology in Computer Graphics. North-Holland Publishing Company, Amsterdam, p 41
WDDC (1981) Proc. of the Workshop on Data Abstraction, Databases and Conceptual Modelling. ACM SIGPLAN Notices vol 16 no 1
Wittgenstein L (1977) Bemerkungen ueber die Farben. Anscombe GEM (ed) McAlister LL, Schaettle M (trans) Basil Blackwell, Oxford, England
Zadeh LA (1975) Calculus of Fuzzy Restrictions. In: Zadeh LA, Fu K-S, Tanaka K, Shimura M (eds) Fuzzy Sets and their Applications to Cognitive and Decision Processes. Academic Press, Inc., New York San Francisco London, p 1

MIX
Papier aus verantwortungsvollen Quellen
Paper from responsible sources
FSC® C105338

If you have any concerns about our products,
you can contact us on
ProductSafety@springernature.com

In case Publisher is established outside the EU,
the EU authorized representative is:
Springer Nature Customer Service Center GmbH
Europaplatz 3, 69115 Heidelberg, Germany

Printed by Libri Plureos GmbH
in Hamburg, Germany